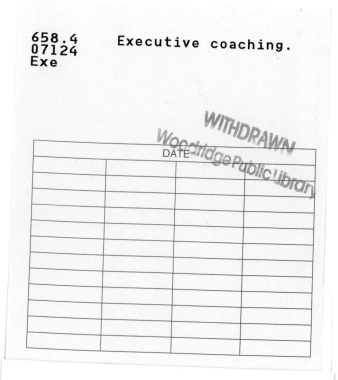

PRAISE FOR EXECUTIVE COACHING

"One of the few books on the market that really gives practices and perspective. The editors have fulfilled the promise in the title. By gathering true practitioners, they have ensured that readers will walk away with real tools, techniques, and practices they can use every day."

Philip J. Harkins, President and CEO, Linkage, Inc.

"A substantive and immensely practical book that makes a critical contribution to establishing the highest standards for this emerging field and should be fundamental reading for practitioners. Supports the learning of all members of the coaching partnership, including executives, coaches, and the companies in which they work."

The Executive Coaching Forum (TECF), author/publisher of
Executive Coaching Handbook (www.theexecutivecoachingforum.com)

"An excellent collection of practical advice about coaching leaders. I highly recommend it as 'must' reading for CEOs and anyone interested in improving his or her organization through leadership development."

Robert L. Reynolds, Vice Chairman and Chief Operating Officer,
Fidelity Investments

"An exceptional resource for those who assist today's business leaders in facing their daunting challenges. Speaking from a vast experiential base, the authors provide theory and wisdom, shedding light on common practices that benefit professional executive coaches and those thinking about employing them."

Lily Kelly-Radford, Ph.D., Vice President,
Leadership Development, Center for Creative Leadership

"An invaluable book that takes the reader to the leading edge of executive coaching. A tool with great promise for firms like ours."

R. Bruce McLean, Chairman, Akin, Gump, Strauss, Hauer, & Feld, LLP

"Provides several essential anchors for a rapidly emerging field. As I read each chapter, the unique potential of executive coaching was revealed, as well as the care that must be exerted to ensure its responsible use in the future."

Eugene Schnell, Director of Organization Development and Diversity,
Johns Hopkins University; author of
The Leadership Report Using FIRO-B™ and MBTI®

"An extraordinarily insightful work that provides frameworks in diverse areas ranging from colliding cultures to managers whose life priorities rapidly change. This book is a tool for effective management in organizations that must be focused in their mission and strategy while encompassing the evolving personal perspectives that leaders and senior executives inevitably experience."

Hank Cauley, Executive Director, Forest Stewardship Council U.S.

"*Executive Coaching* helps move this important profession toward a decision science at a critical evolutionary junction. Combining theory and practice, the editors and contributors bring discipline and rigor to bear on advancing the boundaries of executive coaching. A standard-raising work that assures coaching's future."

John D. Hofmeister, Director, Human Resources, Royal Dutch/Shell

"A powerful, cutting-edge book that brings together the most knowledgeable people in the field of executive coaching. Should be required reading for all professionals interested in enhancing leadership effectiveness."

**Daniel C. Robinson, University Professor and Professor of
Educational Leadership and Policy Studies, Iowa State University;
President-elect, Association for Psychological Type**

EXECUTIVE
COACHING

EXECUTIVE
COACHING

PRACTICES & PERSPECTIVES

CATHERINE FITZGERALD

JENNIFER GARVEY BERGER

Davies-Black Publishing
Mountain View, California

We dedicate this book to our children and grandchildren—
Derek, Naomi, and Aidan—in the hope that executive coaching can
contribute to the development of those who will lead the world
to a just and peaceful future.

Published by Davies-Black Publishing, a division of CPP, Inc., 1055 Joaquin Road, Suite 200, Mountain View, CA 94043; 800-624-1765.

Special discounts on bulk quantities of Davies-Black books are available to corporations, professional associations, and other organizations. For details, contact the Director of Marketing and Sales at Davies-Black Publishing; 650-691-9123; fax 650-623-9271.

09 08 07 06 05   10 9 8 7 6 5 4 3 2
Printed in the United States of America

Library of Congress Cataloging-in-Publication Data
Executive coaching : practices & perspectives / [edited by] Catherine Fitzgerald, Jennifer Garvey Berger.
    p. cm.
Includes bibliographical references and index.
ISBN 0-89106-161-4 (hardcover)
I. Executives—Training of. I. Fitzgerald, Catherine. II. Berger, Jennifer Garvey.
HD30.4 .E938 2002
658.4'07124—dc21

                                       2001054342

FIRST EDITION
First printing 2002

CONTENTS

Part III: Managing Executive Coaching in Organizations

Part IV: Executive Coaching Issues

Part V: Special Coaching Situations

PREFACE

Our goal in this book is to make a serious and substantial contribution to the emerging practice of executive coaching by presenting a rich variety of executive coaching practices and perspectives from experienced and thoughtful executive coaches and human resource managers. The working definition of executive coaching that guided the book's development is that it is one-on-one, confidential work with executives aimed at enhancing their current and future effectiveness and that it

- Is focused on development and not on assessment for promotion or hiring
- Goes beyond specific technical or industry guidance
- Is distinguishable from psychotherapy (while perhaps sharing with psychotherapy some frameworks of analysis and some core skills, such as listening and reflecting)
- Is based on a complex and sophisticated understanding of and focus on both the individual executive and the organizational role and context

The guiding metaphor that shaped our approach to this book is that of a mosaic or a patchwork quilt. The practice of executive coaching is too emergent for any one person or group to have *the* model or *the* right approach, and not enough has been codified or researched for a rigorous and unified model of executive coaching to be in place at this time. Because it is early in the development of standardized approaches to this burgeoning field, we believed that perhaps our best contribution to the expansion and deepening of executive coaching practice would be a collection of the diverse perspectives of a wide variety of practitioners. Our hope is that the collection presented here will be accessible and useful to new and prospective practitioners and human resource managers, while also being of interest and use to experienced professionals.

Contributors

Because we were interested in capturing as many leading-edge practices as we could, we searched broadly for chapter authors. We looked for prospective authors who had substantial hands-on experience as executive coaches or as managers/brokers of executive coaching services, an innovative approach about which they were interested in writing, and a rich combination of client experience, education, affiliations (for example, university teaching affiliations), and organizational roles[1].

We spoke with a wide variety of colleagues in the United States and internationally and asked them to identify highly experienced executive coaches and human resource managers who were managing executive coaching within organizations. We called the coaches and human resource managers these colleagues recommended, told them about our plans for the book, and talked with them about their work. We then asked them who *they* thought highly of, and so on. We also contacted people who had written articles or given presentations at conferences about executive coaching. When we found practitioners whose work was impressive, who had the characteristics we had identified, and who had an interest in writing about their work, we invited them to contribute chapters. The majority of the chapter authors in the book were identified during our broad search: of the eighteen contributors (other than us), we knew only four when the book project began. In addition, several of our current colleagues more than met the requirements for authors, and we invited them to contribute chapters as well.

Overview

The book is divided into five parts, focusing on the following:

- Executive coaching perspectives
- Executive coaching practices
- Managing executive coaching in organizations

- Issues in executive coaching

- Special coaching situations

Part 1, "Executive Coaching Perspectives," consists of three chapters. In Chapter 1, David Coleman distills the lessons he learned as an executive coach and offers general principles for thinking about and taking action with a client, guidelines for engaging in the coaching conversation, and practical suggestions for beginning coaches. In Chapter 2, Jennifer Garvey Berger and Catherine Fitzgerald present a model for understanding complexity of mind in executives and suggest ways to support the development of increasing complexity. Grady McGonagill, in Chapter 3, offers a framework for constructing a model of coaching, describes the evolution of his model of coaching, and provides suggestions to coaches for becoming reflective practitioners.

In Part 2, "Executive Coaching Practices," three chapters describe different approaches to executive coaching. In Chapter 4, Catherine Fitzgerald outlines a framework for understanding the midlife process as experienced by executives and suggests a variety of ways to support development for executives who are in midlife. Chapter 5, by Kathryn Williams, Fred Kiel, Marilyn Doyle, and Laura Sinagra, presents a holistic, in-depth approach to executive coaching that includes a focus on the personal history and current personal life of the client. Robert Goodman, in Chapter 6, proposes a model for executive coaching that draws on adult developmental theory for creating transformative change in executives.

The four chapters of Part 3, "Managing Executive Coaching in Organizations," look at executive coaching from the perspective of senior human resource development and executive development managers who are responsible for developing and managing executive coaching programs within organizations. In Chapter 7, Susan Ennis suggests specific steps for getting executive coaching started in an organization. Chapter 8, by Mary Jane Knudson, explores how executive coaches can support a company's business strategy and how human resource managers can design and implement executive coaching programs that are linked to business strategy. William Hodgetts, in Chapter 9, details what can go wrong in the use of executive coaching in organizations and provides guidelines for minimizing such problems. In Chapter 10, Casey Strumpf analyzes the potential contributions of coaches who are internal to the organization versus coaches who are external and proposes ways to enhance the use and development of internal coaches.

The three chapters of Part 4, "Issues in Executive Coaching," address three important practice topics. Chapter 11, by Catherine Fitzgerald, presents a rationale and an approach for integrating models and concepts of business strategy into executive coaching. In Chapter 12, Sally Carr articulates the implications of motivation based primarily on love rather than fear and explores the impact in executive coaching of motivating clients through love. Richard Kilburg, in Chapter 13, discusses the issue of failure in executive coaching and identifies actions to take to avoid failure.

Part 5, "Special Coaching Situations," contains three chapters that address coaching situations distinguished by a particular problem confronting a client, the kind of client, or the context within which the client works. In Chapter 14, Gae Walters highlights the dilemma of senior executives who get isolated, suggests differences in the causes and effects of isolation in extraverted and introverted executives, and provides guidance for coaching isolated executives. Chapter 15, by Barry Dym, Stephen Jenks, and Michael Sonduck, focuses on coaching entrepreneurs and addresses what is distinctive about entrepreneurs, methods and approaches for coaching entrepreneurs, and readiness and change in executive coaching. Karen Otazo, in Chapter 16, describes in detail a case example of coaching across countries and cultures and illustrates the ways in which executive coaching can be helpful to executives who lead in complex, multinational organizational environments.

Limitations

Although we worked to capture a rich collection of leading-edge—and immediately useful—practices and perspectives in this book, we have no illusions that we have captured the entirety of the complex, multidimensional, and evolving field of executive coaching, for three reasons. First, even for authors whose work is represented in this book, only a very small fraction of their expertise is contained herein. Authors had to carefully (and sometimes painfully!) limit the focus of their chapters to fit within the chapter length constraints.

Second, a number of outstanding executive coaching practitioners were unable to contribute their work because of constraints on their time. Noteworthy examples include Mary Kralj and Ellen Wingard, each of whom is doing important, leading-edge work we would have loved to include. And third, since most of the experimentation, innovation, and refinement of executive coaching practice takes place quietly behind closed doors, as thoughtful and experienced executive coaches develop new ways to help their clients, it is impossible at this point to identify all (or even most) of the leading-edge practices and perspectives. Our hope is that this book will encourage other executive coaches and human resource managers who manage or broker executive coaching services to articulate their views and approaches. [2]

A Personal Note

We thought some readers might be interested in knowing that, although it is not obvious from our names or our pictures, we coeditors share another relationship besides long-term colleagues and collaborators—a relationship with a much longer history. We are mother (Catherine) and daughter (Jennifer). We feel very fortunate to be drawn to related fields and to have professional interests that substantially overlap, and we are delighted to be able to collaborate on this book, as well as on one chapter within the book.

Acknowledgments

We are grateful to many people, without whom this volume could not have been produced. We are especially grateful to the contributing authors for their attention to quality, their willingness to undertake the challenging task of translating their tacit knowledge into words, and their flexibility and patience in dealing with our crowded schedules and changing deadlines. Obviously, this book would not exist without the effort, care, and thoughtfulness they put into their work.

We are also very grateful to the following colleagues and friends who have contributed their ideas, feedback, and support: Sally Carr, David

Coleman, Ben Dean, Susan Ennis, Jim Hammerman, Kathy Karlson, Mary Kralj, Jean Kummerow, Mark Leach, Joseph Mancini, Grady McGonagill, Karen Otazo, Margaret Porter, Geno Schnell, Ellen Wingard, and Joan Wofford. In addition, we would like to thank Sunny Bain, Laura Benedict, and Carol Garner for their invaluable administrative support on the book.

The influence of Lee Langhammer-Law, Divisional Director of Davies-Black Publishing, is noteworthy: this book could not have been produced without Lee's early encouragement, later patience, and overall intelligence, judgment, and support. Jill Anderson-Wilson, Managing Editor at Davies-Black, put an enormous amount of time and care into the complicated production of this book, showed remarkable calmness and thoughtfulness even under great pressure, and applied exquisite judgment to matters large and small. Laura Simonds, Davies-Black's Director of Sales and Marketing, also demonstrated admirable perspective and patience as the book was slowly crafted and readied for publication.

We would like to thank our current and past clients, those leaders and staff within the organizations in which we have been privileged to work who have shared their stories and their insights.

Finally, we are very grateful to our families for their support of and patience with our work on this book. Our husbands, Derek Updegraff, Sr., and Michael Berger, were unfailingly interested in and supportive of our work and took on many additional responsibilities to enable us to complete the book. Our children, Derek Updegraff, Jr., Naomi Catherine Garvey Berger, and Aidan James Garvey Berger (who was born as the book was in its final stages!), also demonstrated remarkable, age-inappropriate patience with "Mom's book." We hope they will all be proud of the resulting product.

Notes

[1] A reader of the Contributors section might note that three authors are currently affiliated with Fidelity Investments. When this book was originally in development, only one author (William Hodgetts) was at Fidelity Investments; the two other authors had other affiliations: Mary Jane Knudson was Director of Executive Development and Succession Planning at Digital Equipment Corporation, subsequently acquired by Compaq, and Casey Strumpf was Senior Vice President of Executive Development at Putnam Investments. In the course of the past two years, both Mary Jane and Casey accepted positions at Fidelity Investments.

[2]There is one important topic we had planned to address that is *not* included in the book. The topic involves the emerging definitions of roles, responsibilities, and standards of practice for executive coaches and for managers of executive coaching. Catherine Fitzgerald and Susan Ennis had planned to write a chapter addressing these issues; however, after much discussion they decided that the scope of the work was beyond what could be accommodated in the book and also that such a topic would be more usefully published in a more broadly participative and faster-evolving form than is possible within an edited volume. Luckily for the field of executive coaching, while this book was in development, a nonprofit group, The Executive Coaching Forum (TECF), was formed to advance the best practices and understanding of executive coaching. (Note: Three chapter authors, Susan Ennis, Robert Goodman, and William Hodgetts, now sit on the TECF board.) TECF has done invaluable work in articulating the state of the art regarding roles, responsibilities, and standards of practice. The result of their work, *The Executive Coaching Handbook,* is available free (at www.theexecutivecoachingforum.com) and will be refined and updated periodically. The *Handbook* has already been widely circulated and has been very well received. Readers are strongly encouraged to look at *The Executive Coaching Handbook.*

CONTRIBUTORS

JENNIFER GARVEY BERGER consults and teaches in the areas of adult development, personality differences, and transformational learning. Her commitment is to offering adults professional development opportunities that not only increase their knowledge about groups and individuals but also transform their ability to implement that knowledge. Berger teaches courses on adult development and complexity of mind at Harvard University and Georgetown University, and she is a faculty member at the Bard Institute of Writing and Thinking. Working with diverse groups—from bank executives to teenage mothers, dotcom gurus to naval officers—she draws on a wide range of theories and research to make complex and important ideas useful and practical. She brings those same values to her writing and research. Berger is coeditor of *Acts of Inquiry in Qualitative Research* (Harvard Educational Publishing Group, 2000). She holds a master's degree in teaching and learning from Harvard University where she is currently completing her doctoral degree in adult development. She can be reached at Jennifer_Berger@gse.harvard.edu.

SALLY CARR is an independent consultant living in Oxford, England, who specializes in helping managers become more aware of their own behavior and work better with people, both in one-to-one coaching and in group settings. She was a founding member of Oxford Psychologists Press, one of the U.K.'s premier sources of psychometric instruments and consultancy. An experienced *Myers-Briggs Type Indicator*® (MBTI®) facilitator, she has led MBTI qualifying workshops for the Association for Psychological Type for eleven years. She also has a long-standing relationship with the Center for Creative Leadership as an adjunct trainer and is a member of the Executive Coaching Roundtable. Carr has a special interest in the potential of meditation and mindfulness practices to help people live joyfully, learn effectively, and access their full wisdom. She has developed and facilitated workshops relating people's experience of such practices to personality differences, recognizing that there are many different paths to the same goal. She holds a master's degree in clinical psychology from the University of London and undergraduate and doctoral degrees in psychology from Oxford University. She can be reached at ssc@gn.apc.org.

DAVID COLEMAN is an organizational psychologist and business consultant to both professional service firms and corporations, primarily in the areas of strategic planning, dispute management, and executive coaching. He is co-creator of the executive coaching program at the International Monetary Fund, has presented to national audiences on executive coaching, and is a highly regarded teacher in the Organization Development Certificate Program at Georgetown University. He has more than sixteen years of experience in coaching managers, from first-line supervisors to CEOs, in both private and public sector organizations. His clients include the World Bank, the International Monetary Fund, and AT&T. He is a member of the Executive Coaching Roundtable. Coleman holds a doctoral degree in clinical psychology from the University of Georgia. He can be reached at dcoleman@atlantech.net.

MARILYN DOYLE is measurement and research manager, clinical psychologist, and technical writer at KRW International in Minneapolis. Her areas of expertise are measurement and psychological evaluation, and her experience draws from clinical work at a community mental health center and a hospital outpatient department, as well as several years of teaching at Augsburg College. Doyle holds a master's degree in counseling psychology from the University of St. Thomas and a doctoral degree in clinical psychology from the Minnesota School of Professional Psychology. She can be reached at doyle022@mninter.net.

BARRY DYM is President of WorkWise Research and Consulting in Newton, Massachusetts. For more than thirty years, he has combined careers in organization development and psychotherapy. Previously he was a founder and director of the Family Institute of Cambridge. Author of two books, *Readiness and Change in Couple Therapy* (Basic Books, 1995) and *Couples* (HarperCollins, 1993), he has also published numerous articles, including "Utilizing States of Organizational Readiness," winner of the Larry Porter Prize as the best article on organization development, 1997–99 (*OD Practitioner*). His clients range from nonprofits, entrepreneurial start-ups, and family businesses to such complex organizations as The Boston Globe, State Street Corporation, Massachusetts Financial Services, Honeywell and Digital Equipment Corporation. His skills include helping to mobilize organizations for difficult change efforts and reviving stalled initiatives, team building and executive coaching, conflict resolution, and strategic planning. He can be reached at bdym@work-wise.org.

SUSAN A. ENNIS is an executive development consultant with more than twenty years of experience. Previously she held executive development positions at Digital Equipment Company and BankBoston where she established a highly regarded executive coaching program. She is a founding member of The Executive Coaching Forum and coauthor of *The Executive Coaching Handbook: Principles and Guidelines for a Successful Coaching Partnership* (2nd ed.) (The Executive Coaching Forum, 2001; for a free copy, go to www.theexecutivecoachingforum.com). She helps companies set up executive coaching systems, along with sourcing, qualifying, and brokering executive coaches. Ennis coaches high-potential managers, newly appointed leaders, and technical managers who need to expand their influence repertoire. She is especially interested in helping people reach their potential, so that organizations can realize the full contribution of executives whose social background, educational experience, or cultural heritage varies from that of their peers. Ennis has presented and published widely on how to execute business strategy through executive coaching, competency-based selection/development, and performance management tools. She holds a bachelor's degree in an interdisciplinary program of psychology, sociology, and social anthropology from Harvard University and a master's degree in education from Northeastern University. She can be reached at Susan@tolead.com.

CATHERINE FITZGERALD is an organizational psychologist and principal of Fitzgerald Consulting, a company that offers executive coaching to senior executives. Her clients have included Fannie Mae, the Inter-American Development Bank, the International Monetary Fund, the National Cooperative Bank, PriceWaterhouseCoopers, and the World Resources Institute. She is coeditor of *Developing Leaders: Research and Applications in Psychological Type and Leadership Development* (Davies-Black, 1997). She has taught advanced courses on executive coaching in the United States and internationally, and she does advanced training and shadow consulting for experienced executive coaches. Fitzgerald is an adjunct faculty member at Georgetown University where she teaches about leadership, adult development, and complexity of mind. She has also taught courses on leadership development and organizational change at the National Leadership Institute of the University of Maryland University College and the School of Public Affairs at the University of Maryland at College Park. A member of the Executive Coaching Roundtable, she received a doctoral degree in psychology from the State University of New York at Buffalo and completed a predoctoral fellowship at Yale University. She can be reached at catherine@fitzgeraldconsulting.com.

ROBERT G. GOODMAN is principal of RGGoodman Associates, a consulting firm offering senior executive leadership development for both for-profit and nonprofit organizations. Trained as a developmental and clinical psychologist, he provides executive coaching, executive team assessment and development, and consulting on the design and implementation of executive development programs, including internal executive coaching networks. Goodman's professional interest focuses on applying principles of adult development and learning to leadership development, so that executives can think and act with the increased complexity necessary for sustained success in today's work environment. His recent clients include Pfizer, Fidelity Management Resources, Thomson Financial, J. P. Morgan, Putnam Investments, Stratus Computer, Kaiser-Permanente, and the Massachusetts Department of Public Health. Goodman is a clinical instructor at Harvard Medical School and a founding board member of The Executive Coaching Forum. He holds master's and doctoral degrees in human development from Rutgers University and Harvard University, respectively. He can be reached at rggoodman@aol.com.

WILLIAM H. HODGETTS is Vice President of Executive Development at Fidelity Investments and cofounder of Hodgetts Associates, an executive coaching and consulting firm. An experienced executive coach, he has more than twenty years of experience in a variety of human resource, leadership, and management development roles in the financial service sector. At Fidelity Investments, Hodgetts has worked closely with the chairman and other senior leaders on issues of organizational change, leadership development, family business, succession management, and the impact of new technology. His current responsibilities at Fidelity include providing executive coaching, developmental assessments, and other resources to senior executives, as well as overseeing executive coaching companywide. As principal of Hodgetts Associates, he has provided in-depth senior executive assessment and coaching to a number of major corporations, family businesses, and professional service firms, including S. C. Johnson and Sons, Corning Glass, Allied Domecq Retailing USA, Dunkin Donuts, Hasbro, and the Handleman Company. Hodgetts is coauthor (with Jane Hodgetts) of "Finding Sanctuary in Post-Modern Life" (in *The Career Is Dead*, edited by Douglas T. Hall; Jossey-Bass, 1996). He has presented frequently at national conferences on executive coaching and leadership development, and has been a lecturer at Harvard Extension School and the Arthur D. Little School of Management. Hodgetts holds a bachelor's degree in government from Cornell University and a doctoral degree in human development and psychology from Harvard University. He can be reached at billhodge@aol.com.

R. STEPHEN JENKS is a management and organization consultant with a special interest in entrepreneurship and issues relating to growing organizations. He is a founder of the Portsmouth Consulting Group, an association of senior freelance consultants that was formed in 1981. He served on the faculty at the University of New Hampshire where he taught a course in entrepreneurial management for twenty years and was the faculty director of the Executive Development Program for four years. Jenks has extensive experience working with presidents of growing entrepreneurial companies on issues of organization structure and design. Much of his work involves executive coaching aimed at helping individual executives and executive teams work as effectively as possible. He is coauthor of *Designing and Managing Organizations* (Irwin, 1983) and *The Feel of the Work Place: Understanding and Improving Organization Climate* (Addison-Wesley, 1977). He received a doctoral degree in organizational behavior from Case Western Reserve University. He can be reached at sjenks@pcgpartners.com.

FRED KIEL is cofounder of KRW International in Minneapolis, a consulting firm specializing in executive coaching and team development. A pioneer in the field of executive coaching beginning in the mid-1970s, he became an adjunct faculty member of the Center for Creative Leadership in 1986. In 1987, he formed, with Eric Rimmer, Kiel Rimmer Associates (renamed KRW International in 1990 when Kathryn Williams joined the organization). KRW's coaching services have been described in such business periodicals as *Business Week, Fortune,* and *Management Review,* as well as *Consulting Psychology Journal.* Kiel received a doctoral degree in counseling psychology from the University of Minnesota. He can be reached at kiel@krw-intl.com.

RICHARD R. KILBURG is Senior Director of the Office of Human Services in the Department of Human Resources and adjunct assistant professor in the Department of Psychology at The Johns Hopkins University. He provides executive coaching services at Johns Hopkins and through his private consulting practice. Kilburg is a fellow of the Consulting Psychology Division of the American Psychological Association. In 1996, he was guest editor for a special issue of the *Consulting Psychology Journal* on the topic of executive coaching. He has published three books, *Professionals in Distress: Issues, Syndromes, and Solutions in Psychology* (1986), *How to Manage Your Career in Psychology* (1992), and *Executive Coaching: Developing Executive Wisdom in a World of Chaos* (2000), all with the American Psychological Association, and more than forty articles and book chapters. He received a doctoral degree in clinical psychology from the University of Pittsburgh.

MARY JANE KNUDSON is Vice President of Organizational Capability at Fidelity Investments where she is responsible for programs and initiatives in leadership development, organization development, succession planning, and management development that support strategic business objectives. She also provides executive coaching as an internal coaching resource. She has twenty years of experience in executive and management development, human resource development, career development, and succession planning. Previously, she was Director of Worldwide Executive Development and Learning at Digital Equipment Corporation (now merged with Compaq Computer) where she also served as an executive coach. Knudson is a frequent speaker at national and international conferences on such topics as executive coaching, competency models, and strategic human resource leadership. With a dissertation on leadership development, she received a doctoral degree in education from Harvard University. She can be reached at maryjane.knudson@fmr.com.

GRADY MCGONAGILL is principal of McGonagill & Associates, an organizational consulting and management development firm specializing in building capacity for learning and change. In the course of his nineteen years of consulting experience, he has served a wide range of enterprises in North and South America, Europe, and Asia. His corporate clients include Aetna Life and Casualty, Johnson & Johnson Products, and Siemens, A.G. His public sector clients include the New York State Board of Regents and the Federal Labor Relations Authority. He also works with nonprofit organizations, such as the Currier Gallery of Art, Amnesty International, and the National Audubon Society. McGonagill's workshops on coaching, leadership, conflict management, team building, and interpersonal skills have been offered through a number of executive programs, including Harvard University's Kennedy School of Government, MIT's Sloan School of Management, Babson College's Center for Executive Education, and Brandeis University's Heller School of Management. He holds a master's degree in German literature and humanities from Stanford University and a doctoral degree in education from Harvard University. He can be reached at gradymcg@aol.com.

KAREN L. OTAZO is a global organizational consultant specializing in executive coaching and assessment. She lives in London and works with clients in Europe, Asia, and the United States, including AlliedSignal, Amgen, ARCO, BankBoston, Chase Bank, Colgate Palmolive, Digital, General Electric, GlobalOne, IBM, Lehman Brothers, Motorola, Sprint, and Time International. Formerly Otazo was Corporate Manager of Executive Development with Atlantic Richfield (now part of BPAmoco). Having lived on four continents, she speaks Spanish, French, Indonesian, and Mandarin Chinese. She is coauthor of "Global Leadership: The Inside Story" (in *Advances in Global Leadership*, JAI Press,

1999), among other publications. She holds both a bachelor's and a master's degree in linguistics from the City University of New York and a doctoral degree in human resources development from the University of Northern Colorado. She can be reached at karen@otazo.com

LAURA SINAGRA is marketing manager at KRW International. She is also a freelance writer whose features and essays have appeared in such periodicals as *Spin, Alternative Press, Request, Blender,* and *Minneapolis City Pages.* At KRW, she coordinates branding strategy and oversees marketing and PR initiatives. Her previous experience includes public policy reporting for the Minnesota State Senate and policy research for the Bureau of National Affairs Publishing Company in Washington, D.C. Sinagra received a bachelor's degree in English literature and history from Ohio's Kenyon College. She can be reached at lmsinagra@yahoo.com.

MICHAEL SONDUCK is a business and organization consultant who has been helping clients understand the relationship between people, organizations, and business success for more than twenty years. In that time he developed his own approach to helping organizational leaders find practical, results-focused solutions to their business problems in balance with the human needs of the organization. His clients describe Sonduck as a "business partner" in their efforts to ensure organizational success. He helps clients achieve results through leadership coaching and education, organization analysis and planning, and ongoing implementation support. Sonduck was formerly board chair of the Ecology of Work Conference, Inc., the oldest annual conference on employee involvement, productivity, and work systems design. A frequent speaker at public and private forums of CEOs and quality leaders, he holds a bachelor's degree in applied behavioral science from George Williams College. He can be reached at sonduckm@leadershipforchange.com.

CASEY STRUMPF is Vice President and Director of Executive and Organizational Development at Fidelity Investments. An experienced executive coach and broker of coaches, she has more than twenty years of experience in a range of industries, including financial management and health care. Previously, she was Senior Vice President of Executive Development at Putnam Investments where she initiated a development program for high-potential executives and served as executive coach to those individuals. Prior to that, as Director of Leadership and Associate Development at Blue Cross and Blue Shield of Massachusetts, she developed an award-winning competency-driven human resources architecture, including training and development, performance management, selection, and succession planning components. At New England Medical Center she built the training, organization development, and total quality management functions. Strumpf has presented at numerous national conferences on executive coaching, HR architecture design, and leadership. She holds a master's degree in education from Simmons College. She can be reached at casey.strumpf@fmr.com.

GAE WALTERS is an international consultant, researcher, and executive coach with expertise in personality assessment and research statistics. She began her research into team dynamics and leadership development while teaching Tests and Measurements at the Rollins College graduate school. Subsequently she joined the faculty of the Center for Applications of Psychological Type, was elected to the board of directors, and served two terms as chairperson. She is also a charter member of the Disney Institute faculty. Prior to establishing her own consulting practice, Walters was Vice President of Organizational Development for the Ritz Carlton Hotel Company where she developed the executive leadership program. She has provided training and consultation throughout Eastern and Central Europe, Asia, the Americas, and the Caribbean. She received her master's degree in behavioral psychology and an educational specialists degree in psychometrics from Rollins College. She can be reached at GaeINTP@cs.com.

KATHRYN WILLIAMS is a partner and Chairman of the Board of KRW International. She has served on the faculties of the Bowman Gray School of Medicine and the Babcock Center of Management Development, Wake Forest University. She also has served as an adjunct faculty member of the Center for Creative Leadership. Williams cofounded Spectrum, a Center for Psychological Services, in 1975 and served as a principal of that organization until she joined KRW in 1990. She has served as an executive coach for the most senior executives in a wide variety of Fortune 500 companies, working with individuals as well as groups and teams. In the past year, she has worked internationally with executives from India, the United Kingdom, and Belgium. She also serves on the President's Advisory Council of the Gorbachev State of the World Forum, co-chairing two roundtables of global leaders, who addressed the issues of uncommon leadership and corporate responsibility for the emotional, spiritual, and economic well-being of the planet in the twenty-first century. Williams holds a doctoral degree in clinical psychology from The Fielding Institute. She can be reached at Williams@krw-intl.com.

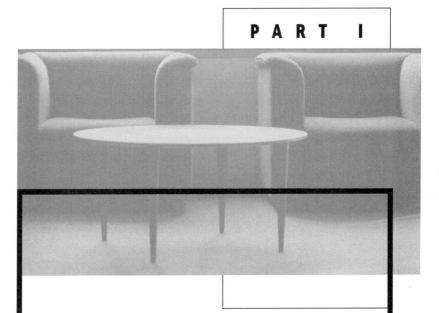

PART I

EXECUTIVE COACHING

PERSPECTIVES

A COACH'S LESSONS LEARNED

Principles and Guidelines for Practitioners

DAVID COLEMAN

During the past fifteen years, I have served as coach to a number of lawyers, economists, accountants, and scientists whose jobs entailed managing the work of others. Some of this work was part of a formal coaching program designed to support the management development of professionals (including those identified as high potential by their organizations). Other aspects were related to larger, organization development interventions, e.g., coaching leaders to prepare them for guiding their organizations through strategic planning processes. Still other aspects involved targeted interventions with key professionals who were highly valued for their technical contributions but were having difficulty managing others.

This chapter distills the key lessons learned through my work as an executive coach. It is divided into four parts:

- General principles to guide thinking about a client's issues
- General principles to guide taking action with a client
- Five paradoxical guidelines for engaging in the coaching conversation
- Practical suggestions that are specifically related to beginning coaches

Throughout, I will illustrate my points with examples from my practice, with names and situations altered to protect clients' confidentiality.

Principles for Thinking about a Client's Issues

There are six principles that inform how I understand my clients and the situations they face (Table 1). Some might describe these as principles of diagnosis, but I prefer to conceptualize them as principles for framing client issues and for identifying areas that may need to be examined more thoroughly as we begin our work together.

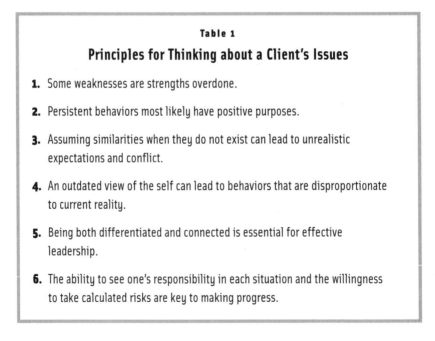

Table 1

Principles for Thinking about a Client's Issues

1. Some weaknesses are strengths overdone.

2. Persistent behaviors most likely have positive purposes.

3. Assuming similarities when they do not exist can lead to unrealistic expectations and conflict.

4. An outdated view of the self can lead to behaviors that are disproportionate to current reality.

5. Being both differentiated and connected is essential for effective leadership.

6. The ability to see one's responsibility in each situation and the willingness to take calculated risks are key to making progress.

Thinking Principle 1: Some Weaknesses Are Strengths Overdone

The very behavior that was key to our survival at some point in our lives often becomes overdone, thereby becoming a deficit (Atkins, 1982). This is my cardinal principle of coaching. I have observed with some regularity that a manager's problems are often caused by some trait or approach that was in the past a strength and a key to success. It makes sense that a manager might overuse an area of strength, that he or she might continue, or even increase, the behaviors that led to positive outcomes and promotions in the past. The dilemma is, of course, that the contexts and the manager's role within those contexts are continually changing. Thus, the behavior that was once essential to survival and/or success may be overdone (used too frequently, across too many contexts, or with inappropriate intensity) or overly relied on to the exclusion of other, more functional skills. As a result, the manager may not be able to grapple effectively with new contexts and new roles. When this happens, the once-productive behavior can actually begin to interfere with the manager's effectiveness and thereby becomes a weakness.

Framing weaknesses as overdone strengths may be comforting to clients as it normalizes the problem for them. Frequently, however, these overdone strengths are somewhat difficult to change because the manager's life experience categorizes this behavior as necessary for survival or success. The coach's goal then becomes to help the manager determine when and how to use this strength. Honoring the value of the strength in past situations while shaping its application in the present can have an enormous effect.

Let's illustrate this principle with an example. Gail, a senior executive, was known for her ability to shut out distractions and focus productively on work for extremely long periods. Only a few individuals truly understood the substantive issues in her highly complex and technical field, and Gail's ability to concentrate had been key to her being recognized and promoted to a managerial level, where she was responsible for other technical professionals. Yet, despite her senior position, Gail was regularly working all night to accomplish tasks. When I was asked to consult with her, her boss explained that she was isolated from her co-workers, did too much of the technical work herself, and was experiencing great personal pain due to problems that had developed with her spouse and three young children. On exploration, we discovered that Gail's focusing strategy had emerged in junior high school as a way to compete with older sisters who excelled socially and academically. Gail chose to become an expert in chemistry and later won first prize in the National Science Fair competition, thus garnering much acclaim from her academically oriented family and the faculty at her exclusive private high school.

Further investigation helped Gail understand how her ability to focus had led her to neglect the concerns of her family and employees as she attempted to maximize her own productivity at work. While exploring her personal and professional goals, it became clear that she hoped to achieve more balance in her life, including time for her family. She also wanted to develop the skills of her direct reports, despite some fears that she might make herself obsolete by training others to do everything she could do. As we explored these risks further, she decided she was willing to test the hypothesis that she would still have an essential role even if she groomed one of her ablest subordinates to handle a key area of her work. In addition, we made three lists:

- What parts of her job required her best focusing
- What parts of her job were adequately served by average focusing
- What parts of her job didn't require her focus at all

In this way, we were able to honor the highly valued strength of focusing and at the same time begin to determine those areas in which her focusing would produce the most value. We also set up a schedule of reminders for Gail to call and check in with her spouse, who worked alone at home.

Thinking Principle 2: Persistent Behaviors Most Likely Have Positive Purposes

I typically assume that even the most destructive behaviors somehow made sense or were useful at some point in a person's life. Identifying the benefits derived from a particular behavior can be helpful in trying to change it (Ferrucci, 1982). I assume positive intent, psychologically speaking, because I think the psyche contains a self-maintaining survival mechanism. The psyche adapts to challenges as efficiently as it can in order to protect and maintain the self. Thus, even an apparently self-destructive mechanism must have served some function critical to the survival or success of the self at some time if it continues to exist. Because colleagues do not always agree with me on this point, I want to offer the two reasons behind my potentially controversial view, one philosophical and one practical.

My philosophical reason for maintaining that even self-destructive behaviors must have produced a good outcome at some point in a person's life is my personal belief that, at the core, most of us see ourselves as good people. This is true regardless of whether we are effective at achieving behavior that others might think of as good.

Let's consider a professor I coached at a major university. Charles was young and very ambitious and had recently joined a rather laid-back graduate program. Students saw him as extremely demanding; for example, he often informed them of short and inflexible deadlines by leaving typed directives in their mailboxes. He could be seen only by appointment and for a limited time. When students were surveyed as part of the tenure decision-making process, Charles was devastated to learn that he was universally viewed as inconsiderate and self-centered, with little or no concern for others. I distinctly remember his tears as he told me, "I'm a good person. I admit I do all the things they accuse me of, but it's because I don't want to waste their time or my own. I want us both to succeed."

Charles had recently come from a school with a high-pressure graduate program where he almost, in his words, "flunked out." He had adopted his "keep to yourself" and "no wasted motion" efficiency as a means of surviving in that context. Indeed, he was convinced that this strategy had enabled him to land his first job, which he considered a prize. He expressed a deep desire to spend more time with students but was afraid that doing so would lead to failure at his new job. So behavior that initially appeared to students as insensitive and self-centered turned out to be more complicated. When he recognized both his effect on his new environment and his own good intentions, he was able to make some changes, and he became more approachable and less isolated.

My practical reason for assuming positive intent is that it allows more latitude in working with clients. The assumption makes it possible to lead with a more open and curious mind about behaviors that others find distasteful or unacceptable. Somehow, this openness and curiosity generates the spaciousness needed to develop new options for dealing with ineffective behaviors.

Thinking Principle 3: Assuming Similarities When They Do Not Exist Can Lead to Unrealistic Expectations and Conflict

Many of us naturally assume that everyone is just like us—in terms of interests, needs, skills, and knowledge. Thus, we operate in the world by trying to treat others as we would like to be treated. That works well when the people around us are indeed like us. Problems arise, however, when this is not the case.

In my experience, this assumption of similarity is particularly resistant to change, perhaps because without it, we must develop a far more complicated formulation of the world—and, for some, such a formulation can be overwhelming. Changing this assumption requires both time and energy, since we must think through our actions instead of responding automatically, as we could before.

In fact, I think most of us have to repeatedly relearn the fallacy of assuming similarity. When some clients become aware of their false assumptions of similarity, the second-level response is "Well, if they're not like me, they *should* be." (I have noticed this reaction repeatedly when, for example, members of the Baby Boom generation talk about those of Generation X.) Nevertheless, complaints of how others *should* be rarely lead to more effective working relationships with them. Recognizing the diverse interests and needs of those around us allows us to tailor our words and actions to our audience and ultimately increases our effectiveness.

This principle applies equally to both clients and coaches. Here are two examples. Clients often assume they should manage their direct reports exactly as they themselves prefer to be managed—with broad clear outcomes defined and with little or no direction or feedback. Such clients are usually surprised that others actually prefer closer supervision or more feedback. Coaches can make the mistake of assuming that clients are as interested as they are in what makes people tick or how interpersonal relationships work. These coaches may be surprised to learn that their clients want only the CliffsNotes™ version or the bottom-line practical idea rather than the whole theory from which the solution is derived.

Thinking Principle 4: An Outdated View of the Self Can Lead to Behaviors That Are Disproportionate to Current Reality

Most of us have an image of ourselves, like a still photograph, that guides much of what we do and how we express ourselves in the world. These images tend to be fixed at critical periods of our development and naturally come to represent our personal definitions of who we are. They organize our experience of self and simplify decision making by allowing us to choose certain courses of action almost automatically, because "that's the kind of person I am."

However, our lives are not like still photographs; they are more like movies—with spontaneous adaptations, growth, and changes brought on by our responses to life's circumstances. The still photographs that provide guides for our behavior can become seriously outdated—so much so that people who interact with us daily might not recognize our pictures of ourselves, which are quite different from their perceptions of us. When our self-images become significantly incongruent with current reality, then our actions may be less than effective. Sometimes 360-degree feedback exercises can help in identifying discrepancies between our internal and external realities. At other times, discrepancies can be discovered by a coach who listens carefully and with curiosity to a client's rationale for actions that may seem surprising or inappropriate. After acknowledging these discrepancies, coach and client can develop strategies to help the client think through actions that were previously automatic.

For example, I recall an executive, Michael, who was known for talking above other people and not listening well in meetings. This behavior did not fit at all with his view of himself as a wimp. Early in his career, Michael was told that he was not assertive enough and that he was going to be overlooked if he did not learn to speak his mind and stand up for himself. He took that criticism to heart and acted on it. Over time, he changed his behavior and became very assertive and outspoken. Nevertheless, he still saw himself as a wimp and compensated for that self-image by talking above others and not listening to them. When Michael realized he was no longer regarded as a wimp, he was able to experiment with new ways of behaving that produced more satisfying results.

Thinking Principle 5: Being Both Differentiated and Connected Is Esssential for Effective Leadership

This paradoxical principle from Bowen's family systems thinking expresses the importance of being clear about who we are and what we want while at the same time maintaining psychological contact with those who are different from us (Friedman, 1985). Most people have a tendency toward either differentiation *or* connection. Personal effectiveness, however, lies in doing both.

When I meet with clients, I often pay attention to how differentiated they are (i.e., how clearly they perceive their thoughts and feelings as separate from others' thoughts and feelings) and how connected they are (i.e., how well they stay in touch, particularly with those who are not like them).

To explore differentiation, I look for the following characteristics:

- The ability to know what one thinks and believes and why, regardless of popular or group opinion
- The ability to take a clear stand in the face of opposition
- Clarity about strengths and weaknesses, as both a manager and a human being
- The maturity to manage emotional reactivity—to act calmly and remain in touch with one's own view when others are upset or in active disagreement
- The ability to act with civility, respect, and courtesy—even when disagreeing

To explore connection, I look for these qualities:

- The ability to make psychological contact with me and with others, at both a human and a professional level
- The ability to demonstrate concern for and provide comfort to others through one's presence and words
- The ability to harmonize and smooth over differences in order to maintain group momentum

Ultimately, I am looking to see if clients can be both differentiated and connected to others, particularly with those who are different.

Thinking Principle 6: The Ability to See One's Responsibility in Each Situation and the Willingness to Take Calculated Risks Are Key to Making Progress

Block (1988) believes we all have two deep psychological needs: for innocence and for safety. Each has a price. The price we pay for innocence is helplessness. If we somehow do not see ourselves as contributing to our own problems (if we think we are innocent), then we have no influence and are unable to change them. The price we pay for safety is being stuck in the status quo. There is no risk-free path; in fact, doing nothing has its own risks. Even though we all want to be safe and comfortable, we are destined to remain in existing situations unless we are willing to take some calculated risks. Consequently, I always ask myself two questions:

- What are clients doing or not doing to contribute to their problems?
- In what aspects of each specific situation, or more generally in their work and personal lives, are they playing it too safe?

When I ask clients the first question, they sometimes respond with a list of actions they have taken to address the problem. To that, I respond, "No, those are your contributions to the solution. What are the ways in which you contribute to the problem itself?" If they still have no answer, then I might suggest that their inability to see how they are part of the problem might be the problem. I am assuming here that unless we can see ourselves inside the frame of the picture of our lives, including the problems we encounter, then we do not have the necessary perspective to make changes in that picture.

In asking clients the second question, I often seek to explore the costs and benefits of taking slightly more risk than is usual for them. In general, I try to encourage them to set challenging but realistic goals that will propel them forward.

Guiding Principles for Taking Action with a Client

In this section, my aim is to provide seven practical principles to guide our actions with clients (Table 2).

Action Principle 1: Listen, Listen, Listen

You have heard it before; nevertheless, I want to remind you again of the ever-increasing need for more and better listening to clients. Sometimes we mistakenly think that our greatest value as coaches lies in sharing our expertise and great ideas. However, in a high-speed world of action, most people are unable to satisfy their deep psychological needs to be seen and heard. Thus, I believe that good listening is increasing rather than decreasing in importance.

Table 2

Principles for Taking Action with a Client

1. Listen, listen, listen.

2. Observe how the client manages you.

3. Begin where the client is.

4. Use and build on the client's ideas.

5. Act as a bridge to what's missing.

6. Formulate changes as hypotheses that must be tested empirically.

7. If stuck, move to immediacy.

In fact, it probably is not possible to listen too much to your clients, especially in the early stages of the relationship. They will tell you what you need to know. Sometimes, when I do not know what to do, I simply try to ask another good open-ended question—just to keep the client talking—in the belief that we will be able to figure things out together if I listen well enough. Your ability to hear between the lines, to make connections among factors that may appear unrelated, is of particular value to them.

Action Principle 2: Observe How the Client Manages You

Your clients' ways of managing you will provide insight into how they conduct the rest of their lives. By noticing my own thoughts and feelings as I work with clients, I often pick up clues as to how others may be reacting to them. In addition, I am able to form valuable hypotheses about what they are doing to handle the problems in their lives.

For example, one client, Barbara, described in painstaking detail the mess she had inherited with her recent promotion. She told me of numerous incidents in which her predecessor had mismanaged both people and situations. As soon as she finished one anecdote, she launched into another about the ineptitude of her predecessor or her bosses. For more than an hour, she described the current state of affairs as being on the brink of disaster. Because this was our first session, I chose to follow the listening principle and not interrupt her. However, while she was talking, I made four observations: (1) that she focused exclusively on the past instead of the present or future, (2) that each situation was described in its worst possible terms, (3) that she allowed little room for my thoughts or reactions to the situations she described, and (4) that as time wore on, I began to feel overwhelmed myself, which is how I imagined she must feel.

By paying attention to our interactions in the moment (what she was saying, how she was managing the conversation with me, and my own reactions to it), I was able to develop hypotheses about this new client and her method of managing her situation. Eventually, I asked some questions with the purpose of determining which of these hypotheses was correct. Each hypothesis was explored for accuracy (was it valid?) and for functionality (did it really serve the client?). I then sought to use that information to work with her to change those aspects of her situation that she wished to change.

Action Principle 3: Begin Where the Client Is

In order to establish rapport with clients, it is important to understand how they see the world and to discover their goals and what they care about. From there, we can begin our work together (Shepherd, 1985). With time, it is possible to gently challenge a client's view and offer other ideas or approaches, but initially it is vital to be on the same wavelength. The metaphor of the tugboat and the ocean liner helps me understand this principle. How is it that a tiny tugboat can alter the course of a huge ocean liner many times its size? First, the tugboat approaches and makes contact with the ocean liner while they are still moving in the same direction. Slowly—very slowly—the tug nudges the liner in a different direction, until, eventually, the liner has taken on a new course.

In the same way, it is important for coaches to make contact with clients while they are moving in the same direction. Once this rapport has been established, coaches can ask questions and make gentle suggestions in order to nudge their clients toward more effective behaviors. (See the example following Action Principle 5.)

Action Principle 4: Use and Build on the Client's Ideas

I look for opportunities to agree with and support a client's ideas and suggestions. If, while struggling with an issue, the client comes up with an idea or suggestion that is generally in the right direction but slightly different from one I have proposed, I actively seek to support and build on that idea, even if I think mine is better. (However, I may attempt to help shape the idea to increase the likelihood that it will accomplish the client's goal.)

I actively support my clients' ideas because I want to build on *their* motivation to move in a more effective direction. Clients are more inclined to take action if they are working on their own ideas. I have observed too many organizations for which consultants have written beautiful reports filled with great ideas that are never translated into action. Since I aim for practical results in the real world, I want to do everything I can to encourage taking action. As a result, I am willing to be a cheerleader for the client's ideas as long as I can do so with integrity. (See the example following Action Principle 5.)

Action Principle 5: Act As a Bridge to What's Missing

One of the coach's key goals is to develop a more complete picture of the situation by filling in the missing pieces in the client's thinking or skills. For example, if the client is focused solely on structure and tasks, the coach might raise questions about process and people. A coach whose client is focused primarily on the external market might decide to explore the internal organizational environment. With a client who tends to concentrate on details in the present, the coach might begin asking gentle questions about the future and the big picture. If the coach does not have the necessary information or skills, he or she could act as a bridge to the appropriate resources and then encourage the client to seek them out.

The following example illustrates how Action Principles 3, 4, and 5 often work in tandem. The senior vice president of a large biotechnology company asked me to work with one of his subordinates, a vice president whom he described as hard-boiled. The vice president, George, was very results oriented, was technically brilliant, and had once been considered a rising star. However, in recent years, he had become sidetracked because of his interpersonal style, which others experienced as abrasive and know-it-all. The senior vice president informed George that he had a good chance at the next senior vice presidency—if he had a successor in place for his present position *and* could demonstrate that he had softened his interpersonal style so that key members of top management saw him as a team player.

In my first meeting with George, I listened carefully to his thoughts on the coaching process. I explored his long-term career goals, what he liked and disliked about his current role, and what results or outcomes he might want from a coaching relationship.

His most immediate concern was "how to put the screws" to his team of four direct reports who, he said, were wasting time and coming up with insufficient results. In line with Action Principle 3 (begin where the client is), I decided to explore this concern. I sought to help him define what "putting the screws" to his team would mean in terms of behavior (what he would be saying or doing) and outcomes (concrete results that could be measured). It turned out that George wanted clearer production targets and accountability. As we brainstormed about how to set clearer goals that his staff would feel obligated to meet, he mentioned that he rarely had time to hold staff meetings and that each of his direct reports operated with relative autonomy. Again, I followed his lead and asked him to explain the agenda and format for the few meetings that had taken place; I also sought his overall assessment of their effectiveness. Eventually, George came up with the idea of briefer but more frequent meetings during which staff members would report on their progress, thereby creating more public accountability among their colleagues.

In line with Action Principle 4 (build on the client's ideas), I actively encouraged George to establish these new meetings by identifying three explicit reasons why his approach was valuable. Having started where the client was, and then building on and encouraging his ideas, I thought I was ready to provide a bridge to what was missing (Action Principle 5). In this case, I saw the following as missing: (1) a more positive reason for setting clear goals and making his staff accountable than "putting the screws" to people, (2) sharing talk time in meetings instead of behaving like a know-it-all, and (3) providing more general support and encouragement to his staff as they sought to achieve their goals. With these ideas in mind, I began to suggest ways for making George's newly established meetings even more effective. By this time, because it was clear to him that I was willing to address an area of interest to him by using and building on his ideas, he was more open to my suggestions for achieving his ends.

Action Principle 6: Formulate Changes As Hypotheses That Must Be Tested Empirically

I believe it is essential to become a coinvestigator of work and life with a client. In taking a collaborative approach, I try to frame changes as hypothetical methods of improving the situation—hypotheses that must be tested by real-time practice. After the client has tried new behaviors, we jointly reflect on the outcome and try to determine whether the behavior led to the desired results. In these circumstances, I often propose that we take the mind of the empiricist, focusing on creating a hypothesis and then gathering data to test it.

An essential first step in implementing this principle is to help the client develop a personal and individual rationale for change. I do this by eliciting the client's response to questions such as "What are you dissatisfied with in your current situation? What's in it for you if you make some changes?" After exploring these questions, I seek to help the client develop a hypothetical idea of the results of the new behavior or approach. Sometimes, but not always, we work together to devise a way of measuring these outcomes. In my experience, if you truly implement this principle with an open mind and notice the results of the changes, then you can help the client fine-tune the changes to fit the unique characteristics of the situation.

Action Principle 7: If Stuck, Move to Immediacy

When I reach an impasse in my work with a client, or realize that we are going in circles, I find it helpful to describe my experience in the moment as neutrally as I can (Block, 2000). This shifts the focus from our immediate task (i.e., *what* we were trying to accomplish) to the process (i.e., *how* we were going about it), thus shifting the emphasis to the relationship between the client and myself and our way of working together. In an organization, the task is usually paramount, since organizations exist to perform a function. However, when the task is not getting accomplished, shifting the focus to the process or method can lead to getting unstuck (Weisbord, 1987).

When I feel the client and I are not making progress on an agreed-on task, describing my own experience in the moment (using neutral language) shifts the conversation to the relationship between the client and me and how we are working together in that immediate moment.

Alternatively, I may explore other aspects of the process that do not seem to be working at that moment: Do we have the right people in the room? Do we have the relevant information? Are we using an appropriate methodology? The shift from task to process accomplishes three things: (1) it broadens the discussion to include the relationship and the process, (2) it is likely to increase the attention and interest of both parties, and (3) it opens the door for more psychological contact by acknowledging our human reaction to our work together. Three brief examples follow.

First, imagine that a client is providing such an excruciating level of detail about each nuance of his situation that you are having a hard time concentrating on the major issues. In this case, you might say something like, "You're giving me more details than I need," and follow your statement with silence. That will usually provoke a discussion of the reasons for the client's behavior or may lead to some change in the process. Second, imagine that the client is talking slowly in a listless monotone about a critical situation that could cause her to lose her job. You find yourself getting bored, and your attention begins to wander. You might say, "It's getting hard for me to pay attention. You're speaking so slowly and without much energy, yet this seems like such a critical issue. What's going on from where you sit?" This will often lead to a deeper discussion about the client's thoughts or feelings. At a minimum, it may result in a temporary change in approach. Third, perhaps you find yourself going over the same points repeatedly without making much progress. You might say, "I think we're going in circles here. Why do you think we're not making progress?" This should lead to a discussion of what might be required in order to make progress.

Five Paradoxical Guidelines for the Coaching Conversation

In this section, I offer five specific—and somewhat paradoxical—guidelines for engaging in the coaching conversation, along with concrete descriptions of how each guideline might look in day-to-day practice. These guidelines may be used as a checklist for evaluating each coaching conversation:

- Lead with warmth as well as professional distance
- Balance challenge with support

- Link hard with soft, and soft with hard
- Focus on yourself to clarify client issues
- Listen well but do not automatically accept the client's framing of the issues

Guideline 1: Lead with Warmth As Well As Professional Distance

Early in an executive coaching relationship, warmth (conveyed through the expression of personal caring and concern for clients and their situations) and distance (conveyed through objectivity) are both necessary to establish an effective working relationship. It is your challenge as coach to determine which side you are most inclined to lead with and then take steps to ensure that the other side is well represented in your early interactions with a new client. If you tend to lead with too much warmth, you can strike a balance with professional distance by taking some of the following approaches:

- Explore the client's reasons for making changes, sometimes even playing devil's advocate if you are given a politically correct rationale.
- Ask questions concerning why making changes is in the client's best interests.
- Refrain from using personal examples, particularly self-deprecating ones, too early in the relationship.

If your tendency is to lead with professional distance, the following procedures will help you demonstrate more warmth:

- Spend more time establishing rapport and learning about the client's history and personal situation.
- Smile and use more head nods than is typical for you in early meetings.
- Express interest about items (for example, pictures, sculptures) you find in the client's office.
- Bring articles or resources of particular personal or professional interest to the client.

Guideline 2: Balance Challenge with Support

The challenges faced by executives in today's fast-paced, highly competitive markets coupled with the fact that most organizations are a "wasteland of support" (Block, 1988) lead to a net shortage of support for most executives in most organizations. Offering support in ways that are acceptable to executives can be a challenge. Successful methods might include the following:

- End meetings by telling clients three things you liked in the day's interaction.
- Send one-sentence e-mails of congratulation for successes both large and small.
- Ask clients what they liked about their performance and what they would do differently.

Other ways to balance support and challenge might include the following:

- Make sure your voice is supportive (use an even tone with no edge, softer volume, slower speed) when delivering tough confrontational messages.
- Hold on to your vision of your clients' "best selves," while recognizing their limitations.
- Suggest that clients "protect their hearts" when you have a hard truth to share.

Guideline 3: Link Hard with Soft, Soft with Hard

I almost never explore soft skills—such as listening, giving and receiving feedback, and confronting others—without exploring my clients' business contexts. Although I think soft skills are important, I seek a business reason for struggling with the difficult process of changing them, because having a practical rationale developed by clients themselves makes it easier to justify the effort. Clients often feel hopeless about their ability to grapple with difficult human problems and may need to be reminded of the concrete business reasons for participating in what may appear to be an emotionally draining activity.

Similarly, I often describe soft skills in harder, crisper language, which often makes them more palatable to many executives. For example, I will say that there are "four predictable steps in emotional reactions to negative feedback" or "three key variables to the Situational Leadership model." Another strategy involves articulating the principles and rationale for trying new approaches whenever possible. For some managers, this seems to legitimize trying new behaviors.

Guideline 4: Focus on Yourself to Clarify Client Issues

Because much of the work of coaching deals with complex and ambiguous situations, coaches must be able to use their own thoughts and feelings as data about what is happening with clients. Through various means, including therapy, twelve-step programs, personal growth workshops, and family of origin work, coaches must explore their own inner lives to calibrate their typical reactions to many different situations. This knowledge will enable them to distinguish between their typical reactions and those that may arise from some aspect of their clients and/or their clients' situations. Coaches can then use their own internal reactions as essential clues to sorting out what is going on and how to proceed.

In addition, Bowen's family systems thinking (Friedman, 1985) has taught me about the strong influence exerted by a calm presence in circumstances of high anxiety and emotional reactivity. Bowen believed that the only way to develop a calm presence is by working on our relationships with our families of origin. This work enables us to focus on the one person in the world we can control, namely ourselves. By doing this, we can clarify what we think, manage our emotional reactivity to clients, and stay emotionally in contact with clients. Thus, paradoxically, continuing to focus and work on *ourselves* deepens our capacity for calmness and enables us to apply our best powers of observation and thinking to our clients and their situations.

Guideline 5: Listen Well But Do Not Automatically Accept the Client's Framing of the Issues

The paradox here is that coaches must listen well in order to see and understand how their clients perceive their own situations while simultaneously keeping in mind alternative ways of framing those situations. Listening so well that clients feel heard and appreciated for themselves adds to the value of the calm presence we discussed above. Often, particularly when clients are confused by complex situations, the active listening skills of paraphrasing and reflecting can help them sort things out.

Alternatively, the ability to offer different views of situations can also be enormously helpful in achieving clarity and/or developing new approaches. Peter Block (1988) says, "We are all born on the wrong side of our eyes." I believe he is alluding to the fact that it is often easier to be objective and clear-sighted about other people's lives than it is to look with similar clarity at our own. Block believed that, even more than our recommendations or remedies, our most important gift to clients consists of offering a different way of thinking about the situations they face. He believed, as I do, that with a different view, clients can develop their own new solutions. Following are some practical suggestions related to this broad guideline:

- As Stephen Covey says, "Seek first to understand; then to be understood" (1989, p. 237).

- Lead with curiosity when confronted with things that are surprising, that seem wrong, or that you don't understand.

Practical Suggestions for Beginning Coaches

In this final section, I want to pass along some lessons learned that I think will be particularly helpful for beginning coaches. I have divided these lessons into two categories: beginner's mistakes and hooks to avoid.

Beginner's Mistakes

Learning any new set of skills requires practice. Sometimes we can benefit from those who have gone before by learning from their mistakes. I describe the following three mistakes, from my early career as a coach, in the hope that new colleagues can avoid repeating them.

Taking on the Wrong Pole of an Internalized Conflict by Showing Enthusiasm Too Early

One of my early mistakes was showing too much enthusiasm, largely through head nods, smiles, and "mm-hms," when executives made socially acceptable statements reflecting good human resources practices because they thought that was what I wanted to hear. By not asking them to articulate their own reasons for changing, I allowed them to put me in the position of having to defend effective human resources practices. This gave them the opportunity to repeat well-rehearsed arguments against change. I believe that in taking one side of a polarized internal conflict, I allowed the clients to argue for the other side. This did not serve them or me. Let me explain with the following example.

Imagine that an executive has received feedback from a 360-degree instrument administered by the coach that she needs to deal with a long-standing personnel issue. The executive accepts the validity of the feedback because she realizes that one situation in particular has gone on for too long and has had negative effects on her group's overall morale. Yet she also knows that the person in question is stubborn, argumentative, and difficult, which means that confronting him will consume an enormous amount of time and emotional energy. Thus, she has already created an internalized conflict about whether or not to have this difficult conversation.

If, as the coach and client begin to explore the situation, the coach expresses too much enthusiasm when the executive first says, "I really should confront this person," then it is quite possible that the client will go on to express all the reasons why such a course of action would be too costly or unsuccessful. This puts the coach in the position of having to repeat the reasons *for* attempting this difficult conversation. Ultimately, the client may be less likely to do what she needs to do. If, however, the coach's initial response is neutral ("Say some more about that") or even skeptical ("Why would you want to do that?"), the executive might feel the need to articulate her own reasons for tackling such an unpleasant task. In my experience, this would probably lead the executive to take action because it was her own idea to do so.

Taking Debate Personally

My second beginner's mistake was to take a client's debate, argument, and resistance as somehow personally directed at me. I have come to realize that many tough-minded managers view debate and argument as their way of processing and taking in new information. Unless they do this, they have not chewed sufficiently on an idea to digest it. I was often astounded, in a coaching session with a manager, to find that the very suggestions the client had vigorously *opposed* in the previous session were already fully implemented. I have learned to think of arguments as a key way by which these managers connect with me. I also have learned not to take personally whether clients follow my advice. Their decisions typically have little to do with my competence or the quality of the ideas I suggest. We all change at our own pace and must be allowed the freedom to do so.

Sharing Opinions Too Early

A third beginner's mistake, which I confess I still make at times, is to share my views, opinions, and/or judgments before clients are convinced that I fully understand the uniqueness of their situations. My intuition frequently serves me well, and, at this stage of my practice, I have often seen situations that resemble those presented by a client. However, if I venture forth too early with my views, without listening fully to the nuances of my current client's situation, I risk being discounted because I have not gotten some important part of it right. As mentioned previously, it is not possible to listen too much in the earliest stages of a new relationship. The more information I have, the more I can tailor my questions and suggestions to the unique situation of the person I am coaching.

Hooks to Avoid

Sometimes coaches get hooked into roles or positions that do not serve them or their clients. In the following section, I describe three ways in which I have been hooked.

Delivering the Performance Improvement Message

The first hook arises in situations of corrective coaching, when I am often asked to communicate the problem as well as work on its solution. Conveying the need to improve performance hooks me into a managerial role at the same time that I must attempt to work in a collabortive coaching role. To avoid getting hooked into dual roles, I usually help the prospective client's manager shape the message that is to be delivered to that client. We then begin the coaching process with a three-way meeting that includes the manager, the client, and myself. In this meeting, I try to have the manager clarify the issues to be addressed by the coaching, how progress will be checked, our timetable, and any limitations to the work.

Offering Advice That Is Outside the Coach's Competence

A second hook to avoid is making decisions or suggesting actions that are really the sole prerogative of the manager. Often, once your credibility is established, clients may begin to ask for your view on issues on which you are not qualified to comment. It takes considerable self-awareness and self-restraint to refrain from offering your views. One noted management consultant, Michael Doyle (Doyle and Strauss, 1984), has asserted that the major shadow issue for facilitators and coaches is the wish to have the power and authority of the managers with whom they work. This hook is tied up with our own needs for power and authority. We may know about these needs, or they may remain in the shadows. Nevertheless, they could hook coaches into making suggestions that overstep their role as coach or exceed the inevitable limits on their knowledge, skills, and abilities.

Confusing Which Issues Belong to the Coach and Which Belong to the Client

The last hook I will mention is, in actuality, a series of hooks to avoid. Coaches must know themselves, and they must be especially cognizant of those lifelong personal issues that will likely come to the fore in their interactions with smart, capable, powerful people. These personal issues have roots in our earliest relationships with our families of origin and with our first teachers. It is important, for example, to know whether your typical response to authority is challenge, compliance, or avoidance of further contact. It is also important to know the psychological reasons that draw you to this work. Are you motivated by getting results in the world, having influence, achieving closeness, or some other need? How do you react to power dynamics such as being kept waiting or being seated in a chair that is lower than the executive's? What do you do when stressed or under pressure?

Being aware of how you react to these types of situations can help you separate what is typical for you and what may be attributable to your relationships with particular clients. Knowing yourself gives you the tools to calibrate yourself as an instrument of change. Through self-exploration and discovery, you can determine which aspects of your responses are yours and which aspects may be providing you with information about your clients. In this way, you can avoid the hook of mistakenly assigning your own personal issues to your clients.

Conclusion

In this chapter, I have tried to articulate some of the lessons I learned in my fifteen years as an executive coach. By offering general principles that guide my thinking and actions, I have attempted to provide a framework that will assist colleagues in their work as executive coaches. The more specific guidelines for engaging in the coaching conversation are meant to illustrate the sometimes paradoxical tactics required in this work. Finally, by offering pointers to beginning coaches, I hope to help new colleagues avoid the mistakes I made as a beginner and prevent them from getting hooked into roles or positions that are not particularly helpful. Executive coaching is a rewarding field that is increasingly valued in organizations. I hope the principles and guidelines articulated here contribute both to the field and to the success of my colleagues.

References

Atkins, S. (1982). *The name of your game: Four game plans for success at home and at work*. Beverly Hills, Calif.: Ellis & Stewart Publishing.

Block, P. (2000). *Flawless consulting: A guide to getting your expertise used* (2nd ed). San Francisco: Jossey-Bass/Pfeiffer.

————. (February, 1988). *Staff consulting skills—Part I: Contracting*. Workshop presented by Designed Learning, Inc., Plainfield, N.J.

Covey, S. R. (1989). *The 7 habits of highly effective people: Restoring the character ethic*. New York: Simon & Schuster.

Doyle, M., & D. Strauss. (1984). *Making meetings work*. New York: Berkeley Publishing Group.

Ferrucci, P. (1982). *What we may be: Techniques for psychological and spiritual growth through psychosynthesis*. New York: Putnam Books.

Friedman, E. H. (1985). *Generation to generation: Family process in church and synagogue*. New York: Guilford.

Shepherd, H. A. (December, 1985). Rules of thumb for change agents. *OD Practitioner*. South Orange, N.J.: Organization Development Network.

Weisbord, M. R. (1987). *Productive workplaces: Organizing and managing for dignity, meaning, and community*. San Francisco: Jossey-Bass.

LEADERSHIP AND COMPLEXITY OF MIND

The Role of Executive Coaching

JENNIFER GARVEY BERGER

CATHERINE FITZGERALD

This chapter concerns a relatively new field of study—the development of complexity of mind in adults and the ways in which understanding that development affects those who work to support adults.

We have all known for some time that children and adults see vastly different worlds. For example, spend fifteen minutes with a three-year-old on an airplane, and you'll discover that, for her, the cars below actually *are* tiny cars, driven by tiny people and parked in tiny garages, and that, after you land, the cars—and the people and garages—grow large again. This kind of "magical thinking," as it has been described (Fraiberg, 1959), disappears fairly early in children's lives. The world changes as children discover that the size of objects is constant, regardless of how far from the objects they themselves move. The world becomes stabler, and we say—sometimes with nostalgia, sometimes with great relief (often with both)—that the children have *developed*.

Those who study adult development, however, are learning that such drastically different ways of looking at the world may well continue throughout a person's life span. The magical thinking of a three-year-old who believes cars grow and shrink may become the magical thinking of a thirty-year-old who watches a report transform from an accomplishment of which to be proud, when his colleague praises it, into a source of shame, when his manager criticizes it. This chapter explores the implications of adult development for executive coaching, arguing that if coaches are to be able to support leaders well, it is vital that they understand the many different worlds these leaders may inhabit.

We have worked with clients from a diverse array of organizations—from Fortune 500 companies to struggling Internet start-ups, from leaders of schools to leaders of the military. We have seen a wide variety of differences in the external worlds these leaders inhabit: in the public, private, and nonprofit sectors; in local and multinational companies; in stable and emerging technologies. One of the most difficult differences to understand, however, is found not in the external world of the executives with whom we work, but in the internal complexity with which those executives view that world. The constructive-developmental theory of Robert Kegan (1982, 1994) offers us a powerful way to understand the complexity of mind of the leaders with whom we work—and to support the development of complexity.

Executive coaches bridge the two different—but clearly interacting—worlds of the executive and the executive's organization. A good coach knows that it is vital to have a sense of the key corporate issues that surround the executive and, also, that he or she must understand those issues both from the executive's perspective and from the perspectives of others in the organization. Often, the way an executive makes meaning of key corporate issues—rather than the issues themselves—shapes the work of the coaching.

Kegan's work focuses on the ways in which people make meaning of the world around them. As a constructive-developmental psychologist, Kegan, like other constructivists, believes not that the world is out there to be discovered but that we create our world through our interaction with and interpretation of it. Like other developmentalists, Kegan believes that humans grow and change over time and enter qualitatively different phases in the process. Kegan's framework is powerful because he joins these two schools of thought and suggests a clear pattern for the development of the systems by which people make meaning.

This chapter focuses on two key aspects of Kegan's work:

- The movement from Subject to Object—the basic process for becoming more complex
- Orders of mind—five qualitatively different ways of constructing reality, which develop from less to more complex

For each of these aspects of Kegan's theory, the following sections define the concepts and explain the theory surrounding them, outline the implications for executive coaching practice, and suggest ways in which executive coaches can support the performance and development of executives through an understanding of these concepts.

The Movement from Subject to Object

The more elements we can see, respond to, and make decisions about, the more complex a view we have. Kegan's theory explicates this idea and suggests ways to increase the number of elements we have under our control.

The Theory

Kegan distinguishes between *informational* learning, which is new knowledge added to the current form of one's mind, and *transformational* learning, or learning that changes the very form of one's mind, making it more spacious, more complex, and more able to deal with multiple demands and with uncertainty. According to Kegan (1994), transformation occurs when we develop the ability to step back and reflect on something that used to be hidden or taken for granted and to make decisions about it. He says transformative learning happens when someone changes "not just the way he behaves, not just the way he feels, but the way he knows—not just what he knows but the *way* he knows" (p. 17). Transformation happens in many ways; the most vital to Kegan is the movement of things from *Subject* to *Object.*

In Kegan's scheme, things that are Subject are by definition experienced as unquestioned, simply a part of the self. They can include many different things—a theory, a relational issue, a personality trait, an assumption about the way the world works, behaviors, emotions—and they can't be seen because they are the lenses through which we see. For this reason, they are taken for granted, taken for true—or not even taken at all. We generally can't name things that are Subject to us, and we certainly can't reflect on them—that would require the ability to stand back and take a look at them. We don't *have things* that are Subject; things that are Subject *have us.*

Things that are Object, however, can be seen and considered, questioned, shaped, and acted on. Something that is Object can be a theory, a relational issue, a personality trait, a belief, behaviors, or emotions. And, while things that are Subject *have us,* we *have things* that are Object. Because it isn't the lens through which we see, something that is Object can be held out and examined. Although we each necessarily have many parts of our world that are Subject, one key aspect of development involves moving more and more things from Subject to Object. The more we take as Object in our lives, the more complex our worldview becomes because we can see, reflect on, be responsible for, and act on more things.

Implications for Practice

Understanding the movement from Subject to Object has profound implications for executive coaching practice for three reasons. First, although executive coaching often focuses on increasing the executive's knowledge or skill, a substantial amount of executive coaching involves helping executives make Subject–Object shifts. In many cases, this happens when coaches help executives surface and examine their hidden assumptions about the world. Uncovering these assumptions can lead to important insights for executives. The following are some examples of insight that involve a Subject–Object shift:

- *I was always the responsible one in my family and I guess I ended up controlling things. I've been talking about empowering staff, but I haven't really been willing to give up control.*

- *I was taught that being loyal to my boss and my company came first, but now I see that doing the right thing can be much more important than loyalty.*
- *I always prided myself on being the smartest and the quickest person in the room. It's amazing to realize that I'm keeping my staff dependent on me by always having the answer first and that by doing so I'm keeping them—and me—from being more successful.*

If coaches can identify when a client is working on a move from Subject to Object and if they are skillful in supporting that move, they will be more successful in helping their clients both be effective and develop.

Second, it is essential for coaches to realize that the movement from Subject to Object is more challenging than it may appear. Clients may have difficulty seeing the limitations of ways of understanding and dealing with the world that have worked well for them and that they experience as coherent. Kegan notes that the first impulse of those who make discoveries about the limited nature of their beliefs, assumptions, or worldviews is *not* to welcome that discovery. Instead, people work to change the shape of the world itself by selectively ignoring data, eliciting particular responses, or making creative interpretations of events such that the belief, assumption, or worldview might remain true.

In addition, no matter how valuable and important it might seem to hold on to and examine an insight as Object, the insight tends to fade and become Subject again. This tendency for insights to be reabsorbed as Subject accounts for the familiar experience of encountering an important new insight and realizing that you made the same discovery in, say, a conflict situation last year, a workshop two years ago, and in therapy five years ago. It also explains why a client can have a critical new insight during a coaching session, and be very taken by and influenced by the insight, and then in a short time be back to business as usual, behaving as if the insight had never taken place. Kegan and Lahey (2001) suggest that we need to consciously build some "psychological muscle" over time so that we can hold out an insight as an Object to be examined instead of reabsorbing it as Subject again. (See the Strategies section on pages 32 to 35 for ways of helping clients sustain the Subject–Object shift.)

This psychological muscle is hard to build because giving up a way of understanding oneself and/or one's world can be painful. Discussions about executive coaching typically pay little attention to the losses that can come with a change in belief or perspective. The adult development literature, on the other hand, explains why giving up an old belief might be associated with loss. Committing ourselves to a new belief means giving up an old one, actually losing our former sense of the world before we have fully articulated our new world (Belenky, Clinchy, Goldberger, and Tarule, 1986: Kegan, 1994; Perry, 1968).

Third, it is important for coaches to understand the Subject–Object shift because it represents an increase in complexity. Although the movement may seem fairly small (and perhaps straightforward and even obvious to the coach), an increase in complexity can shake up a client's way of seeing and dealing with the world, thus affecting the client's self-concept, relationships, goals, and plans. The assumption that the world was flat—which fourteenth-century Europeans accepted as *fact*—made ocean travel terrifying and extremely limited. The simple questioning of that assumption—which seemed ludicrous at the time because the assumption seemed so obvious and *true*—opened up the oceans and greatly expanded the known world. Tiny shifts in what seems possible can literally change the world.

Executive coaches must understand and respect their clients' inclinations to hold on to their previous notions of the way that the world works—even as they try to influence those notions and help make them more complex.

Strategies for Supporting the Movement from Subject to Object

There are two aspects to supporting a Subject–Object shift in executive coaching:

- Recognizing when a client is dealing with a Subject–Object shift
- Providing support for understanding and maintaining a Subject–Object shift

Each is addressed below.

Recognizing When a Client Is Dealing with a Subject–Object Shift

A client may need to make a Subject–Object shift when she reports feeling stuck or at her wit's end, or when a client who is typically articulate, perceptive, and resourceful becomes uncharacteristically tongue-tied, muddled, or helpless.

David, an executive coach, was coaching Jeanne, an executive who was seen as very smart and capable and had risen quickly to a key position in her company. Jeanne talked with David about how burned out she felt and discussed her concerns about neglecting both her health and her life outside of work. After some brainstorming, Jeanne agreed, as a first step, to set some modest limits on her work hours. However, after a number of coaching sessions, she expressed frustration with her lack of progress with setting limits. It became clear that Jeanne was driven by something she could neither name nor see that was making it difficult for her to cut back. David inquired about Jeanne's earlier work history, and after an intense discussion of her aspirations for the future, Jeanne realized that she was driven by the belief that if she wasn't constantly the fastest-rising star, she would lose all of her hard-earned success and quickly sink into mediocrity and failure.

Like Jeanne in the case above, a client may have identified both her central problem (overworking) and a possible solution (setting modest limits on her hours) and—even with the best of intentions and plenty of motivation to make the change—still seem unable to change her behavior. Jeanne is mired in her earlier paradigm and can't seem to keep a clear and constructive view of the problem or move toward resolving it. To help such a client escape the paradigm, a coach needs to be able to recognize that the client is stuck and to support her in both seeing the paradigm and seeing a way out of it.

Providing Support for Understanding and Maintaining a Subject–Object Shift

Once a Subject–Object shift has been identified, the newly recognized existing belief must be treated with seriousness and respect. Kegan (1994) reminds us that, to be a supportive, useful structure, "a bridge must be well anchored on either side" (p. 37). In other words, coaches must have respect for and pay close attention to their clients' current beliefs as well as to the more complex way of understanding the issues at hand they hope to encourage in their clients. (See Chapter 6 for a related approach.)

Kegan (1995; see also Kegan and Lahey, 2001) postulates five steps that may help a belief about the world move from Subject to Object:

- Naming the belief
- Noticing the implications of the belief
- Looking for discrepant evidence
- Charting the history of the belief
- Testing the truth of the belief

Kegan's suggested first step toward making Subject into Object is simply to know that it exists, to name it. Once Jeanne named what she felt was the root of her behavior, she was able to reflect on it. The important change here wasn't discovering the behavior—after all, she knew she had been driven for most of her adult life—but discovering the *root* of the behavior.

Kegan asserts that the second step in changing an assumption about the world is simply to notice how the assumption or belief changes the possibilities available to the person who holds it. Because Jeanne had previously believed—albeit unconsciously—that this behavior was the foundation of her success, she had been unable to make any changes, even though some aspects of that behavior were problematic. As soon as she named her belief, however, she and David were able to take a more systematic look at how it was interfering in her life.

After spending some time simply paying attention to the way her belief worked in her life, Jeanne was ready for the third step—looking for any evidence that might cast even a small amount of doubt on her assumption. She recalled the times she had been compelled to take time off from work—for an illness, for example—and realized that her world had not fallen apart nor had she lost all that she had worked so hard to attain.

The fourth step in Kegan's approach is to go back and look for the roots of our beliefs and try to identify where and when they first began to operate in our lives. Jeanne discovered that her belief came from being one of many children in her family, performing unexceptionally in elementary and high school, and attending a middle-of-the-road state university. Once at the university, she began to push herself hard and found that she could excel. She had continued to push herself ever since.

For the fifth step, Kegan recommends constructing small tests of our assumptions or beliefs, trying to see how our experiences and actions might be different if they were based on different assumptions or beliefs about the world. The shift from Subject (something that is assumed or unexamined) to Object (something that is reflected on and that therefore can be changed) may sound like a small change, but it can open up many new opportunities for the client.

One of the most powerful interventions coaches can provide is simply to help keep critical insights alive for their clients in order to support the movement of a belief from Subject to Object. Without both internal willingness and external support, any insight can quickly become Subject again.

For Jeanne, the Subject–Object shift did not mean that she gained complete control of her world and established an optimal life/work balance. She still thinks of herself as a driven person. But she has realized that she doesn't have to keep such a vigilant watch over things, that she can take time off for a vacation and not worry about job security, and that enjoying her personal life isn't the end of her professional life. She may always work hard, but she now feels more in control of the pace of her work life and less at risk of burning out.

Orders of Mind

In addition to describing the *process* of movement (from Subject to Object), Kegan's theory also describes qualitatively different *stages*—or Orders—along the developmental journey.

The Theory

The most profound example of a move from Subject to Object is when the entire meaning-making system moves from that which unquestioningly runs the person involved to that which the person can actively control. The slow but measurable[1] shift of entire systems from Subject to Object is what gives form to different Orders of mind in Kegan's theory. These Orders involve five ways of constructing reality, ranging from the way of a two-year-old to that of a person well into the second half of life.[2] Each Order represents a qualitative shift in meaning making and complexity from the Order preceding it. In moving from one Order to the next, we do not give up what we've already learned; we transform our relationship to it, moving it from the lens through which we see to one among several possible alternatives to be seen and acted on.

Perhaps the most important thing to remember about the Orders is that, although they become more complex with time, no Order is inherently better than any other (just as a more complex idea isn't necessarily more valuable than a simple one). Our clients can be kind or unkind, just or unjust, moral or immoral while they are at any of these Orders; it is impossible to measure a person's worth—or judge his or her satisfaction with his or her life—by looking at that person's Order of mind. What is more important is the *fit* between the Order of mind and the tasks required of each person.

The five Orders of mind are described briefly below; note especially the ones at which the majority of adults spend most of their lives—the Third and Fourth Orders of mind.

The First Order

Kegan's First Order is made up almost entirely of young children. Executive coaches do not work with those who inhabit this Order, but it serves as a useful reference point because the differences between this world and the others are so easy to see.

People in this Order cannot yet hold the idea that things in the world retain the same qualities over time. They believe they can slip down the bathtub drain because they can't hold themselves as different from the water that slips away. The First Order is a time of magic and mystery, with the world changing inexplicably from moment to moment.

The Second Order

Kegan's Second Order was once thought to belong exclusively to older children and young adolescents, but there is increasing evidence that adults can spend many years here as well. Therefore, while it is unlikely that executives are still operating at this Order of mind, at least some people in their organizations probably live in this world.

When people learn that objects stay the same regardless of their own relationship to them (when I walk away from the car, it looks smaller, but it isn't actually shrinking), their world becomes less magical and more complex. They discover that their beliefs and feelings also remain constant over time (I love chocolate but hate mashed potatoes; I'm good at math even if I can't do this problem). This insight helps them understand that other people have feelings and beliefs that remain constant, too. Second Order children—and adults—are self-centered and see others as helpers or barriers on the road to attaining their desires. If they do not break rules, it's because they are afraid of being caught; when friends don't lie to each other, it's because they fear retaliation.

The Third Order

People can begin to enter the Third Order during adolescence, and there is a great deal of evidence that they can live much or all of their lives in this Order. Studies have shown that a surprisingly large percentage of adults— of all ages, occupations, and socioeconomic classes—inhabit this world (Kegan, 1994, pp. 192–195).

At the Third Order, people no longer see others as simply a means to an end; they have internalized one or more systems of meaning (their family's values, a political or national ideology, a professional or organizational culture). They have developed the ability to subordinate their desires and be guided by the norms and standards of their meaning system(s). Their impulses and desires, which were Subject to them in the Second Order, have become Object. They now internalize the ideas or emotions of others who represent their meaning system and are guided by the ideologies, institutions, or people that are most important to them. They are able to think abstractly, are self-reflective about their actions and the actions of others, and are devoted to something that's greater than their own needs. It is as if, in their growth from the Second Order, those at the Third Order have welcomed a board of directors into their decision making and now have the ideas or voices of important others with them as they make their decisions.

The major limitation of this Order shows up when there is a conflict between important ideologies, institutions, or people. At such times, people at the Third Order feel torn in two and cannot find a way to make a decision. If, for example, someone at the Third Order has internalized—and really believes—some of the culture of his organization (e.g., that levels of power should be collapsed and managers should consult with their staff about decisions) and has also internalized the ideology of his culture (e.g., that consulting with others shows that you do not know the answers yourself and is a sign of weakness), he will feel stuck when it comes to making decisions the Right Way. The person may turn to others to tell him how to best resolve the conflict and will become increasingly bewildered if there is no consensus about the resolution or if others counsel him to decide independently, saying that there is no Right Answer.

Because life often requires us to mediate between different ideologies, institutions, and/or key people in our lives, Kegan suggests that many people in the Third Order feel "in over their heads" much of the time. It is important to remember, though, that the Third Order is not a personality flaw to be corrected with appropriate intervention; it is a necessary point on a developmental continuum. Executive coaches who recognize this can have a vastly different perspective on their clients who are at the Third Order, as well as a more extensive set of tools with which to support them and their development.

The Fourth Order

The Fourth Order seems most familiar to those who work with adults because it is the Order that most closely resembles our modern image of the way adults are *supposed* to be. The most surprising thing about this Order, in fact, is that there are so many adults who have not yet reached this level of complexity.

Adults at the Fourth Order have achieved all that those at the Third Order have, and, in addition, they have created a *self* that exists even outside of its connection to the meaning systems and people surrounding it. The perspectives, opinions, and desires of the meaning systems they have adopted, which had great control over them when they were making meaning at the Third Order, are now Object to them. These individuals are able to examine and mediate among the various rule systems and opinions. The board of directors that was welcomed in the Third Order now undergoes a startling transformation. While the voices and ideas of important others are still internalized at the Fourth Order as they were in the Third Order, the great achievement of the Fourth Order is that the individual becomes the chairperson of the board.

Those at the Fourth Order have an internal set of rules and regulations—a self-governing system—that they use to make decisions and mediate conflicts. Unlike those at the Second Order, people at the Fourth Order feel empathy for others and take their wishes and opinions into consideration when making decisions. Unlike those at the Third Order, Fourth Order adults don't feel torn apart by the conflicts of different meaning systems because they have their own system within which to make decisions. These are the people we read about in the literature who "own" their work and are self-guided, self-motivated, and self-evaluative.

The Fifth Order

Kegan's Fifth Order is never seen before midlife, and then only rarely. Even though it is not commonly seen in the general population, this Order is important to our work because many senior executives are at midlife or beyond, and many of them may be developing toward the Fifth Order.

Adults at the Fifth Order have achieved all that those at the Fourth Order have, and, in addition, they have learned the limits of their inner system—and the limits of having an inner system in general. Instead of viewing others as people with separate and different inner systems, those at the Fifth Order can look across inner systems to see the similarities hidden within what previously looked like differences. Adults at the Fifth Order are less likely to see the world in terms of dichotomies or polarities. They are more likely to understand and deal well with paradox and with managing the tension of opposites. They are also more likely to believe that what we often think of as black and white are just various shades of gray whose differences are made more visible by the lighter or darker colors around them. While they still make use of their Fourth Order board of directors, people at the Fifth Order recognize its inherent frailties. They are more likely to consider the advantages not just of other opinions (which the board might entertain) but of entirely different forms of governing systems. For example, they may realize that their internal system itself contributes to their inability to perceive a wide field of alternatives.

A Historical Analogy for Orders of Mind

According to Kegan (1994), societal demands made at different points in human history are helpful for understanding the different Orders of mind and grasping why so many of us are now in over our heads—not yet developmentally ready to meet the demands placed on us. Kegan explores three historical eras—traditionalism, modernism, and postmodernism—and relates them to the Third, Fourth, and Fifth Orders, respectively. While it is clear that these societal eras are useful mostly as a developmental analogy, it's enlightening to look at the society at large and see how it makes demands on its citizens.

Traditionalism

Traditionalism has been the typical form of society around the world for much of human history. This society requires loyalty to the group and the ability to put the needs of the group before the needs of the self. People in traditional societies tend to live in the same place for long periods of time (perhaps even generations) with people who are similar (from the same tribe, religion, nationality, socioeconomic background). Leaders who espouse their society's ideologies (religious or philosophical leaders, doctors or healers, political leaders, leaders in the workplace) are part of their group. Members of this society look to these leaders or to other representations of the external theology or philosophies (scholarly or religious texts, for example) for the Right Answers to all kinds of problems. These leaders have the authority to help people raise their children, heal their sick, do their jobs, and live their lives by setting out a right action and right belief that others can confidently follow. For the most part, the demands of this society are suited to adults at the Third Order.

Modernism

The modern era began when people became more mobile and society was transformed from small, relatively homogeneous groups to larger, more diverse groups. Instead of belonging to and being committed to a small group, people in modern societies focus on Big Ideas—Science, Democracy, Freedom, Truth. No longer tied down to a single place or job, people move around more and are exposed to new ideas and to different kinds of people.

With the increase in diversity, as well as the increase in communication, group leaders are harder to identify—one of many competing doctors? one of a variety of religious leaders? one of the increasingly mistrusted political leaders? It is also less clear what to do when those leaders disagree. There is general disillusionment with external leaders and so-called heroes because these leaders and heroes are soon shown to be the flawed human beings they are. Because people in modern societies don't have leaders whom they trust, they must turn to other sources of wisdom on raising children, doing their jobs, and being citizens.

In this era, employers demand that people own their own work, become self-motivated, make their own decisions. The self-help section of bookstores continues to expand as people search for guidance. Individuals at the Fourth Order (less than half of all adults) are well suited to the demands of the modern age. The rest of us are in over our heads.

Postmodernism

Some say Postmodernism is here now, but others insist we're still firmly in a modernist world. Those who argue for postmodernism say that the Big

Ideas have failed us, that Truth doesn't exist. Rejecting both the old tribal systems and the search for Big Ideas, postmodern society fosters an awareness that we all belong to greater systems that are linked to one another and to this planet in important ways.

Instead of being enmeshed in a particular philosophy or ideology (which, at the Third Order or in traditional societies might come from external sources, and in the Fourth Order or in more modern societies might be self-constructed), those who exist in a postmodern manner can draw from many philosophies and ideologies, seeing the strengths and weaknesses inherent in all of them or in ideologies in general. They no longer seek to perfect a philosophy or idea; instead, postmodernists look at the ways in which dichotomous philosophies create one another and focus on the system that underlies the dichotomies. The very few who are at the Fifth Order are well suited to the demands of the postmodern age. Thus, in a postmodern world almost all of us are in over our heads.

Implications for Practice

We are still in an early stage in applying an understanding of Kegan's Orders of mind to executive coaching practice. However, we believe that the following observations are relevant to executive coaching:

- The amount of complexity executive roles require is variable.
- The amount of complexity executive roles require is probably increasing.
- The match between an executive's complexity of mind and the requirements of his or her role is critical for both effectiveness and job satisfaction.
- Development requires both challenge and support.

Each observation is discussed below.

The Amount of Complexity Executive Roles Require Is Variable
The complexity of mind an executive role requires is influenced by a number of factors, including the following:

- The characteristics of the role (the kinds of data that need to be gathered and grasped; the kinds of decisions that need to be made; the kinds of relationships that need to be developed; the clarity of objectives; the amount and nature of conflict to manage)

- The expectations regarding coordinated versus independent judgment and action (the amount of consultation and collaboration for decision making that is expected and considered acceptable by bosses, peers, and others; the degree of independence of thought and action that is expected and considered acceptable by bosses, peers, and others)

- The nature of the support provided by the executive's environment (the extent to which the policies, practices, and traditions of the organization provide adequate guidance to the executives; the amount of support for decision making provided by bosses, peers, and others)

We have developed three working hypotheses about the required complexity of mind in executive jobs:

- At a minimum, executive jobs require Third Order meaning making.

- Most executive jobs require Fourth Order meaning making.

- As executives develop beyond the Fourth Order, they may have the capacity to make additional and/or unique contributions to their organizations, but they may feel constrained by and/or dissatisfied with the nature and definition of many executive roles. Moreover, their additional and/or unique contributions may be invisible and undiscussable.

The Amount of Complexity Executive Roles Require Is Probably Increasing

There are a number of trends within organizations and marketplaces that are likely to lead to higher requirements for complexity in executives. These include

- An increase in the occurrence and speed of change

- An increase in the span of control of executives, which results in less time and attention for supporting their direct reports

- Greater ambiguity and uncertainty in decision making

- Less focus within many organizations on tradition and continuity in management and executive careers

The Match between Complexity and Role Requirements Is Critical

The match between an executive's complexity of mind and the require-ments of her role is critical for both effectiveness and job satisfaction. A role will be a poor match when it requires an Order of complexity that is higher or lower than the executive's capability.

When the role is over the head of the executive, she is likely to feel over-whelmed and inadequate. Executives often respond by trying harder; work-ing longer hours; and using all the skills, abilities, and resources at their command in an attempt to meet the expectations of the role. If the issue is a mismatch in complexity, however, additional effort is unlikely to be suc-cessful. (See pages 48 through 52 for suggestions about coaching executives who are in over their heads.)

When the role requires less complexity than the executive is capable of, the executive may be perceived as effective and successful but over time may begin to feel underutilized and unchallenged. A growing but often vague sense of dissatisfaction and frustration may occur, which can be difficult for both the executive and the organization to understand and resolve. (See pages 52 through 56 for suggestions about coaching executives who have outgrown their roles.)

Development Requires Both Challenge and Support

Development is difficult, so people tend not to develop unless they are chal-lenged in some way. Such challenges are presented by anything that prompts us to question whatever we take for granted. Some are self-created (moving to or spending time in another country, changing careers, going back to school as an adult, going into therapy); others result from external events (being fired, being promoted to a more complex position, losing a parent or spouse, going through a long illness). None of these events or situations causes development; in fact, it is quite possible to engage in nearly all these events without developing at all. Challenges such as those described will be experienced differently by different people and by those at different Orders of mind. Yet each new challenge, as long as it is combined with support, makes development possible.

Support is also a necessary ingredient in development. Because develop-ment can be filled with uncertainty and discomfort, people tend to slip back into more comfortable roles and ways of thinking—at least at first. Supporting people in their new ways of experiencing the world can help them hold on to the developmental aspects of these experiences and test their previous assumptions about the way the world works. Support, like challenge, can come from many different places (and people at different Orders of mind will probably be supported by different things). In a perfect world, each challenge would come with its own kind of support. In reality, however, people often have to be resourceful—and perhaps lucky—to get support that matches the challenges they are facing. For example, someone who gets a promotion at work—but not the necessary support on the job—could seek coaching to deal with the new challenges.

Strategies for Supporting the Performance and Development of Clients at Different Orders of Mind

Different executive coaching strategies may be appropriate for different situations:

- When there is a reasonably good fit between the complexity of mind of the executive and his or her role and environment
- When the executive's complexity is less than that required by his or her role or environment
- When the executive's complexity is greater than that required by his or her role or environment

Before describing possible strategies to use in these three circumstances, we offer a note of caution. In our view, it is never appropriate for an executive coach to insist that a client develop in a particular direction or manner or even that he or she develop at all. While development may have some advantages for a client, it also invariably comes, as mentioned earlier, at a cost. The executive coaching approaches we present here illustrate interventions we have found to be useful to clients in circumstances similar to the ones described. These interventions were developed to respond to dilemmas and concerns that the clients brought to the coaching relationship and were not imposed on clients because of our attachment to this, or any other, theory.

Additionally, we don't believe that this—or any other—chapter on Kegan's theory will enable anyone to determine a client's Order of mind; such determination requires the administration of a Subject–Object

Interview (Lahey, Souvaine, Kegan, Goodman, and Felix, 1988). Our intent in this section is to offer a sufficiently clear view of the Orders of mind so that the patterns we describe are illuminated in a new way, allowing coaches to see new solutions to old concerns. We have used this theory to build tools with which to help executives be more effective and happier in their positions—not to diagnose or label them.

When There Is a Good Fit between Complexity and Role

When there is a reasonably good fit between an executive's complexity of mind and his or her role and environment, an executive coach can look for opportunities to support the executive's development in a way that enables him or her to take on more complex challenges. Because the developmental issues around complexity of mind are different at different Orders of mind, this section addresses separately the strategies for supporting development in Third Order clients and in Fourth Order clients. For each, a description of the key developmental issues involving complexity of mind and strategies for executive coaching are discussed.

Supporting Development in Third Order Clients The key developmental issue in moving from the Third Order to the Fourth is the development of a self-authored system: the appointment of the individual as chairperson of his internal board of directors. Before the executive can begin to listen to and trust his internal guide, he first needs to recognize the limitations of the meaning systems—the external guides—on which he has relied thus far. The executive discovers that the internalized voices of external ideologies, institutions, or people cannot make all of his decisions; this may become especially clear when two important others disagree. Over time, the person learns to pay attention to and trust his own emerging voice. As mentioned earlier, a move to the Fourth Order doesn't mean that a person has abandoned key meaning systems—it reflects instead an ability to mediate across meaning systems.

An executive coach can support the development of a Third Order executive by

- Giving the executive opportunities to explore his view of critical events and issues, by asking questions such as What did *you* observe, think, feel? What's most important to *you* in the situation? What would *you* prefer to have happened?

45

- Noticing and pointing out even subtle differences between the executive's perspective or reaction and that of another person (a boss, a peer). For example, the coach might say, "So your boss thought Joe was out of line, but you thought Joe had some good points— although you agree with your boss that Joe's timing was a problem."

- Exploring with the executive relevant aspects of his key meaning systems (the values of his family, ethnic group, or religion); the perspectives of his profession (law, economics); the assumptions and implicit code of conduct of his organization

- Paying particular attention to issues and situations in which key meaning systems disagree and helping the executive develop strategies for mediating such disagreements

- Recommending activities that can help the executive identify his own views (journaling, taking time off alone for reflection)

- Using psychological instruments, such as the *Myers-Briggs Type Indicator* instrument, that portray individual differences as normal and natural and that support a differentiated approach to individual perspectives, interests, and reactions

- Helping the executive identify bosses, peers, and others who are especially good at articulating an independent perspective while taking into account the organization's culture and brainstorming about ways to observe and interact with bosses, peers, and others

Supporting Development in Fourth Order Clients In moving from the Third Order to the Fourth, the challenge is to *question the infallibility of external guides* and learn to trust the internal, self-authored guide. In the move from the Fourth Order to the Fifth, in contrast, the key task for the client is to *question the infallibility of her self-authored system* and see the need to transcend her reliance on that system.

Just as those moving from the Third Order to the Fourth retain the internalized voices of others as they develop their own voice, those moving from the Fourth Order to the Fifth retain their own self-authored system even as they recognize the need to link their system with those of others. Now, instead of having a hierarchical board of directors with herself as chair, the emerging Fifth Order executive might search for new metaphors. She might work to see herself as a member of a council of elders, for example, with each member representing his or her own internal and external constituencies and *at the same time* listening to the ways other council members shape and create the available options.

One of the most valuable ways in which a coach can support a client's movement from the Fourth Order to the Fifth is to make note of any thinking and behavior that demonstrate increasing complexity, as well as any positive effects of such thinking or behavior. The transition to Fifth Order might manifest itself in an executive in an increased ability to

- Understand and integrate the perspectives of other people and/or groups: *We've always dismissed that view of things, but I can see now why it looks that way to them.*

- Integrate apparent opposites: *I told them we weren't going to announce a solution until we had one that provided some structure and closure so that _____ can do their job, but that also has flexibility for our staff and our customers.*

- Take a fresh look at taboos or undiscussable issues: *The practice in my profession has always been _____ , but I'm beginning to see that we need to rethink our approach.*

- Tolerate contradictions (in themselves or their work) instead of denying, ignoring, or trying to fix them: *I always thought I was one of the good guys, but I'm beginning to see that what I always held as my altruism is really another form of selfishness.*

- Demonstrate awareness of their own meaning systems: *I'm increasingly recognizing that my training as a lawyer has accustomed me to see things in adversarial terms, which in this case has caused some real difficulty for the project.*

- Make connections across levels: *As I was listening to the two sides argue at the meeting, I was struck by the fact that I have some of those same arguments inside my head and that I sometimes feel both ways about that issue at the same time.*

- See the influence of their mind-set and expectations on their view of reality: *I realize that I went in there determined to see them as the bad guys and my expectations helped lead us to an impasse.*

When appropriate, executive coaches can highlight and reinforce such examples of increasing complexity and can discuss with clients their implications and potential positive effects on the organization.

As clients become more complex, they may begin to voice somewhat vague concerns about the inadequacy of processes and practices with which they previously had been comfortable: *I know we've always done it that way, but I'm starting to see more of the downsides.*

Executive coaches can help clients articulate what seems to be lacking and brainstorm about alternative approaches. Coaches also can help normalize the situation for clients, as clients often feel torn about their criticisms. Their sense of the inadequacy of the process or practice in question may be strong and insistent, while at the same time they may feel that they are being unreasonable, overly critical, even harsh: *I'm sure they're thinking, "How come he's so picky all of a sudden?" And it's not as if I have a lot of great ideas about how to change things. I don't blame them—I don't like it when people just criticize and don't offer solutions.*

When the Executive's Complexity Is Less Than Required

There are, of course, times when executives are themselves in over their heads as their jobs require more complex ways of making meaning than they possess. This can happen to Third Order clients whose roles have Fourth Order expectations as well as to Fourth Order clients whose roles have Fifth Order expectations.

Supporting Third Order Clients Whose Roles Have Fourth Order Expectations Executive coaching clients can be in over their heads when the expectations they face from their boss, peers, staff, organization, or others are that they be able to make meaning at the Fourth Order (that is, that they be self-authoring) when their level of complexity—like that of much of the adult population—is at the Third Order.[3] For example, changing jobs can create strain for Third Order executives by increasing the level of complexity expected or decreasing the available support. Such job changes can involve promotions, changes in scope and scale, and a move from a more structured to a more ambiguous part of an organization.

Third Order executives can experience similar dilemmas due to a change in the nature of or circumstances surrounding a current job, such as getting a new boss. We have seen clients who were very successful under one boss struggle and even fail under another boss who wanted the client to take more ownership of the process. In addition, changes in an organization resulting from mergers, reorganizations, transitions in top management, strategy redirection, or technological changes can disrupt a work setting that has provided a sense of coherence and clarity about roles, relationships, work practices, and operating procedures, thus creating challenges for Third Order executives.

A Third Order executive who faces Fourth Order expectations is likely to feel overwhelmed, strained, and uncertain. He may have excellent skills and a great capacity to respond to the demands of a situation. However, the Fourth Order requirement typically involves not just *meeting the demands* but also *identifying and deciding among them*—in essence *choosing* the demands. Third Order executives in this situation are likely to try in a variety of ways to get clarity (from their bosses or others) about what they and their part of the organization should be doing, and they may feel intensely frustrated and confused when the message comes back as some form of "You decide." They may expend a great deal of effort trying to get results and be successful, and they may experience heightened confusion and anxiety when their hard work doesn't pay off, sensing that somehow they're not getting it. They can become resentful of their bosses and other people in authority for not providing enough direction, for being vague and unclear about what they want.

Bosses and others in the environment who are expecting Fourth Order meaning making (usually without being aware of the real nature of their expectations) may interpret the executives' behavior as indecisive, risk-averse, dependent on authority. They may give messages, directly or indirectly, that say in effect

- *Take some initiative.*
- *Don't be so dependent on others.*
- *Why are you unwilling (or afraid or unable) to decide?*

Conversations across Third Order–Fourth Order differences can lead to increasing frustration on both sides. A Third Order client might complain, *I don't know what she wants and whenever I try to get some clarity, she's elusive (or not helpful or vague or dismissive).* A Fourth Order boss might assert, *I can't figure out why he isn't getting on top of his assignment. He's a smart guy—it's not asking that much for him to take the initiative and start things moving.*

An executive coach can support a Third Order executive who is facing Fourth Order demands by

- Helping to identify and articulate the expectations that are causing strain and confusion

- Brainstorming with the executive about sources of information, expertise, and judgment that might support the executive's decision making; these sources might involve people (peers, subordinates, experts) or frameworks, policies, or research

- Helping the executive craft an explicit decision-making process that can be used (with helpful resources) to make difficult decisions

- Proposing ways to have constructive discussions with bosses, peers, and others

- Reframing the situation as a valuable developmental opportunity

Supporting Fourth Order Clients Whose Roles Have Fifth Order Expectations Executive coaching clients can be in over their heads even when they meet the modernist expectations of complexity—the Fourth Order—if their role and environment require meaning making that goes beyond the Fourth Order. The same kinds of events (a job change or a change in the circumstances surrounding a current job) that lead Third Order clients to be strained and overwhelmed can affect Fourth Order clients. A new role that requires an executive not simply to deal with but to really integrate a wider range of perspectives or to demonstrate substantial subtlety and flexibility in mediating among different constituencies or domains (e.g., economics, law, and diplomacy) can be experienced as over-whelming or even impossible by a Fourth Order executive. A new boss or changing organizational circumstance (e.g., a merger) that requires these or similar capabilities could also lead to an executive's being in over his or her head.

Fourth Order executives who face Fifth Order expectations are likely to feel frustrated. It may be very clear to them what needs to be done and, when a suggestion is made about integrating other perspectives or kinds of considerations, they may be defensive ("I know what they want and I've considered their views in my decision") or stymied ("I've come up with a plan that takes all the factors into account, but my boss seems to think I'm not going far enough in understanding and representing all the different views. I don't see how anyone could go farther than I have in giving people what they want").

Fourth Order executives are likely to try to explain the coherence and logic of their decision making and to be frustrated or even angry when their logic is not seen as sufficient or perhaps is not even engaged with. They may struggle to find a better, more finely tuned internal system that allows them to have a better grasp of the situation. They may not realize, however, that what is needed isn't a better system, but rather an awareness that no single system is complex enough to deal with the circumstances.

Bosses and others in the environment who are expecting Fifth Order meaning making from a Fourth Order executive may see the executive as arrogant, too cut-and-dried, and/or unable to reach beyond her own way of thinking. Interactions can have a broken-record quality, with the executive reiterating the underpinnings of her approach and others continuing to suggest that she include other perspectives in her thinking and decision making.

An executive coach can help a Fourth Order client who is facing Fifth Order expectations by

- Helping her enhance her ability to understand the relationship between her own system and the systems of others (see Chapter 6 for strategies for helping clients increase their perspective-taking ability)

- Reviewing with her conversations she has had that were unsatisfying and looking for opportunities to reframe others' perspectives and reinterpret interactions with others such that the executive can see those different perspectives as ones that she holds—at least a little bit—as well

- Helping the executive see that even belief systems that are very different from hers can have their own admirable internal coherence; the experience of being able to admire the coherence of another's system while holding an awareness of the deficiencies of that system may increase the executive's ability to understand both the strengths and the limitations of her own system and ultimately to see that any one system is limited

- Looking for circumstances—however minor or peripheral to the points that are in contention—in which she can identify with or admire another system of meaning making, especially when it is very different from her own

- Encouraging her to identify peers or bosses who are especially effective in mediating across different perspectives or domains and then to find opportunities to interact with or observe such people in action

- Reinforcing that the process of growth and discovery, however difficult, is a valuable one that will enhance other skills and add important competence for future, more complex roles

- Supporting her in managing her frustration (and perhaps anger) and maintaining a sense of equilibrium and patience with the process

When the Executive's Complexity Is Greater Than Required

A different set of dilemmas are created and different opportunities for executive coaching are presented when executives have developed beyond what is expected in their roles. This can happen in Fourth Order clients whose roles have Third Order expectations as well as in Fifth Order clients whose roles have Fourth Order expectations.[4]

Supporting Fourth Order Clients Whose Roles Have Third Order Expectations Fourth Order executives can encounter Third Order expectations either when they develop and therefore outgrow their roles or their parts of the organization or when their jobs or the circumstances surrounding their jobs change. In the latter case, a change in bosses, a move to a more tradition-based part of an organization, or an organizational change that results in a more constrained, rule-bound, or "back-to-basics" approach can result in placing Fourth Order executives into Third Order roles and environments.

Fourth Order executives in Third Order environments are likely to feel constrained, controlled, and frustrated. They may experience a lack of freedom to act and make decisions, and may feel that they are being prevented from exercising their own judgment and being successful in their own way. In such circumstances, executives may consciously try to exercise self-control to hide their discomfort and frustration. They may go underground with their initiative and work around the rules so that they can feel at least somewhat in charge of the situation. They may drop out psychologically and go through the motions of the job, while seeking satisfaction in other parts of their lives. They are likely to feel stuck, sensing that they've lost any forward momentum in their development, or even feel that they're slipping backward in their capacities and achievements.

A boss with Third Order expectations may experience a Fourth Order subordinate as insufficiently respectful of authority and/or tradition, as an upstart, as undisciplined, or even as insubordinate. Concerns can be expressed in the following ways:

- *He's a capable guy, but he's not with the program.*

- *She thinks she can just make up her own rules.*

- *I don't know what he wants—I've given him a lot of responsibility, but he's always complaining that he doesn't have enough authority to really take the initiative.*

Interactions between the executive and others can be strained, with each side seeing the other's expectations and behavior as off-base, offensive, or even outrageous. Unless there is a compelling reason to stay (intense commitment to the mission, a skill or knowledge base that can't be attained elsewhere, great attachment to the people involved, extraordinarily unattractive alternatives), Fourth Order executives will often do whatever they can to leave Third Order environments as soon as possible because being there is so uncomfortable and unsatisfying.

An executive coach can support a Fourth Order executive who is facing Third Order demands by

- Supporting the executive in describing and understanding the situation, the issues the situation raises for him, and his reactions to various aspects of the situation

- Brainstorming with the executive about language that supports the rules but makes a case for an exception and about actions thatallow independence of thought and action but aren't seen as insubordinate

- Helping the executive identify and avoid specific settings and events (e.g., awards ceremonies) that are particularly frustrating, demotivating, or offensive

- Brainstorming with the executive about ways to increase his freedom of action (e.g., by taking on leading-edge assignments or engaging in cross-functional projects)

- Encouraging the executive to identify and try to expand the more satisfying parts of the job (e.g., mentoring staff, working with customers, learning a new skill or knowledge base)

- Proposing ways to continue growing and developing, both within and outside of the job, to counteract the sense of being stuck or regressing

- Helping to manage the frustration that stems from the situation and providing an outlet for the executive to express his negative reactions or feelings

- Supporting the executive in articulating the kind of role or environment that would be a better fit and in seeking to find and move toward that role or environment

Supporting Fifth Order Clients Whose Roles Have Fourth Order Expectations As discussed previously, modern expectations for adults involve Fourth Order meaning making; Fifth Order meaning making is far less common and far more difficult to understand or describe. As a result, executives who develop past the Fourth Order are likely to operate in roles and environments that are primarily Third and Fourth Order. Exceptions are roles and environments in which a leader is highly developed and over time both supports and calls for post–Fourth Order development or in which the work is particularly complex, requiring, for example, mediation across different perspectives and domains.

When an executive grows in complexity of mind beyond the Fourth Order, she begins to develop perspectives and capacities that are elusive and that are mostly undiscussable—because we do not have adequate language to talk about Fifth Order phenomena—and invisible—because the sensibilities and capacities of the Fifth Order are *Subject* to the vast majority of people.

Post–Fourth Order perspectives and capacities may enable the executive to make unique contributions to her organization (e.g., by dealing with diverse perspectives or by crafting solutions that integrate apparent opposites). However, the executive may find the environment narrow and constraining and may feel that there is a lack of understanding and recognition of her most developed—and most interesting—capabilities. As a result, there can be a tension between a sense of satisfaction and accomplishment and a subtle dissatisfaction or discomfort with not really being heard or understood, in all of the executive's developing complexity. The executive may experience others as too cut-and-dried in their views and as lacking in flexibility, subtlety, or depth.

- *It's not a simple as my boss (or peer) thinks.*
- *They don't see the limitations of their perspectives.*
- *I basically agree with them, but there's somehow more to it.*

Others in the executive's environment may see him or her as capable, but may think that he or she sometimes makes things too complicated.

- *He's not always good at laying down the law about things—he listens too much sometimes to _____.*
- *The solution is really simple—why does she always have to make things so complicated?*

Others may also sense a vague unhappiness or dissatisfaction.

- *She's hard to please sometimes. I've given her a lot of recognition, but she still doesn't seem very happy with my response to her work.*
- *I'm trying to be supportive, but I can't figure out what he really wants.*

An executive coach can support a Fifth Order executive who operates in a Fourth Order role or environment by

- Supporting the executive in articulating the dilemmas and dissatisfaction she may be experiencing

- Brainstorming with the executive about aspects of his or her current role or about possible new assignments that might be rewarding and could contribute to her development

- Helping the executive accept that there may be things that the boss (or peers) may never really understand or appreciate and lower her expectations for such understanding and appreciation

- Supporting the executive in identifying the ways in which she would love to develop, as well as specific strategies for pursuing that development

- Encouraging the executive to develop or expand a "kitchen cabinet" of diverse, wise colleagues, former bosses, and others that will support her development

- Brainstorming with the executive about ways to explain, frame, or justify post–Fourth Order perspectives, approaches, and achievements in ways that are persuasive and accessible in a Fourth Order environment

- Highlighting the developmental nature of the dilemmas and dissatisfactions she has been experiencing, as well as the value of possible future contributions based on her ongoing development

Conclusion

In previous centuries, adults thought of children as little adults—people who could understand and interact with the world in the same way adults could as soon as their physical capacities were mature enough. As researchers and teachers discovered more and more about the internal worlds of children, they were able to create environments far more supportive of the growth and development of those children. Similarly, people often think of adults as being generally all the same developmentally—with differences in skills or intelligence. While such variables as skills and intelligence are clearly important, we believe that understanding the different worlds adults inhabit is a key factor in helping them be more successful and effective in their work. The constructive-developmental theory of Robert Kegan offers shape to these worlds, and this chapter has attempted to apply Kegan's theory to the evolving field of executive coaching. Our hope is that executive coaching that is informed by Kegan's theory can help both leaders and their organizations be more effective.

Notes

[1] Order of mind can be measured by the Subject–Object Interview (SOI; Lahey, Souvaine, Kegan, Goodman, and Felix, 1988). This measure, an intense, hour-long qualitative interview administered, transcribed, and scored by a skilled practitioner, identifies the meaning-making system of the interviewee.

[2] This system actually begins at birth with babies and toddlers at a kind of Zero Order, which has its own way of constructing the world.

3 Actually, most of our lives are spent in the transitional spaces between the Orders. Kegan has identified four such places between each of the major poles (there are four poles between Third Order and the Fourth Order). Therefore, we may have many clients who are not yet *fully* Fourth Order who have characteristics of both Third and Fourth Order meaning-making systems.

4 Another caveat about the Fifth Order: In the following sections we'll talk about Fifth Order clients and also about Fourth Order clients in Fifth Order roles or environments. It is unlikely that there are many clients who are fully Fifth Order, and it is even less likely that any organizations have demands that are universally Fifth Order. What does seem likely is that there will be some clients who are beginning the journey toward the Fifth Order and there are some organizations that, because of their global orientation or diversity of ideas or complexity of missions, will have some Fifth Order demands.

References

Belenky, M., B. Clinchy, N. Goldberger, and J. Tarule. (1986). *Women's ways of knowing: The development of self, voice, and mind.* San Francisco: HarperCollins.

Fraiberg, S. H. (1959). *The magic years: Understanding and handling the problems of early childhood.* New York: Scribner.

Kegan, R. (1982). *The evolving self: Problem and process in human development.* Cambridge, Mass.: Harvard University Press.

———. (1994). *In over our heads: The mental demands of modern life.* Cambridge, Mass.: Harvard University Press.

———. (1995). *Supporting our development at work: An interactive and reflective workshop.* Paper presented at Collaboration and community building: New approaches to violence prevention, Harvard University Graduate School of Education.

Kegan, R., and L. Lahey. (1984). Adult leadership and adult development. In B. Kellerman (ed.), *Leadership* (pp. 199-230). Englewood Cliffs, NJ: Prentice-Hall.

———. (2001). *How the way we talk can change the way we work: Seven languages for transformation.* San Francisco: Jossey-Bass.

Lahey, L., E. Souvaine, R. Kegan, R. Goodman, and S. Felix. (1988). *A Guide to the subject-object interview: Its administration and interpretation.* Cambridge, Mass.: Laboratory of Human Development, Graduate School of Education, Harvard University.

Perry, W. G. (1968). *Forms of intellectual and ethical development in the college years.* Cambridge, Mass.: Bureau of Study Counsel, Harvard University.

[3]

THE COACH AS REFLECTIVE PRACTITIONER

Notes from a Journey without End

GRADY McGONAGILL

I f we don't move forward on this, someone is going to wind up in the hospital." So ended a team meeting led by Alan, the vice president of a global corporation's product division. Such declarations were typical of Alan, whose intimidating style left him isolated from his team and who was the object of occasional reproach from his boss. As a consultant to the team, I had become convinced that Alan's enormous leadership strengths were limited by his proportionally long shadow. Although I established a good initial base for working with him, I was unable to build on it to bring about meaningful change in behavior. Why, I wondered?

Eventually, questions like this prompted me to begin reflecting systematically on my practice as a coach.[1] All too often, I had found myself winging it—while of course pretending that I knew exactly what I was doing. I realized that I was engaged in a primarily intuitive method of working with my clients. As I thought about my practice, the serious limitations of relying on an intuitive approach became clearer. My reflections have given me insight into the limits and accomplishments of my work with Alan and other clients. This in turn has made me more aware of my core practices as a coach and helped me identify areas in which I need to grow. I came to understand that the best way for me to review my practice was to begin creating a model that made explicit the various influences on my coaching practice.

In this chapter, I offer a general framework for constructing a model of coaching and describe my efforts to apply it in my own practice. In doing this, my goal is to encourage other coaches to review their own practices and to provide a tool that might be useful as they build their own personal models. The chapter is organized around an introductory rationale for and presentation of the framework, followed by an account of how I have used its various elements to reflect on my coaching practice and begin building a coaching model. In order to make concrete the practical implications of a model, I report on my investigation into my work with Alan and two other clients, describing how these experiences both reflected and informed my core practices.

Becoming a Reflective Practitioner

As I began thinking of how to construct a model, Donald Schön's (1982, 1987) studies of the reflective practitioner came to mind. His research on professionals in action lends support to the notion that coaching is more art than science. In studying professions as diverse as architecture and psychotherapy, he found that, when faced with the challenge of choosing among competing theories to deal with unique cases, practitioners create artistic performances in which they respond to complexity in simple, spontaneous ways. Schön gives that artistry a name—*reflection-in-action.* When exercising this artistry, practitioners frame problems, devise and experiment with solutions, and reframe as the situations talk back. They make sense of the situations not through rote application of a theory but with reference to a "repertoire of examples, images, understandings and actions" (Schön, 1982, p. 163).

There is an irony in Schön's work. Although the professionals he studies are reflective in that they make nonroutine decisions in the moment, his research suggests that they tend to exercise their artistry in an unself-conscious and therefore relatively unreflective way (Schön, 1987, pp. 119–56). In such interactions, practitioners who are aware of their methods have an edge over those who are naive about their craft. A coach with this awareness is more likely to recognize the limits of his or her approach and treat it as a set of hypotheses, subject to continuous testing and revision. Such a coach will also be more able to invite a client into a partnership and employ methods that are transparent and subject to mutual influence.

For these reasons, coaches would do well to aspire to being truly reflective practitioners, capable of displaying the following qualities:

- Awareness of their own filters for making meaning of coaching interactions
- Awareness of their own assumptions, methods, and tools
- Commitment to an inquiring stance toward their effectiveness
- Ability to regard each new client as a fresh challenge to models that are continuously in evolution

I see the creation of a personal model as a means to becoming a reflective practitioner of this kind. Reflecting on my model is a way to think about my practice outside the moment of client contact and allows me to be more conscious of making choices from a range of theoretical and methodological repertoires that, in turn, inform and deepen my core practices. Ultimately, to be a reflective practitioner is to see in the moment of client interaction everything one would see if one were to step out of the moment and reflect. Clearly, this is an unobtainable goal, but one may take small steps toward it by routinely allowing time to adopt a posture of inquiry. This stance distinguishes the reflective practitioner from the intuitive one.

Recognizing that others might approach the challenge of model building in a different way, I concluded that the best way to review my practice was to create a framework that identified three influences that inform a coach's core practices: the coach's *vision,* the coach's *frames for understanding human behavior,* and the coach's *personal profile.* Together these elements

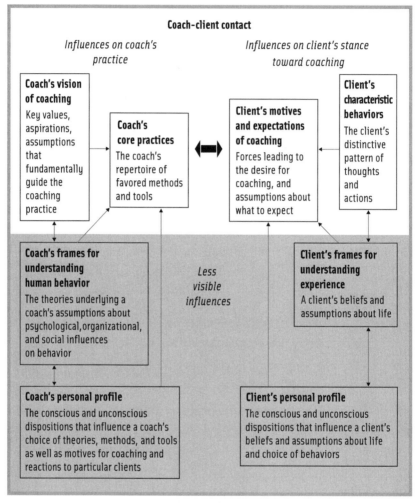

Coach-client contact

Influences on coach's practice

Influences on client's stance toward coaching

Coach's vision of coaching

Key values, aspirations, assumptions that fundamentally guide the coaching practice

Coach's core practices

The coach's repertoire of favored methods and tools

Client's motives and expectations of coaching

Forces leading to the desire for coaching, and assumptions about what to expect

Client's characteristic behaviors

The client's distinctive pattern of thoughts and actions

Coach's frames for understanding human behavior

The theories underlying a coach's assumptions about psychological, organizational, and social influences on behavior

Less visible influences

Client's frames for understanding experience

A client's beliefs and assumptions about life

Coach's personal profile

The conscious and unconscious dispositions that influence a coach's choice of theories, methods, and tools as well as motives for coaching and reactions to particular clients

Client's personal profile

The conscious and unconscious dispositions that influence a client's beliefs and assumptions about life and choice of behaviors

FIGURE 1 · FRAMEWORK FOR MODEL BUILDING

constitute a framework for model building (Figure 1). Fleshed out to describe a particular practice, these elements, interacting dynamically with one another, constitute what I mean by a model. It is critical to conceive a model with explicit reference to how the coach and client jointly shape the coaching relationship, so that is also reflected in the framework. In the remainder of the chapter, I use this framework to document my reflections on my practice and describe the model that has evolved—and will continue to evolve.

Vision

Until I began reflecting on my model, I would have been hard pressed to articulate my vision of coaching. I have come to believe that making one's vision explicit is a critical element of a coaching model. A coach necessarily has an image of the enterprise that guides what he or she is doing, whether explicit or tacit. Without the awareness of that vision and how it is formed, coaches will be blind to at least some of their motives for intervening in certain ways. This idea came home to me when I heard Peter Block advocate an approach to executive coaching based on helping people "become the authors of their own experience."[2] On hearing this view, I recognized it as a tacit vision of coaching toward which I had been moving for some time; this conscious acknowledgment proved quite helpful to me. Indeed, it led me to recognize conflicting tensions in my vision of coaching between advocating such an aspiration versus accepting a client's goals even when they are more limited. I address this tension below.

Origins of a Practice

David Kantor suggests that all practice begins through imitation.[3] Consciously or unconsciously, we all begin by appropriating approaches from others—parents, teachers, and role models of other kinds. After reflection, I saw that my methods of practice had their seeds in my graduate education. I was inspired to become a consultant by exposure to the work developed by a renowned theorist/practitioner, Chris Argyris, in conjunction with Donald Schön and others—work known as Action Science (Argyris and Schön, 1975; Argyris, Putnam, and Smith, 1985; Fisher, Rooke, and Torbert, 2000; Torbert, 1991).

With a background in Action Science, it is no surprise that, while proposing a coaching relationship in a conversation with Alan, I made the following statement: "It appears that you send mixed messages to the team. On the one hand, you frequently make statements about the value of openness and participation. On the other, you are seen as a leader who sometimes goes around subordinates to solve problems." I then gave examples from the interviews to support the perception and went on to ask, "What's your reaction to this view?"

The statement is a typical Action Science intervention, calling attention to a gap between Alan's *espoused theory* (i.e., individual and team empowerment) and his *theory-in-use* (i.e., unilateral intervention to solve problems).

Implicit in my approach is a vision of the coach's role: I present a *challenge* to Alan by pointing out gaps between intentions and actions, offer to provide *support* by developing his awareness of the sources of this gap so that he can unlearn old ways of thinking and acting and proceed to learn new ways, and hold out the implicit *vision* of congruence between aspirations and actions.[4] In adopting this approach, I was essentially imitating Chris Argyris and other senior practitioners of his method whom I had experienced personally as classroom teachers, seminar leaders, and coaches.

Evolution and Conflicts

Reflecting on my model has made me aware, not only of this original tacit vision, but of other aspirations I hold for clients that—evolving over time, due to a variety of influences—could possibly conflict with this vision. Increasingly, I see myself encouraging clients to become aware of the conscious and unconscious influences on their behavior, to take ownership of those influences and their consequences, and to use this expanded commitment and awareness to envision and act on a wider range of choices. Such aspirations for clients are potentially more ambitious than the aim of merely reducing the gaps between their intentions and their actions.

This raises a disturbing question. What if the client has no interest in the kind of learning required to become the "author of his or her experience" but has much more pragmatic goals (which in fact turned out to be the case with Alan)? Is it appropriate for a coach to confront clients with what he or she perceives as limited aspirations on their part? My current view—which I continue to examine—is that I wish to take a stance with my clients that openly advocates an ambitious vision for their development, yet respects their right to decide for themselves the level of aspiration they think makes sense. (I will pick up this thread later when I review my personal profile and core practices, the two other elements of the framework.)

At the same time, there is a synergistic parallel between holding high aspirations for my clients and my commitment to being a reflective practitioner. By aiming to coach in ways that reflect an explicit awareness of and openness to learning about the consequences of my underlying assumptions and influences as well as a willingness to explore new options, I am trying to do for myself as a coach what I desire to help my clients do for themselves—to become, as Block might phrase it, the author of my practice. The coaching model (see Figure 1) attempts to capture this parallel.

In summary, by using the framework to investigate the source of my vision, I gained several insights. Least surprising was the realization that I could trace much of my vision to role models from my graduate training—models whom I continue to imitate. Most interesting was determining that my vision was largely tacit, and the effort to make it explicit has raised some serious tensions that I would do well to resolve. In general, reflecting on my vision and its sources confirms my intuition that vision is a significant influence on a coach's core practices.

Frames for Understanding Human Behavior

A model of coaching will inevitably entail assumptions about why people behave as they do. The task coaches face is to become conscious of those assumptions and assess their strengths and limits. Are they robust enough to survive an encounter with the wide range of situations presented by different clients facing different organizational and personal challenges? My general framework led me to examine two overlapping sources of influence on a coach's assumptions: *psychological influences on behavior* and *individual differences*. I found on reflection that in each area I had extended my range of core practices and identified a wider range of options for being responsive to clients.

Psychological Influences on Behavior

Action Science gave me some basic assumptions about human behavior, but it did not offer a comprehensive and systematic way to understand how individual experience shapes behavior. I soon discovered a need for such theories.

In working with particular individuals, each of whom had his or her own rich history of family and other influences on their development, I intuitively drew on learning assimilated from a decade of exposure to therapy. My therapists came from no single school of thought. However, my principal coach and mentor articulated in one of our sessions a perspective that seemed to characterize an unstated common assumption: "Any face-to-face work is about linking internal structures to the creation of external structures, linking internal imagery and critical events in one's life to how one imprints and creates structures in the external world." I tacitly took this internalized sensibility to my encounters with my client Alan.

In my work with Alan, I naturally sought opportunities to probe for information about his family background that might help me understand his ways of approaching his role and interactions with others. After several sessions, he was willing to talk about his childhood and revealed some important information. He was the oldest of seven children who were abandoned by their father when Alan was nine. From that point on, Alan acted as a surrogate parent, taking responsibility for himself and his siblings.

Alan acknowledged that what he learned from this experience was to take a high level of personal responsibility while distrusting the help of others. Indeed, he experienced profound ambivalence when he needed help. At the conscious level, he truly believed in the company rhetoric of empowering individuals and teams, but his history led to a deeper set of beliefs, which made him feel that he could not count on others to fulfill their responsibilities. These deeper beliefs undermined his commitment to the espoused management philosophy. From this information, I constructed the following intervention:

> I feel that I'm in a double bind in my relationship with you, and I sense that others do, too. You are a person of great strength and power. Your team members experience the possibility that this power may be used against them [Alan laughs here], and they fear you. What they don't see is that you use some of that power against yourself, by putting yourself in double binds that prevent you from getting help from others. As I try to help you by bringing up these kinds of issues, you will have an instinct to push me away, so my double bind is that if I work with you in the way that has the greatest potential payoff, you're likely to fire me. If I don't pursue them, I may not get fired, but I'll deliver less than maximum value, and at some level you'll be disappointed, as will I. I'd like to get your reaction as to whether any of this rings true and, if it does, to see whether you'd like to pursue this with me.

Alan responded,

> You underestimate me and don't give me enough credit. I see your comments as pointing to a weakness on my part, which I recognize. . . . I do some things that create problems without knowing it. For example, I recently said to my wife, "I wish the kids would come to me more often to talk about things instead of always going to you." She said, "If you could see the look on your face when something simple happens, like a glass of milk spills, you'd know why the kids don't talk to you." So I know I've got an issue there. . . . [But] I'm interested. Some of the things you said I'd be interested in talking more about.

In order to work with Alan, I supplemented my Action Science approach with loosely formulated theories of the effect of psychological development on behavior. I was moving beyond imitation of my original role models to broaden my theoretical base. In so doing, I was imitating earlier role models (my therapists) and a new one (my coach), albeit rather intuitively.

Reviewing the above interaction as part of my current examination of my model has helped me see aspects of the encounter that escaped my attention at the time. I was so relieved by Alan's willingness to move forward that I was blind to some of the more obvious problems inherent in his response. It is now clear that there were limits to his understanding of the double bind I had mentioned above. But I was satisfied with the chance to proceed and did not catch the dismissive quality of his response, which was later pointed out by my coach. Thus I missed clues to the challenge that lay ahead and to the potential need for other approaches in working with him.

At about the same time, another client, Bill, the manager of a semi-independent subsidiary of a large company, posed a very different challenge, requiring me to reach further beyond the theories of Action Science. Bill's boss engaged me to address issues that had led him to put Bill on probation. Before the engagement began, with participation strictly voluntary for Bill, we conducted three-way negotiations to establish the nature of the coaching relationship. During the meeting, we identified and wrote down our expectations regarding improvement in three areas: profitability, customer service, and an environment that supported the development of team members. We attached quantitative measures to the first two issues and agreed to stay in touch regarding the third, softer one. In probing the concerns of his boss and team members in this third area—which involved micromanaging, a tendency to focus on the negative in dealing with subordinates—Bill revealed thought patterns heavily oriented toward negative self-evaluation ("I'm just no good"). Along with recurrent self-critical thoughts, Bill experienced a good deal of what he termed anger ("I'm like a crab, all hard on the outside") and what sounded like depression ("I'm just down, no energy"). He saw himself as a failure in both his professional and personal lives. At work, he felt ineffectual in his efforts to influence his boss and more generally in maneuvering within a "political" organization. At home, he was having trouble coping with his two teenage children.

From the outset, Bill was open and revealed his self-critical thoughts and the apparently related feelings of anger and depression. Action Science provided me with no particular tools for understanding or addressing these issues. Instead, I pursued an approach based on cognitive therapy (Beck, 1979; Burns, 1989), a perspective to which I had been introduced by a colleague and which I had found helpful in understanding myself. Aaron Beck and his followers had made more explicit some of the notions that seemed to underlie Action Science, such as the linkage between thoughts and action, and offered more explicit assumptions regarding thoughts as the cause of moods and feelings. Practitioners of this approach had identified a range of typical dysfunctional thought patterns, along with a range of tools for helping people recognize and overcome their blind reactions to such inner thoughts (Burns, 1989).

Bill was quite willing to accept homework assignments consisting of cognitive therapy exercises in which he explored the linkage among triggering events (a hostile comment from his son), automatic thoughts ("my son hates me"), and the consequences (believing he is an inadequate parent and therefore an inadequate person). After identifying particular powerful and recurrent automatic thoughts, he would ask himself,

- Are there distortions in these thoughts?
- Are there any counterarguments to these thoughts?
- What if these thoughts are true? What is the underlying assumption about the consequences?

This and other forms of reflection seemed to be helpful for Bill. Team members reported that the overall climate had become favorable to development. His boss began to hear similar reports and consequently was pleased with the coaching. Several years later, I checked in with Bill to see what, if anything, of long-term value he had gained from the coaching. He said he had learned to "think more in gray rather than black and white" and he recognized that he had been "personalizing things that were not personal." He felt he was "more open to other viewpoints" and "intolerant of narrow-mindedness." Bill attributed this to the exercises he had done and to the challenges I had made to his thought process.

Looking back on this interaction, I see that I discerned a need to expand the core theoretical base from which I was operating and found that in this case cognitive theory served my purposes well. No doubt there are other ways in which a coach might have diagnosed and responded to Bill's concerns. My reponse simply reflected my having by chance become aware of and attracted to cognitive therapy. This illustrates the intuitive and potentially arbitrary ways in which a coaching practice may evolve and underscores the importance of periodically stepping back to reflect on one's practice to ensure that it is evolving in coherent ways.

Incorporating Theories about Individual Differences

Although Bill responded well to the methods of cognitive therapy, I discovered that many of my clients—like Alan—were not promising candidates for such tools, let alone the more reflection-oriented methods of Action Science. Based on these and similar experiences, I had already concluded that the failure to take individual differences into account was not simply a problem with the pedagogical tools associated with Action Science but a limitation of the theory itself. In essence, this school of thought does not explicitly encourage a coach to treat one person differently from another. In addition, it does not allow for the possibility that some people may not react positively to its methodological approach.

As a result, I was attracted to a theory of personality differences. I found the *Myers-Briggs Type Indicator* (MBTI) inventory—a tool based on such a theory and grounded in the work of Carl Jung—an effective instrument for understanding common differences among people and for understanding myself and my reactions to others. It also seemed highly complementary to Action Science. The differences indicated by the MBTI personality inventory offer clues to the preferences that inform a person's particular theory-in-use. Although it relies on self-reported data, always inherently suspect from an Action Science point of view, one could consider type a hypothesis to be explored. And I found that the MBTI tool could sometimes provide more rapid and direct insight into behavior than did Action Science.

The MBTI instrument was of great value with Chris, a partner in a professional services firm, whose leadership style appeared to be contributing to the company's problems with retaining the loyalty of younger colleagues. Interviews with members of the firm revealed a number of concerns about Chris's style: he was seen as indirect to the point of dishonesty in his dealings with employees ("People doubt that they are ever hearing the true story"), chronically unable to give negative feedback ("You sense that something is wrong but don't know where you stand"), unable to say no to clients ("He'll agree to deliver more than we originally promised and then leave it up to us to do the work"), too willing to sacrifice his standards to please clients ("He'll always go for the second-best solution if that's what the client wants"), and chronically unable to keep commitments ("He works to keep his options open and constantly double- or triple-books"). Chris's MBTI profile indicated ENFP, a people-oriented style with a tendency to see the big picture, place a high emphasis on values and feelings, and exercise great flexibility. Like most ENFPs, Chris was reluctant to hurt other people's feelings, which caused him to avoid conflict and withhold negative evaluations. His tendency to overcommit resulted from the same pattern: he did not want others to be disappointed. Of course, his strategies only worked in the short run. Using the MBTI personality inventory to understand the motives underlying his behavior helped Chris improve his ability to say no in order to avoid even greater pain later on. Chris also found his MBTI profile useful in highlighting a key personal value—his integrity—which is extremely characteristic of ENFPs and was reinforced by his firm's values. The importance of maintaining his integrity led him to identify two areas in which he felt he needed to bring about change: "Being bolder, in terms of where I take a stand on things . . . and making sure I can deliver what I promise."

While many colleagues share a preference for the MBTI instrument, some are attracted to Human Dynamics (Seagal and Horne, 1997), and others prefer the Enneagram (Riso and Hudson, 2000). My attraction to the MBTI personality inventory has been reinforced because clients consistently like it and it often generates useful insights. A considerable body of research also supports the instrument's basic validity and reliability (Fitzgerald, 1997).

There is no clear limit to the types and number of theories that are relevant to understanding individual behavior. In brief, I have also found it useful to supplement my theoretical base with systems perspectives (Oshry, 1995; Senge, 1990) and theories of the influence of culture (Harrison, 1995, pp. 147–282; Schneider, 1994). And I'm increasingly mindful of the importance of a firm grounding in theories of the effects of ethnicity, class, and gender (e.g., McGoldrick, Giordano, and Pearce, 1996).

In using the framework for model building to review my frames for understanding human behavior, I came to several conclusions. First, drawing on multiple schools of thought, rather than a single favored paradigm, clearly increases a coach's capacity. Second, my inability to see the initial signs of the barriers I had faced with Alan was most likely due to the limits of my intuitive application of psychological theories and to insufficiencies in my personal profile and core practices, which I explore below. This has helped me identify areas that require further attention as I continue my model-building process, as detailed at the end of the chapter.

Personal Profile

To an even greater extent than most practitioners, the coach is his or her own primary instrument. Thus, personal qualities must be part of a coach's model. David Kantor has long advocated this view and he has created a set of tools for therapists and consultants that is explicitly designed to help them identify their "boundary profile," areas of potential synergy and friction in the match with individual clients and client systems (Kantor and Neal, 1985; Kantor, 1997; Kantor, 2001a).[5] The concepts and instruments of the boundary profile are equally helpful as a diagnostic tool with clients. I have also found several additional sources of support as I attempt to increase my awareness of my own profile as a coach.

Gaps between Espoused Theories and Theories-in-Use

Consultants and coaches are as vulnerable as their clients to gaps between their espoused theories and their theories-in-use. Even coaches who are committed to self-knowledge are at risk of remaining systematically blind to their own limitations.

Argyris provides an interesting example of such a gap in the coaching practice of a renowned source of advice on effective behavior, Stephen Covey. Argyris (2000) analyzed the transcript of a coaching interaction between Covey and his son contained in the widely read *The 7 Habits of Highly Effective People* (1989), in which Covey reports feeling "upset and disillusioned" (p. 177) by his son's failure to honor his commitments regarding yard work. Yet he suppressed those feelings and instead "faked a smile" and asked how the yard work was going, despite obvious evidence that the answer was going to be negative. Argyris points out that, as a coach, Covey behaved in ways that are inconsistent with his recommendation to act authentically, apparently in the interest of being "positive." Argyris concludes that "Covey employs two mutually inconsistent theories of effective action: the one that he espouses and the one that he actually uses" (p. 22). In being vulnerable to such inconsistencies, Covey is no different from the rest of us.

Action Science predicts—and years of observing the practice of managers and my own practice as consultant and coach convince me—that such discrepancies are inevitable and human. Discovering such discrepancies is a powerful clue to one's model of oneself as coach, to reflecting on areas where one is ineffective and discovering areas where one is blind.

How to discover such discrepancies? I have acquired the habit—typical of practitioners of Action Science—of taping my consulting and coaching interactions whenever possible. Sometimes simply listening to segments of a tape (or reading a transcription of the segment) generates insight into interactions that seem not to have gone as well as I would have liked for reasons I cannot explain. With especially puzzling interactions, learning cases are a powerful albeit more labor-intensive tool for self-reflection. The coach begins by writing down *spoken dialogue* between two parties in one column and his or her *internal dialogue* in a parallel column. Simply writing out such a case often leads to subtle insights into the framing of the situation and the resulting options. However, used as the basis for a consultation with a colleague or one's personal coach, it is even more powerful.

Support from a Coach or Mentor

Ultimately, a coach is simply unable to see what he or she cannot see. Clinical supervision, or having one's own coach, is the classic model in training psychotherapists, and I have found this technique to be enormously valuable in becoming cognizant of my patterns of reflection-in-action. I initially engaged a coach who was a highly skilled practitioner of Action Science. Subsequently, I have used an individual of more eclectic background for many years in the unusual combination of coach, mentor, and therapist. Having a coach who knows me well allows me to present complex challenges with the confidence that I will be supported in recognizing blind spots and in seeing how I may be getting stuck in the self-reinforcing interplay of vision, theories, methods, and personal proclivities. In addition, I find that scheduling regular meetings with a coach has the advantage of building reflection into my routine by making it a task, which more successfully competes with other tasks for my scarce time.

My interaction with Alan was sufficiently challenging that I decided to use it as the basis for reflection with my coach. He helped me think about the link between Alan's internal structures and his ways of creating structures in the external world. After reviewing with me the transcript of key interactions with Alan, my coach framed the challenge in terms of helping Alan recognize that "he uses his structure to keep himself in power and eliminate the possibility of surrendering to help. He doesn't see how he creates double binds that prevent him from getting what he wants." This helped me shape the intervention that I documented earlier.

Even as I felt that I had—with my coach's help—successfully shifted my coaching of Alan to a deeper level, subsequent reflection with my coach helped me realize that I had missed an opportunity to show Alan his own pattern in action. Pointing to Alan's statement that I had underestimated him, my coach saw a "maneuver of neutralizing your power by devaluing your input. . . . That's how he works." I came away from this discussion with the mixed feelings that were typical in my work with my coach: I believed I was gaining insights that could improve my ability to see a broader range of options in the moment of client contact, but at the same time I also felt rather dull-witted and overwhelmed. Such, I suppose, is the hidden tuition we pay on the path of continued learning.

Knowing Your Type

As already illustrated, I have found the MBTI personality inventory quite useful in identifying ways in which my natural inclinations might align or conflict with those of a particular client. It also served to highlight some of the strengths and weaknesses of my characteristic tendencies when coaching.

For example, I learned that, as an INTP, I may lack appreciation for detail and structure and be less attuned to the possibility that some clients (with Sensing and Judging preferences) would like me to be more prescriptive. It also reminds me that I will feel the most passion when working with clients who—like me—view life as a never-ending search for meaning. And because I have only a mild preference for Thinking as opposed to Feeling when it comes to decision making, the MBTI assessment tool has also made me aware of my internal struggle between being an observer/bystander who enjoys solving problems and being a passionate advocate on behalf of my values; this tension is directly reflected in the ambivalence I feel regarding my vision for coaching as well as my coaching practices.

Core Practices

A coach's vision of coaching and theoretical orientation is one step removed from actual practice. The distinctiveness of a practice emerges in face-to-face interactions with the client. I have found it instructive just to inventory my core practices. In assessing my core tools and methods, I noticed a continuing prominent role for tools I had seen modeled by my Action Science teachers, such as the distinction between *Model I* and *Model II* behavior (the skills corresponding to unilateral versus collaborative interactions), the *ladder of inference* (a method of mapping specific steps in the reasoning process that lead a person from concrete data to assumptions, beliefs, and conclusions that influence action), and the learning cases described earlier.

I can now see that I also developed—partly through imitation and partly through adaptation—a less explicit underlying methodology that reflects an Action Science perspective. As I reconstructed the common features of my coaching interactions with Alan, Bill, and Chris, I identified the elements presented in Table 3.

In broad outline, these features of my approach to coaching may well resemble the practice of other coaches or even therapists. The potential distinctiveness of the approach lies, I believe, in my self-conscious balancing of advocacy and inquiry, an orientation I share with other practitioners of Action Science.

Balancing Advocacy and Inquiry

The relative balance of advocacy and inquiry in my practice is guided by the underlying Action Science principle of bilateral or shared control. Coaches inevitably make choices—explicit or otherwise—about the desired balance of control within the coaching interaction. The fundamental questions are

- Does the coach have an agenda, and, if so, how does he or she manage it?
- Should the coach make this agenda explicit, or keep it in the background to guide the interaction?

Action Science encourages practitioners to make their intentions and hypotheses known and to test them openly with clients. It also recommends equal emphases on *inquiry* (listening, asking questions that increase clarity

---

Table 3

Core Coaching Method

- Begin the coaching relationship by establishing goals, boundaries, and preferred modes of working together, usually based on some external source of data on the client's behavior.

- Conduct individual sessions by drawing on the following elements:

  - Encourage the client to give examples of the challenges he or she faces, with concrete data regarding thoughts, feelings, attributions of others' motives, and other factors.

  - Explore the ways in which the client frames examples, using active listening—asking clarifying questions and reflecting back key thoughts and feelings—to test your understanding of what you have heard and to create a climate of safety in which the client can identify thoughts and feelings that lie beneath conscious awareness.

  - Explore options for handling the particular challenge, inviting the client's suggestions and selectively offering your own when you see choices beyond the client's awareness.

  - Clarify implications for action on immediate challenges.

  - Look for opportunities to probe more deeply into the factors shaping the ways in which the client frames challenges, including personal history.

  - Look for opportunities to offer alternative ways of framing challenges and use those reframings as a way to help the client become more aware of how he or she constructs meaning.

  - Generate and test hypotheses about characteristic patterns in the client's way of framing challenges and acting on those frames, based on examples presented and from other available data.

- Conclude the coaching relationship, taking stock of what has been accomplished and eliciting feedback.

Source: This simple threefold framework for organizing the method was influenced by Landsberg, 1997, pp. 122–23.

and understanding) and *advocacy* (offering assessments and interpretations, making suggestions, or asking questions that encourage the client to reflect in a particular way).

I have found that many other coaching methods deviate from Action Science's approach of coupling advocacy with inquiry while giving equal weight to both. Some, for example, favor advocacy over inquiry in pursuit of transformational changes in the client.[6] Such approaches encourage a coach to view a client's defenses against frontal assault as obstacles to be beaten down in the interest of the client's liberation. Equally prevalent is the tendency to favor inquiry over advocacy, typically on grounds that power to resolve problems resides within the client. At its best, this approach leads coaches to reflect back what they are hearing and ask facilitating questions to which they do not have predetermined answers (see examples below). Such questions can be genuinely helpful and are highly useful for the coach when a client is more knowledgeable about a given area. However, taken in its pure form, this strategy needlessly undermines the coach by rendering invalid his or her own perspective.[7]

I developed the template shown in Table 4 in order to reinforce a conscious choice between advocacy and inquiry and to maintain a balance between the two. Originally, this framework was meant to provide a structure for inquiry only (Whitmore, 1992), but I adapted it to express my beliefs. As the template suggests, my approach—at least as espoused!—combines the active listening/support orientation of a client-centered method with the willingness to make direct challenges. It's worth commenting on both ends of this continuum.

Reflective Listening and Mind-Sets

By incorporating an emphasis on reflective listening, I have been able to moderate in myself a default tendency toward advocacy. In my colleagues Barry Jentz and Joan Wofford (Jentz, 1999), I found a powerful set of role models who showed me what it means to use, and teach, reflective listening, a skill that is consistent with the inquiry of Action Science but which does not receive special emphasis in that theory. Using this tool, in contrast to inquiring by asking direct questions, not only helps me test the accuracy of my listening but gives clients more freedom to take our conversations in directions that may be more helpful to them.

While I feel no conflict in committing myself to fully listening to the client, I find myself struggling to decide on my stance at the other end of the

Table 4

Balancing Advocacy and Inquiry with the GROW Model

	Goal	Reality	Options	Wrap-up
Reflect	It sounds like you would like to focus on. . . (?)	So the project is going well overall but you're concerned about. . . (?)	What I'm hearing is that you see three options . . . (?)	So you're now feeling confident of being able to follow through. . . (?)
Ask clarifying questions	What would a successful outcome look like? What specifically should we focus on?	What reasons did they give for the change? How would you account for your success?	What would be involved in pursuing that option?	When would be a realistic target date for completion?
Ask facilitating questions	What do you want? What would you like to get out of this session?	Where are you now? What's working? What's not working?	Have you faced anything similar before? If so, did you learn anything about how to handle it?	What specific steps might you take? What obstacles might you face?
Ask challenging questions	What would be a goal that would represent a breakthrough for you?	What prevented you from saying what you thought directly to your boss?	If you knew the answer, what would it be?	Given what you know about yourself, how might you sabotage this commitment?
Assert	Given what you've said, I think we should focus on . . . (What do you think?)	I see you making an assumption that you may not be aware of . . . (What's your reaction?)	I see another option that I'd like to put on the table . . . . (What do you think?)	I think it would make more sense to do A first, then B, for the following reasons . . . . (Does that make sense?)

Inquiry

Advocacy

continuum: how much of an advocate should I be? As already mentioned, I am attracted to a view of coaching that aspires to help clients be the "authors of their experience," which involves making them aware of any limits to recognizing their freedom.[8] Yet I recoil at the aggressive methods of the transformational schools ("Are you willing to have a breakthrough in this conversation?").

I have tentatively reconciled this dilemma by building on the work of Evans and Russell (1989), among others; through them, I came to appreciate the concept of *mind-sets* as a means of describing the beliefs and assumptions that drive behavior; I also gleaned particular ways of encouraging awareness of tacit mind-sets. Kegan and Lahey (2000) developed a compatible exercise in which they lead clients through a set of questions that can generate potentially deep insights into the basic assumptions underlying tacit commitments that conflict with espoused beliefs. Both approaches illustrate methods that enable clients to gain deep insight into the degree to which they are the authors of their experiences yet allow them to control the depth of the inquiry and their aspirations for change.

As I reflected on my core practices, I saw clearly how deeply Action Science continues to inform my approach to coaching—particularly my commitment to creating a balance between advocacy and inquiry. I also came to appreciate the importance in my model of reflective listening as a tool for inquiry. These insights were useful but not surprising. The most valuable insight was a surprise and builds on the insight I gained from examining my vision: my uncertainty regarding how much of an advocate to be and how I manage that dilemma in my practice through the use of mind-sets. Consequently, I have identified this dilemma as the focus of continuing reflection.

Continuing to Build One's Model

If my experience is any guide, the challenge of developing one's approach to coaching is never over. Even for those who have arrived at Kantor's third and highest stage of model building—a model that is one's own and is internally consistent—the task of modeling the complex world of a coach is ongoing. The reflective coach adopts a posture of humility, bringing full commitment to bear on any given coaching interaction while remaining only half sure of the approach, which is subject to continuing reflection and refinement.

Examining my practice has given me ready access to humility. Although I experienced moments of genuine pride as I reviewed notes and transcripts, I was more frequently plagued by doubts and self-criticisms. For example, I felt reasonably satisfied with my sessions with Bill and Chris, since they both came to an understanding of their own behavior and began making changes in their personal and professional lives. However, I did not feel good overall about coaching Alan. Although I believed I had positioned myself for potentially powerful work with him through the intervention analyzed above, I did not succeed in working with him in ways that would have resulted in deeper learning on his part. Alan subtly resisted reflecting on his contributions to interactions, and I saw no pattern of improvement. While I was occasionally able to point out ways in which his framing of events led him to reduce his options or reinforced self-limiting beliefs, he did not seem to internalize these lessons. After I helped him and his team identify long-term priorities and solve short-term challenges, his perceived need for my services waned, and the coaching relationship faded out over time. I was frustrated because my aspiration had been to help Alan learn a set of attitudes and behaviors that would not only resolve current conflicts but prevent new ones. In particular, I wanted to enable him to smooth off the rough edges on his commanding but overbearing style. My incomplete documentation of our subsequent interactions makes it impossible to go back and determine the points at which I might have done things differently.

Collaboratively Setting Goals
I had not realized until this recent reflection that I never fully shared with Alan either this goal or my sense that we were failing to achieve it. It was implicit in my double-bind confrontation with him, but I had never explicitly returned to our interpretation of our contract for working together, and I had never let him know that he was failing to live up to my expectations. Without knowing it, I had fallen into a posture of holding an untested agenda for his improvement. This was an explicit violation of my model. How was I to account for this?

These reflections led me to contact Alan, with ironic results. He had been promoted to a new position, managing a budget twenty times the one he had been handling when we worked together and overseeing a workforce of many thousands of people. Clearly, my shortcomings had not held him back much. When I summarized my concerns about my failure to capitalize on our mutual awareness of the influence of his personal history on his current behavior, Alan was amused. He said,

> I think what you got was pretty much what you were going to get. You sensitized me to some issues, and I made some changes. But at a certain point, you are who you are and it's a two-way street. It's also up to other people to accommodate me. You may have missed an opportunity, but not by much.

He went on to describe the impact of my consulting work with his team, which had resulted in their commitment to a vision of operational excellence. This vision led him to master new methods that produced tremendous gains in efficiency, for which he was promoted to his current position. I had unknowingly succeeded in an area that was Alan's highest priority. Where I fell short was in neglecting to clearly express my own differing aspirations and negotiate the goals for our coaching relationship in a collaborative way. This was a deeper failing, but one that led me to recognize the importance of resolving my ambivalence toward being an advocate and of including my clients in setting goals for the coaching relationship.

I have also concluded that I need to keep working on my ability to assert myself with extremely strong personalities like Alan. It was already a stretch to challenge him as I did. To continue challenging him was apparently beyond my capacity at the time.

Clarifying Stages and Boundaries

I believe I might have maintained a more potent stance had I been equipped with a better-developed model of the stages of a coaching relationship. My thinking about this had not gone beyond recognizing the three stages of a coaching relationship: establishing the relationship, working together, and concluding.

This model now strikes me as too limited. Kantor (1985) argues persuasively that the therapist-patient relationship—and by extension the coach-client relationship—is most fruitfully viewed from a developmental standpoint, with different stages of development representing choice points for the continuation, or dissolution, of the relationship. I am beginning to explore the possibility of applying Kantor's approach to my practice, although I recognize that his framework requires some adaptation from the therapy context.

In this connection, I am working to clarify my beliefs about the boundary between coaching and therapy. Currently, I feel that while there are likely to be differences in the client's motivation to pursue deeper issues, there is no inherent difference in the range of relevant material. Nonetheless, I do believe that a therapist may be of more help with in-depth work in some cases, due to superior training and specialization. How do I recognize the boundary where my effectiveness diminishes and the help of a therapist would be more appropriate? Under what circumstances might parallel coaching and therapy make sense? These are questions I intend to pursue.

Understanding Adult Development

It has also become clear to me that I would do well to expand my model to more explicitly include theories of adult development. Laurent Daloz (1999) illustrates the value of such perspectives by summarizing three developmental schemes (Kegan, 1994; Levinson, 1978; Perry, 1968) and applying them to his mentoring of adult learners. I find Kegan's approach particularly compelling. He posits a path of development that leads to greater consciousness of responsibility for how one constructs the world and acts in it. (See Chapter 6 for an overview of this approach and its implications for coaching.)

Kegan's scheme provides a rigorous conceptual framework for understanding the vision that I now recognize I have been tacitly holding—that of helping clients become "the authors of their experience." This capacity essentially corresponds to the fourth of Kegan's five stages of development. Reflecting on this framework has also enabled me to recognize that I have begun to hold a related yet deeper aspiration for my clients, corresponding to Kegan's fifth stage—that of helping clients see the limits of their self-authorizing systems and find ways to constructively interact with others who make meaning in different ways.

As I begin to incorporate Kegan's framework into my coaching practice, I face the unresolved dilemma of how to reconcile the use of that framework with my commitment to making aspirations explicit and collaboratively setting goals. Practitioners of Kegan's approach tend to keep their methodology tacit, not making it known to clients. My own inclination, consistent with others who have integrated Action Science with a developmental approach (Fisher, Rooke, and Torbert, 2000), is to be transparent with clients about my methods. However, this requires finding ways to introduce a hierarchical scheme of development that could appear evaluative and create defensiveness. Meehan (1999) has taken a significant first step in mapping this dilemma by comparing the risks and benefits of the differing approaches recommended by practitioners of Action Science versus those who use Kegan's model when encountering limits in a client's framing of choices.

Conclusion

The main goal of this chapter has been to demonstrate the value of building a model of one's coaching practice in order to facilitate the transition from primarily an intuitive practitioner to more reflective one. The ideal end state of being a reflective practitioner—one who is able to see in the moment of client interaction everything he or she can see after stepping back and reflecting—is unattainable. However, investing in systematic reflection will move one incrementally in this direction.

By using a framework to assess the state of my own model development, I hope I have stimulated others to invest in the time-consuming work of self-reflection and illustrated one approach to constructing a model. The technology for model building is at a primitive stage of development. The more pilgrims who take this path and are willing to report on their progress, the more quickly we can bring light to an area that is woefully unmapped and which it is our professional obligation to explore. Although reflecting on one's practice is often difficult and sobering, it is also rejuvenating—an antidote to boredom and stagnation.

I hope that this account of my journey will encourage other coaches to come forward with their accounts of building their models and sustaining ongoing reflection.

Notes

[1] I have received enormous support in these reflections by participating in the seminar "Leadership Model Building," led by David Kantor and B. C. Huselton of the Leadership Model Building Company (www.leadershipmodelbuilding.com).

[2] Remarks by Peter Block made during the presentation "Executive Coaching," May 1, 2001, in Cambridge, Mass., at an event sponsored by the Executive Coaching Forum.

[3] Kantor offers a three-stage model, of which the second and third stages are *constraint* (i.e., as we imitate, we begin to add to, subtract from, or amend the model according to our own experiences, testing the model's limits and experimenting with the incorporation of elements from other models) and *autonomy* (i.e., we develop an internally consistent set of principles for our practice that is comprehensive enough to deal with all the typical challenges).

[4] Laurent Daloz (1999) suggests that mentors provide these three elements, which helped me recognize them in my practice.

[5] A comprehensive description of Kantor's "boundary profile" tools is not yet publicly available. However, William Isaacs provides an excellent summary of three of them— Actions Positions (the Four Player Model), Communication Domains, and System Paradigms—in *Dialogue* (1999), pp. 192–229.

[6] Fernando Flores is a particularly dramatic representative of this movement. See Harriet Rubin's (1999) description of him.

[7] Carl Rogers (1961) is the grandfather of this approach, which continues to attract followers.

[8] An intriguing theoretical question, which I do not pursue here, is whether a coach can truly enable clients to become the authors of their experience when the coach's choice of methodological approach is the stimulus for framing such authorship and therefore plays a shaping role.

References

Argyris, C. (2000). *Flawed advice and the management trap.* New York: Oxford University Press.

Argyris, C., R. Putnam, and D. Smith. (1985). *Action Science.* San Francisco: Jossey-Bass.

Argyris, C., and D. Schön. (1975). *Theory in practice: Increasing professional effectiveness.* San Francisco: Jossey-Bass.

Beck, A. (1979). *Cognitive therapy and the emotional disorders.* New York: New American Library.

Burns, D. D. (1989). *The feeling good handbook.* New York: William Morrow and Company.

Covey, S. R. (1989). *The 7 habits of highly effective people: Restoring the character ethic.* New York: Simon & Schuster.

Daloz, L. (1999). *Mentor.* San Francisco: Jossey-Bass.

Evans, R., and P. Russell. (1989). *The creative manager.* London: Unwyn Hyman.

Fisher, D., D. Rooke, and W. R. Torbert. (2000). *Personal and organizational transformations.* Boston: Edge Work Press.

Fitzgerald, C. (1997). The MBTI and leadership development: Personality and leadership reconsidered in changing times. In C. Fitzgerald and L. K. Kirby (eds.), *Developing leaders: Research and applications in psychological type and leadership development.* Mountain View, Calif.: Davies-Black Publishing.

Harrison, R. (1995). *The collected papers of Roger Harrison.* San Francisco: Jossey-Bass.

Isaacs, W. (1999). *Dialogue.* New York: Doubleday.

Jentz, B. (1999). *Soft skills for a hard world.* Unpublished manuscript.

Kantor, D. (1985). Couples therapy, crisis induction, and change. In A. Gurman (ed.), *Casebook of marital therapy.* New York: Guilford.

————. (1997). *Boundary profile description.* Unpublished manuscript.

————. (2001a). *Boundary profile and structural imprint.* Unpublished manuscript.

————. (2001b). *The model building matrix.* Unpublished manuscript.

Kantor, D., and J. Neal. (March 1985). Integrative shifts for the theory and practice of family systems therapy. *Family Process* 24: 13–29.

Kegan, R. (1994). *In over our heads: The mental demands of modern life.* Cambridge: Harvard University Press.

Kegan, R., and L. L. Lahey. (2000). *How the way we talk can change the way we work.* San Francisco: Jossey-Bass.

Landsberg, M. (1997). *The tao of coaching.* Santa Monica, Calif.: Knowledge Exchange.

Levinson, D. (1978). *The seasons of a man's life.* New York: Knopf.

McGoldrick, M., J. Giordano, and J. Pearce (eds.). (1996). *Ethnicity and family therapy.* New York: Guilford Press.

Meehan, E. S. (1999). *On the mutually informing potential of Action Science and constructive-developmental psychology.* Ph.D. diss., Harvard Graduate School of Education.

Oshry, B. (1995). *Seeing systems.* San Francisco: Berrett-Koehler.

Perry, W. (1968). *Forms of intellectual and ethical development in the college years.* New York: Holt, Rinehart & Winston.

Riso, D. R., and R. Hudson. (2000). *Understanding the Enneagram.* Boston: Houghton-Mifflin.

Rogers, C. R. (1961). *On becoming a person.* Boston: Houghton-Mifflin.

Rubin, H. (January, 1999). The power of words. *Fast Company* 21: 142.

Schneider, W. (1994). *The reengineering alternative: A plan for making your current culture work.* New York: McGraw-Hill.

Schön, D. (1982). *The reflective practitioner.* New York: Basic Books.

————. (1987). *Educating the reflective practitioner.* San Francisco: Jossey-Bass.

Seagal, S., and D. Horne. (1997). *Human dynamics.* Waltham, Mass.: Pegasus Communications.

Senge, P. (1990). *The fifth discipline*. New York: Doubleday.

Torbert, W. R. (1991). *The power of balance: Transforming self, society and scientific inquiry*. Newbury Park, Calif.: Sage Publications.

Whitmore, J. (1992). *Coaching for performance*. London: Nicholas Brealy.

PART II

EXECUTIVE COACHING

PRACTICES

[4]

UNDERSTANDING AND SUPPORTING DEVELOPMENT OF EXECUTIVES AT MIDLIFE

CATHERINE FITZGERALD

Because most executives are in midlife (late thirties and beyond), executive coaches may find that an understanding of the midlife process enhances their effectiveness. Our purpose in this chapter is twofold: to help executive coaches understand the midlife process and to provide strategies with which to support that process.

My son turned thirteen as I began to write this chapter, so adolescence has been very much on my mind. In adolescence, we can't help but see the enormous changes that take place; in midlife, the changes are less visible. But I'm convinced—after talking to hundreds of clients, colleagues, and friends about their experiences of midlife, and from immersing myself in the theoretical and research literature on the topic—that midlife is a natural epoch in human development.

Understanding Midlife

This chapter offers two components for understanding the midlife process: a theoretical framework for midlife, based on Jung's theory, and a description of the three stages of midlife.

A Theoretical Framework for Midlife

There are many different ways to conceptualize what happens at midlife (see Lachman and James, 1997; Levinson, 1978; Vaillant, 1993). This chapter presents a framework for understanding midlife that I feel best fits and gives conceptual coherence to the wide variety of experiences people have at midlife. The framework incorporates—and integrates—two different aspects of the work of Carl Jung: his distinction between the first and second halves of life (1971b) and his identification of robust individual differences, which he called psychological types (1971a).

The First and Second Halves of Life

Jung (1971b) asserted that the goals of the first half of life (through approximately age 35 to 40) are qualitatively different from the goals of the second half. The goal of the first half of life is to make your way in the world, to "win for [yourself] a place in society" (p. 12). The focus is on being a specialist—specializing in a family role (for example, the older, responsible one), a profession or business, a way of life, and so on.

In the second half of life, in contrast, the focus is on being a generalist, on revisiting and incorporating all of the parts of yourself that you had put aside in order to make your way in the world in the first half of life. The goal of the second half of life is individual integration and wholeness—which necessarily includes all of your neglected, disowned, and rejected parts, the characteristics that are described, for example, as follows:

- *My sister is like that, but I'm not.*
- *That dishonest person is like that, but I'm not.*
- *Some people are tolerant about situations like that, but I'm not.*

In Fitzgerald (1997a), I described midlife as a time when people begin to get "inklings, 'taps on the shoulder' with a subtle but increasingly clear message: 'We're back!'" These inklings come from a variety of ideas and emotions that we may experience as old, primitive, and perhaps unsettling, because they feel as if they don't really belong to us.

According to Jung, this period is one of preparation for a significant, although not necessarily conscious or obvious, change that is about to take place. He characterized the process as "a matter of indirect signs of a change which seems to take its rise in the unconscious. Often it is something like a slow change in a person's character; in another case certain traits may come to light which had disappeared since childhood; or again, inclinations and interests begin to weaken and others take their place" (1933, p. 104).

When we accept these developments into our awareness and expand our sense of who we are, we initiate a rich, although not usually easy, process of integration within ourselves. Through this process, we become more open to other perspectives and increase our awareness both of the necessary tension between opposites (e.g., between practicality and vision) and of the need to accept and work well with that tension (Fitzgerald, 1997b).

The midlife process involves a gradual expansion of the sense of self to include these neglected, disowned, and rejected parts. The goals of the midlife process are paradoxical and involve developing yourself as much as possible as a unique individual, with a unique history and set of experiences, *while at the same time* seeing yourself as more and more "cut of common cloth," as more and more being very human, very much like other people.

Psychological Types

The other aspect of Jung's work that is relevant to midlife involves his identification of psychological types—robust differences in individuals. Jung identified three dimensions of individual difference,[1] with each dimension consisting of two opposite preferences:

- Extraversion–Introversion
- Sensing–Intuition
- Thinking–Feeling

Jung believed that each person has natural preferences for one side of each of the three dimensions.[2]

He considered the preferences of the second and third dimensions (Sensing, Intuition, Thinking, and Feeling) to be the basic human *cognitive* functions. (Table 5 describes the four functions.) The second dimension

---

Table 5

Jung's Four Cognitive Functions

Two Forms of Perception

- *Sensing (S)* perception relies on data from the five senses. Because of its basis in the senses, it focuses on what exists in the present moment and is linked to concrete, practical, verifiable, and specific ways of knowing.

- *Intuition (N)* perception relies on insights, patterns, and hunches as a way of viewing the world. It involves perception that focuses on possibilities for the future. Intuition is linked to imaginative, conceptual, abstract, and future-oriented ways of knowing.

Two Forms of Judgment

- *Thinking (T)* judgment is focused on objective, impersonal, and logical ways of deciding. It is associated with an analytic and critical stance and an emphasis on fairness and justice.

- *Feeling (F)* judgment is focused on subjective, personal, and values-based ways of deciding. It is associated with a focus on the human (rather than the technical) aspects of problems and an emphasis on relationships, harmony, and kindness.

Note: For a more detailed description, see Myers, McCaulley, Quenk, and Hammer, 1998.

(Sensing–Intuition) involves *perceiving* (taking in information about the world); the third dimension (Thinking–Feeling) involves *judging* (making decisions).

Jung's theory, elaborated by Myers and Briggs, who developed the *Myers-Briggs Type Indicator* (MBTI) personality inventory (Myers, McCaulley, Quenk, and Hammer, 1998), asserts that individuals have a robust and enduring preference for one of the perceiving functions (Sensing or Intuition) and will tend to use that function to the relative neglect of its opposite. As a result, one of the perceiving functions typically becomes well developed, refined, and conscious, while the other remains less developed, less refined, and more unconscious. A similar process occurs with the judging functions (Thinking and Feeling), with similar consequences.

As a result of their preferences for one each of the perceiving and the judging functions, plus their experience in making a great deal of use of these preferred functions, individuals tend to exhibit characteristics of the combinations of these preferences (Sensing and Thinking, Sensing and Feeling, Intuition and Thinking, or Intuition and Feeling).

Psychological Type Differences in Midlife

In attempting to understand the midlife process, it is important to integrate psychological type into the notion of the first and second halves of life. First, psychological type has a great influence on what we neglect, disown, and reject in the first half of life and these aspects are often a key focus of development in the second half. Second, because psychological type greatly influences our characteristic ways of dealing with the world—and with ourselves—it may also influence the ways in which we perceive and judge the challenges of midlife and will have some impact on our approach to dealing with them.

Jung's idea that the first half of life is focused on being a specialist and the second half on being a generalist applies to psychological type as well. In the first half of life, individuals tend to specialize in their two preferred functions; in the second half, the areas of greatest development and growth typically involve their two less-preferred, more neglected functions.

This theory implies that if development has basically gone well, individuals enter midlife with two well-developed, *adult* functions, one for perceiving the world (either Sensing or Intuition) and one for making judgments (Thinking or Feeling). However, people will also have two much less-developed, *childlike/childish* functions, which are the opposites of their preferred perceiving and preferred judging functions. So we could say that while the adult functions have spent the first half of life establishing our place in the world, the childlike/childish functions have been quiet and unobtrusive, perhaps helpful at times if their skills were required, since we develop and use skills as necessary, across all functions. Then in midlife, our childlike functions intrude and begin to demand much more attention.

At midlife, the less-preferred functions typically display the following characteristics:

- They have an unrefined, idiosyncratic, and young quality.
- They feel at least a little strange and different, sometimes in a good way and sometimes in a worrisome way.
- Unlike our preferred functions, they are not under our conscious, refined, deliberate control.

- Given some time and attention, they become more familiar and somewhat more manageable.

Attending to our less-preferred functions—unruly and ill-mannered as they can be—can really pay off. Integrating them with our preferred functions can greatly enhance our capacity to use the gifts of both sides of the dimensions, understand and appreciate a wider range of personality types, engage in paradoxical thinking, and move toward personal integration and wholeness. Developing and integrating our less-preferred functions can also provide a sense of rejuvenation, a recovery from a subtle and puzzling feeling of stagnation that can occur at midlife. Table 6 contains a brief description of the less-preferred functions at midlife. The appendix has lengthier narrative descriptions of the less-preferred functions at midlife.

The Three Stages of Midlife

Most work settings operate on the assumption that the people in them will behave in calm, logical, and predictable ways. There is little recognition of and support for developmental transitions that may be confusing, distracting, and even turbulent—particularly ones that might affect the leaders who are responsible for ensuring calm, logical, and predictable work environments. As a result of this lack of recognition and support, the midlife process—in which individuals integrate neglected, disowned, or rejected parts of themselves into a larger sense of self and which is likely to be confusing and distracting—generally takes place quietly and behind the scenes.

My work with executives—which has involved both conducting intensive leadership development programs and coaching many executives, sometimes over a period of years—has convinced me that although executives in midlife may look even and unchanging on the surface, there is often a great deal of development taking place. And there are often periods of confusion, disorientation, and even turbulence—reactions that the executive must try to understand and deal with privately, while maintaining a calm, confident, and collected public demeanor.

My experiences coaching executives in midlife has led me to see the midlife process, as it is experienced by executives, as typically occurring in three stages: getting inklings, going underground, and bringing the larger self out into the world. These stages seem to be of variable intensity and duration in different executives.

Table 6

Descriptions of the Less-Preferred Functions at Midlife

Midlife Intuition for Sensing Types

In midlife, Sensing types are drawn—at times—to

- Paying attention to their hunches and the patterns they see—even those that are not yet supported by facts

- Focusing on possibilities and seeking new and different ways of understanding and approaching the world

- Engaging in artistic or creative activities (visiting art museums, writing poetry, painting), even when they have no practical value

Midlife Sensing for Intuitive Types

In midlife, Intuitive types are drawn—at times—to

- Staying present moment-to-moment in the real world, rather than focusing on associations and the future

- Appreciating the history, reality, immediacy, and temporal quality of things

- Experiencing the sensory world in a more direct way (feeling the soil while gardening, focusing on what a chair really feels like)

Midlife Feeling for Thinking Types

In midlife, Thinking types are drawn—at times—to

- Focusing on what they care about and value, rather than on what's logical

- Considering their personal reactions to, not their analysis of, a situation, and taking into account the personal reactions of others

- Viewing a situation from a more attached and subjective perspective

Midlife Thinking for Feeling Types

In midlife, Feeling types are drawn—at times—to

- Being separate from others—even others about whom they care deeply

- Viewing a situation with more detachment and objectivity

- Being assertive and taking their own interests and needs seriously even when they conflict with those of others

Getting Inklings

This first stage of midlife occurs early in the process, as executives begin to notice new and surprising reactions and desires that often do not easily fit into their existing ways of seeing and dealing with the world. Typically, the clients with whom I work are living busy, engaged lives when they start to notice unexpected shifts in focus and direction. The challenges of the first stage are to pay attention to the new reactions and desires (even if they are distracting and uncomfortable) and to observe these new developments with interest and curiosity.

This stage can involve the following reactions:

- New and inexplicable interests
- Loss of interest in what was once exciting and compelling
- More complicated reactions to events and decisions
- Need for time alone, to putter and daydream

New and Inexplicable Interests When discussing their interests and how they're spending their time, clients in midlife often mention that they are drawn to activities and pursuits that don't make much logical sense to them. Such activities and pursuits take many forms, but what is characteristic is that the new interests really draw the person, involve a strong longing, and don't seem logical or sensible to them. Clients often speak a bit sheepishly about their new interests, using phrases such as "Nobody knows about this, but . . . ," "You're going to think this is really strange, but . . . ," or "This really isn't at all like me, but . . . " At the same time, they may use a different tone when describing these new interests, one almost of reverence coupled with a little embarrassment.

Clients in this stage have identified interests that include reading religious or spiritual books, painting or drawing, riding horses, putting together family photograph albums, reading or writing poetry, collecting a certain kind of art, spending time in a particular natural place, or gardening. The nature of the interest is frequently related to their less-developed MBTI functions. Sensing types often develop interests in more *abstract* areas such as art or poetry, Intuitive types may turn to *real* things like gardening or nature, and Thinking types may pursue *spiritual* or *relationship-based* interests.[3]

Loss of Interest in What Was Once Exciting and Compelling   Clients in midlife have reported with concern that things that had been exciting and compelling—and sometimes greatly wished for (such as a promotion or a plum assignment)—were losing their appeal. The situations described are different from situations in the past when one interest or focus was replaced by another, which was then pursued enthusiastically. In the new situation, there are no new interests or focus, except perhaps ones that seem irrelevant or even weird (such as described in the last section).

The loss of interest creates dilemmas and difficult questions for clients. They may wonder, for example, "Am I losing my edge?" "What's going on with me?" or even "Should I force myself to get over this?" They may begin to ask themselves whether they were ever genuinely interested at all, but discussion of their history usually confirms a robust and very real past interest or even passion.

If the client is facing a decision, the situation can be excruciating. Say, for instance, that an executive has been offered a dream job, and everyone involved (often both at work and at home) assumes that he or she will be thrilled and will jump at the opportunity. When the executive expresses reservations, others might react with shock and/or disapproval:

- *This is what you said you wanted.*

- *Are you too big for your britches that this isn't enough (or good enough) for you?*

- *What's going on with Mary that she's hesitating?*

- *Is John really not up to the challenge?*

The client may be torn between excitement about the potential job and a feeling of flatness about or even aversion to it.

The situation is usually much less painful and urgent when the client is not facing a decision about a new job or other life changes. Executives then may just notice declining interest over time:

- *This job doesn't engage me the way it used to, but it's not as if I'm drawn to doing anything else.*

- *I can't figure out what's going on with me—my boss is really supportive, we're doing great, I should be really excited and happy.*

- *I'm having a hard time getting myself geared up—it's like pulling teeth and I'm not giving it my best effort.*

- *This isn't fun anymore and it's still a great job and a great opportunity, so the only thing that's changed is me.*

More Complicated Reactions Clients in midlife often report that their reactions to events are not as clear-cut and comprehensible as they had been. These executives may experience themselves as unexpectedly restless and distracted, pulled in two different directions at the same time, or prone to overreact emotionally in ways that are hard for them to understand.

Decisions, especially those concerning job or lifestyle changes, can seem more complicated. Executives who pride themselves on their clarity and decisiveness may feel unexpectedly hesitant, uncertain, or even paralyzed. When exploring their reactions in coaching, clients often realize that such situations usually involve a conflict between what they *should* want and what they *really* want.

Need for Time Alone, to Putter and Daydream Clients in midlife report a desire for solitude—but not for the purpose of engaging in focused and productive work. They're drawn to being by themselves, but they often don't really know what to do with themselves when they are alone. They may take long walks or putter around their home, garden, or office. They may be drawn to go through old papers, letters, books, or photographs. They may experience a desire to go someplace alone—an old neighborhood or city, the ocean, the desert, and so on.

Going Underground

The second stage of midlife comes after a person has responded to the inklings of the earlier stage by privately pursuing developmental activities of some kind. In this stage, the initial sense of surprise and disorientation about shifting interests and focus has evolved, so that, on the surface, life appears to be proceeding as usual even as personal development is quietly, but deliberately, pursued. The activities and interests are very variable across executives and are usually pursued, not for logical reasons, but because they satisfy a vague but insistent desire.

Over the course of the second stage, a calmer, more confident, and more deliberate conviction of the value of these developmental activities may begin to emerge, along with an increasing recognition of an expanded sense of self. The challenge of this stage is to pursue a variety of developmental activities with curiosity and an open mind, while maintaining a high level of performance at work.

People in this stage may experience the following reactions:

- Private exploration of areas of interest

- A search for meaning, for a sense of past and potential identity

- Shifts in relationships with others

Private Exploration of Areas of Interest Many midlife executives with whom I have worked have chosen to privately—but intensively—pursue their personal development outside the workplace. This stage of the midlife process usually seems less turbulent and confusing than the first stage, when changing interests and new reactions are often startling or upsetting. In this second stage, emerging interests can be explored in a calmer and more intentional way.

Such interests may include reading of spiritual or personal growth books, artistic pursuits (such as painting or drawing), collecting art or artifacts, writing of various kinds (poetry, journaling), physical activities, and reflection. The following characteristics distinguish midlife developmental activities from the hobbies or interests of the first half of life:

- The pursuit of interests seems emotionally charged. Clients do not discuss their interests in a matter-of-fact way but are serious and quietly excited.

- They are somewhat hesitant, even embarrassed, about their interests.

- These interests are very private; clients don't discuss them widely because they feel they are somehow personally revealing.

- Clients are passionate about their interests, even though they typically don't feel their devotion can be justified logically.

- The nature and form of the interest is very often related to the executive's less-preferred MBTI functions (see Table 6 for specifics).

Because executives in midlife are devoting energy to interests that are not work-related, they may experience themselves as less ambitious and less driven, and they may begin to question long-held career goals.

Search for Meaning During this stage of midlife, clients are often quietly driven by a search for meaning, for what's most unique and valuable about them and for what's most important to them. Some common elements of the process include

- Focus on exploring a more comprehensive and meaningful sense of personal history and, sometimes, family history

- Recollection, reconsideration, and reinterpretation of key life and work events and people

- An increasing sense that there may be a higher purpose to life and that it would be valuable and comforting to understand it

- A tendency to look for—and often find—significance in chance events: *I haven't seen him in years—isn't it amazing that I should run into him just when I've been thinking about the impact of that incident on my life?*

The kinds of activities in which clients engage in their search for meaning include reflecting, journaling, paying attention to their dreams, reviewing written material from the past, reading, and visiting people and places from earlier times in their lives.

Shifts in Relationships with Others As clients develop in midlife, they often report shifts in their relationships. They may be drawn to other people, either those who are themselves going through a process of growth or those whose characteristics or interests match those that the executive is developing or pursuing. Time spent in conversations with such people can be experienced as rich and valuable, as well as somehow affirming.

On the other hand, clients may be less drawn to—and may even actively avoid—peers and friends who think of them in a static way and who assume that they are exactly the same people they have always been. Clients, in fact, can be taken aback when they encounter others' views of them—views that seem dated and outgrown. They are grateful to those who don't assume they are the same as always, like George Bernard Shaw who liked his tailor because "he takes my measurements anew each time he sees me, whereas others expect me to fit old measurements." Yet clients sometimes find that they are caught in a dilemma, since they know that the unhappiness they feel when people don't notice they are changing may be due in part to the fact that they have not spoken freely about their new interests.

Shifting relationships, especially those that involve outgrowing previously valued connections, are often indicators of the degree and scope of the changes that are under way.

Bringing the Larger Self into the World

The third stage of midlife occurs still later in the process, after a considerable amount of development and integration has taken place underground. The challenge of the third stage of midlife is bringing the development that has been occurring into both work and life. Clients at this stage often experience the following reactions:

- Increasing clarity about who they are and what they want

- An increasing desire to have their work and their life fit who they are now

Increasing Clarity about Identity and Goals At this stage, clients report becoming increasingly clear about who they are and about the kinds of work they want to do and the kinds of relationships they want to have. Clients describe being more settled with and more confident in their sense of themselves. At this stage, clients generally appear to have a more down-to-earth—and usually more accurate—sense of themselves, a sense that includes recognition of both strengths and weaknesses. They typically focus less on having to prove themselves to others and more on satisfying their own standards.

An Increasing Desire for Work and a Life That Fits Them Now As development occurs in midlife, some aspects of the expanded sense of self may be demonstrated in the workplace, but often the executive appears quite unchanged on the surface. As the development becomes more and more consolidated, clients report desires to

- Be seen for who they are *now*

- Have work and lives that fit them

- Make a contribution that's in line with what's most important to them

Some executives have sufficient flexibility in their work and their lives to allow them to work toward what feels like a good fit. Others find some aspects of their work or their lives constraining and face difficult decisions about making changes.

Strategies for Supporting Midlife Development

Poet e. e. cummings addressed—in vivid terms—the pressure placed on people to conform and the challenge of developing as an individual:

> To be nobody but yourself in a world which is doing its best, night and day, to make you everybody else, means to fight the hardest battle which any human being can fight, and never stop fighting.

There are a variety of methods executive coaches can use to support the battle to which cummings refers and to nurture midlife development in a way that enhances both the executive's current performance and his or her future development. Possible strategies can involve supporting clients in

- Pursuing the search for personal meaning
- Maintaining high performance at midlife
- Making decisions about the future

Pursuing the Search for Personal Meaning

The search for personal meaning is one of the key aspects of the midlife process and, because midlife is not commonly discussed or understood in either work or personal settings, executives typically have little or no support for their search for meaning. When appropriate, an executive coach may provide information and guidance that can make the process less turbulent and episodic and more valuable and satisfying for the executive.

There are a number of ways in which coaches can support the search for personal meaning, including

- Encouraging reflection
- Helping to identify and make sense of emerging and evolving interests—and encouraging their pursuit
- Helping to identify key themes and deeper patterns in a client's history, interests, talents, values, contributions, and commitments
- Providing resources that support the search for meaning

Encouraging Reflection

One of the most valuable things that people in midlife can do is to take regular time for reflection—through such activities as quiet walks or drives, meditation, journaling, engaging in spiritual or religious activities, visiting museums, and pursuing avocations (gardening, woodworking, sailing), if they are done at a reasonably reflective pace. Unfortunately, many executives find it difficult to take time out for reflection, both for situational reasons (they are extremely busy people) and for psychological reasons (the reflective process may seem too slow or unproductive to those accustomed to an action-oriented, problem-solving approach).

I often encourage clients to brainstorm about

- The kind of setting or situation (taking a long walk, visiting an art museum, sitting on their back porch by themselves) that would be most palatable and bearable (at first) and most engaging and rewarding (a little later)

- When they might be able to get *some* time, perhaps even just an hour a week to start

In terms of personality, Introverts are more likely to be familiar with the process of reflection than are Extraverts. However, Extraverts are often very interested to find out that people with a preference for Extraversion tend to turn inward in midlife, to seek more private time, and that this leaning is a normal and potentially beneficial part of the midlife process. However, many Extraverts often don't know what to do with themselves once they are alone, and they may end up feeling uneasy—which could cause them to avoid spending further time alone. Suggesting that clients start with small amounts of time and gradually lengthen their periods of solitude can be helpful.

Occasionally getting away from the everyday routines of work and personal lives can provide invaluable new perspectives. Clients often say that they really need to take several weeks off, but they are often satisfied with brief respites of a day or two.

Identifying, Understanding, and Pursuing Emerging and Evolving Interests

When clients identify an emerging interest they experience as surprising, somewhat illogical, or even weird, I often inquire about why they think they are drawn to it and what they experience when they pursue it. Answers to these questions typically are vague and sometimes ironic:

- *I'm not really sure and I don't really have the time, but it just feels satisfying.*

- *I really liked to do it when I was young; maybe I'm going into my second childhood.*

- *It's somehow comforting and calms me down.*

- *It engages me in a way that most other things these days don't.*

I frequently identify the developmental aspects of a client's new interests in terms of his or her particular MBTI type. For example, with Intuitive types, I might explain how gardening or horseback riding draws on—and contributes to the development of—their less-preferred Sensing function; with Sensing types, I'll point out how writing poetry or visiting an art museum does the same for their less-preferred Intuition function.

Since I strongly believe that engaging in activities related to a client's less-preferred MBTI functions contributes substantially to his or her type development, which in turn enhances leadership capacity, I'll often make that case and encourage the client to pursue emerging interests.

Identifying Key Themes and Deeper Patterns

One common aspect of the midlife process involves the search for one's own unique identity, for what William James called "character."

> I have often thought that the best way to define a man's character would be to seek out the particular mental or moral attitude in which, when it came upon him, he felt himself most deeply and intensely active and alive.

Clients seek answers to questions such as Who am I anyway? What's unique or special about me? What do I want to do with the rest of my life? What contributions do I want to make to my work, my family, the world? What legacy would I love to leave?

A first step toward answering these questions often involves revisiting a client's work and life histories and identifying important influences and patterns that have shaped and characterized both professional and personal lives. In the course of my coaching, I typically ask clients about their work and life histories, and, while helping them to reflect on and identify key influences and patterns, we sometimes discuss the implications for future choices and development.

One means of gaining this perspective is to revisit past key players. I therefore often suggest that clients contact and meet with former mentors and peers; such meetings are invariably useful, often poignant, and may lead to a valuable reconsideration of past experiences, repeating themes, enduring talents, and current status.

My approach at this stage has been influenced by James Hillman, who suggests in *The Soul's Code* (1996) that there is an ultimate purpose for which each person is born and that the circumstances, successes, and hardships of life act as preparation for achieving that purpose. Although Hillman seems to believe this in a literal way, I prefer to think of it metaphorically. I frequently ask myself, and then perhaps my client, "If your life— with its unique history, successes, failures, talents, values, and interests —were preparing you to make a unique and valuable contribution to the world, what might that contribution be?" Clients often have extremely interesting and personally meaningful responses to this question. The answers may be quite vague at first but usually become clearer over time.

A similar method has been helpful to clients who are dealing with severe disappointment, hardship, or loss (the failure of a major effort, a long-anticipated promotion that went to someone else, a rupture in an important relationship, getting fired). After providing support, jointly analyzing the possible options, and acknowledging that the situation is less than ideal, I sometimes ask, "If you were to think that the universe has a plan for you, and that there are some things of great importance that you are meant to learn and understand now, perhaps through the current situation, what do you think these lessons might be?"

I have been impressed with the clarity and speed of my clients' replies, which are typically poignant and seem accurate in terms of their development.

- *I've always succeeded and have become somewhat arrogant—now I guess it's important that I realize that I can't always get what I want.*

- *I've always hated whining and I haven't been sympathetic with people who were having problems—now I know what it's like, and I think it will make me more compassionate.*

- *I've had some doubts about whether this was really the right direction for me—so a part of me is disappointed and a part of me is relieved that I can now really consider other possibilities.*

- *I've been losing interest in this job for a long time, but I was too comfortable to make any changes—I'm scared now, but I'll be forced to find out what I really want to do.*

Finding meaning in the face of painful situations seems to provide clients with a sense of comfort and purpose that has a sustained positive impact on them.

Providing Resources That Support the Search for Meaning

Clients vary greatly in their appreciation of reading as a resource. Some find it helpful, and others do not. For those who express interest, I have recommended a number of books. In some cases, biographies of inspirational figures (Winston Churchill or Eleanor Roosevelt) may be comforting and instructive. For others with some appetite and tolerance for a more psychological approach, books such as *Callings* (Levoy, 1997), *The Middle Passage* (Hollis, 1993), *Owning Your Own Shadow* (Johnson, 1991), *The Soul's Code* (Hillman, 1996), and the unlikely named, but terrific, *Swamplands of the Soul* (Hollis, 1996) have been helpful. Bridges's *Transitions* (1980) is a book that a wide variety of clients have found to be valuable and I recommend it often.

Maintaining High Performance at Midlife

One of the key challenges for executives at midlife is to function at a high level in their demanding jobs, while responding to the psychological and emotional demands of midlife described earlier. The ways in which executive coaches can support clients in maintaining high performance at midlife include

- Helping them pay attention to—and intentionally manage—their energy, focus, and drive
- Helping them minimize "dutiful" activities and identify—and use— their individual high-performance patterns

Helping Them Pay Attention to Energy, Focus, and Drive

Executive coaches can help clients by paying attention to—and encouraging their clients to pay attention to—the fluctuations in energy, focus, and drive that may occur in midlife. These fluctuations take a number of common forms:

- *A loss of energy when confronted with responsibilities, situations, and sometimes even people that the executives feel represent old, outgrown, "been there, done that" aspects of themselves.* The reaction clients describe is a feeling of being pulled back into a less-developed time, which is uncomfortable, draining, and deadening. When discussing such situations, clients often apologize for overreacting; they may feel mystified and annoyed with themselves for not being able to perform in these situations with their usual energy and effectiveness. Their confusion and annoyance with themselves can increase their sense of feeling drained and deflated.

- *A sense of anxiety, sometimes surprisingly intense, when confronted with situations about which they are torn.* Clients who have expressed great reservations about having their careers go in a particular direction have reported feeling anxious—and really knocked off-balance—by hearing about the promotion of a peer in that direction. Clients who are beginning to see certain kinds of recognition and reward as *not* what really satisfies them can have strong reactions to hearing about someone else's receiving such recognition or rewards. When asked if, on reflection, they wanted the promotion or recognition, clients are likely to say that they really did not but that their reactions show them how much conflict they are still experiencing about what they *do* want.

- *A surprising sense of energy, enthusiasm, and optimism resulting from being involved in certain kinds of assignments, conversations, events.* Clients have reported—with excitement but also some puzzlement—that an unusual new assignment, a brief conversation, or a particular event has sparked their energy and triggered their creativity, drive, and optimism about the future. On reflection, clients can typically relate those situations that spark their energy to their emerging interests and their evolving development.

Executive coaches can help clients analyze such situations and understand the developmental roots, as well as the developmental implications, of their unexpected reactions. With regard to situations that drain their energy, coaches can help clients become more aware of which kinds of situations affect them and can brainstorm with them about ways to avoid or minimize their involvement with such situations. *Work responsibilities* they have outgrown, or at least substantial portions of such responsibilities, can often be delegated, sometimes resulting in valuable developmental assignments for others. It can be harder for clients to extricate themselves from *social responsibilities* that have become draining and deflating (e.g., Friday afternoon get-togethers, monthly lunch meetings) because there are often many expectations and attachments that accompany them. However, finding ways to take a temporary time-out from such activities (e.g., three months) can help clients eliminate sources of energy drain, while allowing time to explore their reactions and their desires for the future.

When clients describe situations that increase their anxiety, coaches can help them explore their reactions and articulate what they *do* want, perhaps comparing what they *used to* want or what they think they *should* want. Supporting clients in articulating what's most important to them in their work and in crafting a picture of a desired future—in terms of the kind of work they are drawn to, the way they would like to develop, and the contributions they would love to make—can be extremely valuable.

Coaches can also help clients understand and capitalize on unexpected positive reactions. Such reactions can indicate new directions and new arenas of work that can be both energizing and rewarding and in which the executive's evolving development can make substantial and unique contributions. The form of pursuit of such new directions and arenas can vary. Common forms include

- An expansion of an existing role (e.g., more focus and time spent on mentoring staff)
- Further development of a component of the executive's organization (e.g., an innovative approach or increased focus on serving a particular customer segment)
- The crafting of a different approach to a current role (e.g., working in a more team-based way or in more collaboration with customers, peers, and others)
- Volunteering to participate in a new role (e.g., working on a cross-organizational task force or an international assignment)

Overall, helping clients stay on a relatively even keel, while learning and finding meaning from their unexpected reactions, can contribute enormously to their effectiveness.

Helping Minimize "Dutiful" Activities and Identify High-Performance Patterns
Once work practices in organizations and professions get established, they can be extraordinarily difficult to change, even when they are reducing the

effectiveness of some or even all of the people involved. Departing from such established practices can be seen as heretical, risky ("What if everyone were to do that!"), and/or presumptuous.

The problems with such practices may be that they were initially adopted for arbitrary reasons or that, even if once quite effective, they may have been made obsolete by the enormous amount of change in the workplace. Moreover, they rarely accommodate the range of individual differences that are typically found in a work setting.

Executive coaches can help their clients be more effective by encouraging them to notice and respond to their own natural style of working. Two different areas of focus can help executives identify their natural styles:

- Paying attention to activities that the executive is doing in a dutiful way—and identifying different approaches to those activities

- Exploring the specific, even idiosyncratic, characteristics of situations in which the executive is at his or her highest performing—and working to incorporate key elements of such situations into the executive's work practices

Executive coaches can pay attention to the activities and tasks executives describe in dutiful or even burdened ways and can raise questions such as

- Is there any aspect of that activity that interests or engages you?

- Was there any time or situation in which that activity was more engaging or interesting?

- What is the overall goal of that activity? Are there other ways to accomplish that goal?

- Are there any ways that the activity could be done differently that would be more engaging, more efficient, or more effective?

- How would you describe the particular value that you are adding to the accomplishment of that activity?

- Is there any way that you could delegate or at least minimize the time that you spend in that activity?

Activities in which executives are engaging in a dutiful or burdened way are usually *not* the activities in which they are making critical value-added contributions; in fact, they tend to be the places in which they are making the *least* real contribution. And, if their attention is drawn to it, executives can often quickly identify many options for doing things differently. In many cases, they have all the authority and latitude they need to depart from established practice.

Approaching the issue of work style from the opposite direction—by focusing on an executive's individual high-performance pattern—can also be valuable. Asking executives to describe in detail two or three situations in which they performed at their highest level can elicit valuable information about the approaches to work that are likely to be most effective. Executive coaches can encourage clients to customize work as much as possible to match their natural high-performance patterns—even if elements of that pattern are somewhat unconventional. Focusing attention on—and implicitly giving clients permission regarding—the development of a work style that is highly customized to them can make clients much more effective.

An example of an executive's discovering and honoring her natural work style involved the general counsel of a large organization who realized that she was better informed through discussions with involved staff than through reading the legal briefs of pending cases. Her staff was initially surprised when she indicated her preference because it went against traditional practice. Over time, staff members began to look forward to the discussions, as they gained valuable time with and exposure to the general counsel. The executive freed up time for focusing on strategic and policy-related issues and also got more in-depth contact with staff.

For a systematic and comprehensive approach to identifying an individual's high-performance pattern, see Fletcher (1993).

Making Decisions about the Future

As noted earlier, decisions about the future can get more complicated during midlife, for two reasons. First, midlife is a process of integration, and integrative decision making—combining reality and vision (Sensing and Intuition) and mind and heart (Thinking and Feeling)—is more complex. Second, particularly in the early part of the midlife process, the decision maker may be trying to decide something important, while he or she is in the midst of a confusing transition.

Executive coaches can support clients in making decisions about the future in the following ways:

- Provide a framework for a more complex decision-making process
- Help to expand the options being considered

Provide a Framework for a More
Complex Decision-Making Process

It can be helpful for clients to know that there is a good reason—in fact, a reason that has to do with the increasing sophistication and complexity of their decision making—why decision making may feel more tortuous, frustrating, and protracted in midlife. When appropriate, identifying the developmental issues that are specific to a client's psychological type can be useful, in that executives are likely to be drawn to include their less-developed functions more than previously, with the following possible effects:

- Sensing types may pay attention, not just to the reality of the situation, but also to the Intuitive aspects of the situation (what their hunches may indicate, what a sense of the future that is not just experience-based may lead to, what their imagination may suggest).

- Intuitive types may pay attention, not just to their hunches and inspirations, but also to Sensing aspects of the situation (what a realistic, practical, down-to-earth approach may be; what the facts may suggest; what a careful look at experience—separated from imagination—may reveal).

- Thinking types may pay attention, not just to the logic of the situation, but also to Feeling considerations (what's personally important to them, what they care about, and also what others who are involved in the situation care about and see as important).

- Feeling types may pay attention, not just to what they and others involved care about and see as important, but also to Thinking considerations (what an objective perspective might suggest, what a logical analysis might indicate, what a critical eye might notice).

The following exercise may be valuable for executives with a preference for Thinking (the overwhelming majority of executives) who are faced with making a difficult choice. First, ask the executive to identify the benefits and costs of each of the options under consideration. This step, which calls on the Thinking function, is usually very familiar and might in the past have led to a clear-cut decision. In midlife, however, a second step is often helpful and sometimes essential: ask the executive to look over the benefits and costs of all options and identify the ones that matter most, that are personally most important, *without regard to the logic of the situation or to what anyone else in a similar situation might care about or think is important.* This step often reveals key Feeling considerations that were suppressed by the stronger and more familiar Thinking function:

- *This sounds foolish, but being in a place where I can be ten minutes away from my house and my kids is worth giving up the prestige of the other job.*

- *A lot of people would think I was nuts to give up the money and a promotion, but my work with John is going great, I really trust him, and I think we have a good chance of doing work that will have a real impact.*

Help to Expand the Options Being Considered

Many executives can substantially underestimate the options available to them, both within and outside their organizations. Executives who, after a period of development that has been privately pursued, find their current position to be unsatisfying and narrow, often feel stuck and can be afraid that any request for a new direction or a new challenge will be seen as inappropriate and/or unreasonable.

Executive coaches can help clients explore options and can raise questions about negative assumptions. Coaches can also help clients develop plans for collecting data and perhaps for conducting some careful inquiry about options. In addition, helping clients identify people within current and past environments who could safely provide different perspectives and could act as sounding boards can be valuable. In my experience, after a little encouragement from a current or former boss or after discovering that other executives have made similar transitions, most clients begin to explore possibilities with more energy and optimism.

Guidelines for Discussing Midlife Issues

If executive coaches have a coherent way of thinking about midlife, they can help clients better understand their experiences at midlife and be more effective—and more satisfied—as leaders. However, a topic like midlife—which is personal and somewhat psychological—needs to be introduced with care. I propose the following guidelines for executive coaches with regard to discussing the issue of midlife:

- Don't raise midlife issues until you have developed a good working relationship with your client and have substantial credibility with him or her. With some clients, a working relationship and credibility can be established fairly quickly and easily; with others, a great deal of time and effort may be required.

- Introduce midlife issues in the context of a real, immediate business problem that the executive is trying to solve.

- Present information about midlife and its applicability to the client's situation as a hypothesis and then be sure to get the client's views about whether it fits and whether it's potentially helpful.

- Watch your language: try to present information in everyday language and avoid jargon and language that may be too "touchy-feely."

Although having a model for midlife can be helpful, the use of such a model should never lead coaches to stereotype clients, dictate to them the "right" way to approach their work and their development, or reduce clients' interests and experiences to a formula or equation.

Conclusion

For executives in midlife, an executive coach who understands—and has strategies for dealing with—the midlife process can help them navigate the complexity of development while maintaining high performance as leaders in their organizations. Executives who move through midlife supported by a knowledgeable guide will be better able to find—or create—their own paths toward a full and productive second half of life.

Appendix

Narrative Descriptions of the Less-Preferred Functions at Midlife

Midlife Intuition for Sensing Types

For Sensing types, midlife Intuition involves a new desire to pay attention to hunches and to patterns and a new interest in things that they had previously thought were irrelevant or tedious. In one-on-one conversations, midlife Sensing managers have revealed a new—and to them surprising—interest in such areas as art, poetry, or psychology. An ESTJ (Extraverted Sensing Thinking Judging) government manager talked about being drawn to visit art galleries and noted that when she was younger, such places were alien and uninteresting. A Sensing manager in a manufacturing organization talked about being drawn to write poetry, which he had never shown to anyone else. An ESTP (Extraverted Sensing Thinking Perceiving) oil company executive talked with great enthusiasm about recently developing an interest in psychology—a way of thinking about things that he had thought earlier to be irrelevant and weird. What these examples have in common is the midlife Sensing type's new fascination with abstract things that have no immediate practical value.

Intuitive types are familiar with paying attention to their hunches, but Sensing types tend to focus instead on the facts of a situation. In midlife, Sensing types sometimes report paying more attention than previously to their hunches with some surprising—to them—results. An ISTJ (Introverted Sensing Thinking Judging) executive reported, with some enthusiasm, the midlife emergence of his "hunches." Early in the process, he recalled his staff's bringing him a table or chart and his getting a sense—*without the facts*—that something was wrong with it. Because he did not have facts to support his hunches, he thoroughly researched each hunch and found that hunches frequently led him in a useful direction. At the time of our discussion, he declared with pride, "When I tell my staff that I have a hunch about something, they will instantly pursue it!" In general, Sensing types seem to experience midlife Intuition as unsettling, somewhat foreign, but often interesting.

Midlife Sensing for Intuitive Types

For Intuitive types, midlife Sensing involves a desire at times to be more present in the immediate time and place. It seems to take the form of just wanting—for pretty much the first time—to *be*, to sit in a place and just look and hear and touch and smell. It may involve increased interest in physical comfort (how a chair really *feels*) and in sense activities (touching). It may involve a focus on money as something suddenly *real* and not just a concept. Midlife Sensing sometimes involves a new interest in activities such as gardening, with Intuitive types reporting great delight and a quiet satisfaction in feeling the earth, moving things, and just physically experiencing the garden environment. One Intuitive management consultant, unfamiliar with the manifestations of midlife Sensing, confessed that she was drawn to being in her backyard and was spending her time there just looking—with great interest and involvement—at the bark on one particular tree. Intuitive types report this new focus on being more immediately present as both difficult and exciting.

Midlife Feeling for Thinking Types
For Thinking types, midlife Feeling involves discovering their "softer side" and, in the process, Thinking types often experience a new desire for intimacy with others and a new tendency to be emotionally touched by certain expressions of feelings. In midlife, Thinking managers may develop a new focus on people issues. An ST (Sensing Thinking) manager with a strong technical background told me, "The technical issues are less important and much less interesting to me than they were earlier. The people issues are what I care about and am primarily focused on now; I realize how much I have to learn." Thinking types can become unexpectedly—and embarrassingly—tearful about depictions of feelings, even when these depictions are conventional (long-distance telephone ads). A Thinking manager told me, "I've become an old softy. I really care so much about these guys [the other members of the top management team], but they still think I'm a tough guy." At a leadership development program, an ESTJ (Extraverted Sensing Thinking Judging) military officer heard about my interest in midlife and cautiously raised the topic with me. When I generally described the midlife process and some of its possible signs, he confessed, "I can't sing the 'Star Spangled Banner' anymore." Whenever he started to sing the national anthem, he got choked up and started to cry—a reaction that greatly embarrassed him but that also showed him how much he cared about what the "Star Spangled Banner" represented for him. His story illustrates what I often observe and hear from Thinking types about midlife Feeling: that Thinking types can tend to feel somewhat overwhelmed and out of control when they encounter their midlife Feeling.

Midlife Thinking for Feeling Types
For Feeling types, midlife Thinking involves discovering their tougher side, what Jung (1933) called their "sharpness of mind" (p. 108). Feeling types discover an inner push to be, at times, more objective and more

separate from others and to focus on "what I want for myself" rather than feeling obliged to respond to others' needs. In midlife, Feeling types are often drawn to be assertive and competitive in a new way in the world. They may begin to feel a greater sense of their own personal power and authority and let themselves be more challenging. Feeling types report feeling guilty about the urge to do things for themselves rather than doing things for others they care about. A manager with a preference for Feeling told me, "I used to be a nice person"—and then described what sounded like appropriate, assertive setting of limits with others. In addition to occasional guilt, Feeling types report experiencing a new sense of capability and possibility for influence in the world.

Source: From "Type Development and Leadership Development," by C. Fitzgerald. In C. Fitzgerald and L. K. Kirby (eds.), *Developing Leaders: Research and Applications in Psychological Type and Leadership Development* (pp. 311–35), 1997, Palo Alto, Calif.: Davies-Black Publishing. Reprinted with permission.

Notes

[1] *The Myers-Briggs Type Indicator* (MBTI) inventory, which is based on Jung's psychological types, includes a fourth dimension, Judging–Perceiving, that was added by Myers and Briggs based on their interpretation of Jung's work (Myers, McCaulley, Quenk, and Hammer, 1998).

[2] Recent empirical research has provided compelling support for the accuracy of Jung's observations about these robust individual differences. Using traditional statistical methods to identify key domains of difference and to assess them across individuals, psychological researchers have repeatedly identified five factors of personality—now called the *Big Five*. Research comparing the Big Five and the MBTI instrument shows strong correspondence between four of the Big Five factors and the four MBTI dimensions. The fifth factor, Neuroticism, is not assessed by the MBTI instrument. (See Fitzgerald, 1997a for more information.)

[3] No example of the emerging interests of Feeling types comes to mind, which is probably because my clients, like most executives (McCaulley, 1990), have been overwhelmingly Thinking types.

References

Bridges, W. (1980). *Transitions: Making sense of life's changes.* Reading, Mass.: Addison-Wesley.

Fitzgerald, C. (1997a). The MBTI and leadership development: Personality and leadership revisited in changing times. In C. Fitzgerald and L. K. Kirby (eds.),

Developing leaders: Research and applications in psychological type and leadership development (pp. 33–59). Mountain View, Calif.: Davies-Black Publishing.

———. (1997b). Type development and leadership development: Integrating reality and vision, mind and heart. In C. Fitzgerald and L. K. Kirby (eds.), *Developing leaders: Research and applications in psychological type and leadership development* (pp. 311–35). Mountain View, Calif.: Davies-Black Publishing.

Fletcher, J. L. (1993). *Patterns of high performance: Discovering the ways people work best.* San Francisco: Berrett-Koehler.

Hillman, J. (1996). *The soul's code: In search of character and calling.* New York: Random House.

Hollis, J. (1993). *The middle passage: From misery to meaning in midlife.* Toronto: Inner City Books.

———. (1996). *Swamplands of the soul: New life in dismal places.* Toronto: Inner City Books.

Johnson, R. A. (1991). *Owning your own shadow: Understanding the dark side of the psyche.* San Francisco: HarperCollins.

Jung, C. G. (1933). *Modern man in search of a soul.* San Diego, Calif.: Harcourt Brace Jovanovich.

———. (1971a). *Psychological types* (H. G. Baynes, trans., revised by R. F. C. Hull). *The collected works of C. G. Jung,* Volume 6. Princeton, N.J.: Princeton University Press. (Original work published in 1921.)

———. (1971b). Stages of life. In J. Campbell (ed.), *The portable Jung* (pp. 3–22). New York: Penguin Books.

Lachman, M. F., and J. B. James (eds.). (1997). *Multiple paths of midlife development.* Chicago: University of Chicago Press.

Levinson, D. J. (1978). *The season's of a man's life.* New York: Alfred A. Knopf.

Levoy, G. (1997). *Callings: Finding and following an authentic life.* New York: Harmony Books.

McCaulley, M. H. (1990). The Myers-Briggs Type Indicator and Leadership. In K. S. Clark and M. B. Clark (eds.), *Measures of leadership* (pp. 381–418). Greensboro, N.C.: Center for Creative Leadership.

Myers, I. B., M. H. McCaulley, N. L. Quenk, and A. L. Hammer. (1998). *MBTI manual: A guide to the development and use of the Myers-Briggs Type Indicator* (3rd ed.). Mountain View, Calif.: CPP, Inc.

Vaillant, G. E. (1993). *The wisdom of the ego.* Cambridge, Mass.: Harvard University Press.

[5]

BREAKING
THE BOUNDARIES

Leveraging the Personal in Executive Coaching

KATHRYN WILLIAMS

FRED KIEL

MARILYN DOYLE

LAURA SINAGRA

When *Fortune* magazine published the cover story "Why CEOs Fail" (Charan and Colvin, 1999), which investigated the seeming paradox of bright, achievement-oriented people derailing at the apex of their careers, the insights came as no surprise to our executive coaches. We see cases similar to those described all too often in our consulting work. Based on our experience, we could have predicted the magazine's findings: *Fortune*'s "failures" received dismally low marks in areas requiring interpersonal wisdom and emotional competency, the abilities necessary for effectively leading and developing others, building loyalty, and increasing leadership bench strength. At KRW International, we have worked with hundreds of senior executives to help them develop those needed behaviors and avoid the pitfalls that brought down *Fortune*'s unfortunates.

Successful executives, we have found, often run into trouble when the very behaviors that brought them to the top are no longer appropriate. Over the years, high achievers develop their own winning formulas—the particular mix of behaviors they have used along the way and to which they credit their rise in their organizations. Changing these formulas to meet new challenges is indeed difficult. Even when an executive recognizes the need to develop a new approach, old habits die hard. Rational understanding of the need for change rarely is sufficient, and altering a formula that has been rewarded repeatedly over the years can seem too great a risk, even when there is abundant information to suggest that it is no longer working.

The Need for In-Depth As Well As Skills-Based Coaching

Executive coaches have tended to address the need for change with approaches similar to those they would use in coaching for business performance—skills development. At KRW, we have found that, while it is invaluable as a component of the process, pure skills-based coaching seldom results in long-term change. Instead, sustainable change seems to require that the client recognize and understand the deeper motivators of his or her behavior.

Our work with high-achieving executives led us to develop an in-depth, holistic coaching approach that allows for consideration of the ways in which a client's current personal life and personal history influence his or her behavior. This approach involves extensive interviewing of the client and of individuals in the client's work arena and in his or her personal sphere, as well as psychological testing and the more typical measures of executive effectiveness. It examines the relationships between workplace behavior and identity outside of work, emotions, and events in the past. Awareness of the larger context and of deeper motivational drivers provides a foundation on which executives can begin to truly build behavioral flexibility and thus conduct their lives more consciously.

Since the advent of executive coaching, strict boundaries have distinguished it from psychotherapy. It has most often focused on high-level skills training, and any resemblance to therapy has been disavowed. This kind of coaching confines data gathering, discussion, and intervention to the context of the workplace, and its emphasis is on teaching the executive new performance-related skills and strategies. The skills-based coach is careful not to probe into the client's personal or emotional life or early family history. However, the skills framework does not provide the scope for addressing the underlying factors that drive behavior, nor does the skills-based coach typically have the specialized training or experience to do so.

We have found that long-term success and sustainable change frequently require a different approach, one that carefully crosses the boundaries of traditional executive coaching and looks beyond the workplace to help the individual achieve a more lasting understanding of the self and an opportunity for what we might call alignment of head and heart. This approach—which requires an executive coach who has achieved credibility through a solid grounding in the business world, who can preserve objectivity by remaining outside the client's organization, and who is experienced in the psychology of individual dynamics—can mean the difference between a fleeting fix and sustainable change.

Getting Personal:
The Unique Characteristics of the In-Depth Approach

The in-depth executive coaching approach adds five unique elements to the typical coaching process: the psychologist-coach, collection of current personal life data, examination of personal history, exploration of emotions, and increased self-awareness.

The Psychologist-Coach

Rather than focusing on traditional yardstick measures of performance skills, our approach to executive coaching begins by studying the individual as a whole, as a person whose strengths and weaknesses extend into all areas of his or her life. We draw on the field of psychology in assuming that individual effectiveness can be enhanced most strongly by identifying and understanding the internal motivators—beliefs, emotions, and unconscious assumptions—that drive behavior, often outside one's awareness. We believe that this psychological understanding permits deeper and more lasting behavioral change.

Such in-depth work is the province of coaches who have extensive training in both leadership coaching and psychology. It involves collecting data from many areas of the executive's life. Standard workplace interviewees include superiors, peers, and direct reports. Beyond this typical workplace pool, the coach conducts interviews with friends about current personal life interactions and with the client and family members—spouse, parents, siblings, teenage children—exploring both existing family relationships and early family history. Psychological training allows the coach to safely and effectively cross the boundary between work setting and personal life in order to guide the executive in processing powerful data, considering the relevant associations, and then ultimately using self-awareness as a foundation for achieving more behavioral flexibility.

The Scope of the Now: Current Personal Life Data

Current personal life information enriches the coaching process by allowing coach and client to compare work data with personal life data for the purpose of identifying similarities or differences that corroborate or contradict work findings. Information about a client's current personal life may reveal that problems at work also exist outside of the office—making it even more important to address them. Alternatively, the data may show that problematic work issues do not occur elsewhere, which raises a number of possibilities, including the likelihood that certain strengths in the client's personal life might be put to good use in the work environment or that environmental cues in the workplace trigger useless responses.

As previously noted, successful executives can have particular difficulty accepting suggestions for workplace change. However, we have found that when the same or similar issues are reflected in their personal lives as well, there is far less "wiggle room," as one of our clients put it. For example, although the client's work data repeatedly stressed the importance of reducing negative behaviors such as bullying and being dismissive, he rejected these suggestions, saying that his behavior was acceptable and even necessary because of the competitive and political nature of the workplace. He did not question his style until he read verbatim interviews with his teenage children and his siblings, who used the same words to describe him as had his workplace critics. Faced with this new information, he finally took seriously the need to change.

Sometimes, behaviors evidenced in an executive's personal life, which are discovered through interviews with family and friends, are exactly the ones *needed* to solve workplace problems. Consider the situation of another executive, who was notoriously nonempathetic at work. He had created such a strong culture of fear in the workplace that his people would not bring him any bad news. Unfortunately, his anger increased when he was surprised by unexpected problems. Good people were leaving, unhappy with this culture of anxiety and discouraged by the boss's seeming inability to recognize anything done well. Although our client had received feedback about the effect of his approach on the business and his people, he discounted and rationalized this feedback and continued his negative style.

Interviews with this client's family members and friends, however, revealed a different picture of the executive—that of a caring, empathetic grandfather. According to the family members and friends that we interviewed, he regularly showered warmth and praise on his grandchild, who flourished as a result of this attention.

In comparing the client's work life and personal life data, we helped him identify his unconscious belief that "a kick in the seat of the pants" was needed to achieve results in the work setting, while at home, empathy, patience, and encouragement were his preferred methods of motivation. Through this comparison, he gained a deeper understanding and was able to update his belief system to include the possibility of using his nurturing skills in managing his employees. A skills-based approach of teaching interpersonal behavior would not have been enough to cause him to alter his style; without understanding the larger context and examining the underlying beliefs that drove his behavior, he would have been unwilling to change. Equipped with his updated belief system, he began to empathize, and his people felt safer and were more timely in reporting problems. As a result, productivity and retention increased.

The Hidden Power of the Past: Personal History

Although the notion of the unconscious is generally accepted in the field of psychotherapy, referencing it in the context of executive coaching has typically been thought inappropriate. However, when an executive coach has the training to explore the past with the client in pursuit of a better understanding of present behavior, the benefit to the process is undeniable.

Psychologists continue to debate the influence of conscious intent on actual behavior. A recent article asserted that "most of a person's everyday life is determined not by their conscious intentions and deliberate choices but by mental processes that are put into motion by features of the environment that operate outside of conscious awareness and guidance" (Bargh and Chartrand, 1999, p. 462). While we do not espouse this extreme view, we do believe that at least some behaviors diverge sharply from intentions.

Recent research suggests that "we perceive ourselves to have far more control over our everyday behavior than we actually do" (Park, 1999, p. 461). In her introduction to the July 1999 *American Psychologist* issue on the role of conscious intent on behavior, Park described the article's uniting theme in this way:

> There are mental activations of which we are unaware and environmental cues to which we are not consciously attending that have a profound effect on our behavior and that help explain the complex puzzle of human motivation and actions that are seemingly inexplicable, even to the individual performing the actions. (p. 461)

We all do things that we ourselves don't understand at times. In coaching, a person may describe a seemingly isolated behavioral reaction, perhaps an outburst of anger, and say, "I don't know why I did that." Or perhaps an executive, even after acknowledging the validity of repeated feedback about truly listening to people or being less autocratic in decision making, will be unable to make the necessary long-term changes. At least in part, this inability to follow through on making needed changes in behavior can have roots in early life experience, when such decisions were made and relegated to the unconscious.

Early Childhood Events
We form many of our behavioral templates in childhood. The behaviors we initially try out are either effective or not and thus are positively or negatively reinforced. Over time and with continued reinforcement, the reasons that once necessitated certain behavioral choices are often lost and the behavior becomes simply an automatic response to an environmental cue. In this way, we build our style and approach to the world along with complex systems of justifications and rationalizations for our behaviors. Even when those old behaviors lose their effectiveness in the present, we continue to repeat them in response to situations or cues that tap into that early learning.

Early life and emotions had exerted an enormous unconscious effect on another of our clients, a senior leader who had been receiving the same performance criticism for many years. Although he obviously had the technical brilliance to fuel an impressive ascendance through the ranks, colleagues pegged him as a loner, highly introverted and noninclusive in decision making. He typified the kind of maverick leader who takes charge and gets results but keeps his office door perpetually closed. He did not allow time for others and never made any real effort to build relationships. When he went through our coaching program, the qualitative workplace feedback he received contained a great many comments to this effect.

As we gathered his personal history, we found that, for a variety of reasons, his upbringing had been shifted to a grandmother. He grew close to her over the years, rebuilding the trust he had lost when separated from his family of origin. However, when he was ten years old, his grandmother died in a household fall, and he was the one who discovered her body. When we asked him how he had dealt with this as a child, our client told us, "I remember I sat out on the front porch and said, 'I'll never talk to anyone again. I'm alone. I'll never talk to anybody again.'" He lost his trust in people and decided he could rely only on himself.

After discussing this story, which he had never told anyone before and had effectively forgotten, the executive had an "aha" moment—he realized that his current behavior was self-protective and that he used his introversion to avoid the possibility of further abandonment and loss. The underlying unconscious rationale for his loner style—that if he did not let anyone in, he would not have to fear losing them—had long since become outmoded. He was finally aware of the connection to his past and could admit, "I'm still living off that old decision."

Behaviors That Have Outlived Their Usefulness

We worked with another executive whose automatic behaviors came from a long-held formula for success that involved being the smartest person in the room, and his outstanding intelligence made him quite effective at meeting that goal. Once he reached the highest levels of the company, however, the style that had brought him so far no longer fit with the needs of his position. Now, success was not *being* the winner but rather *developing* winners. The competitive style on which he had relied in the past became counterproductive, for it did not allow those beneath him to grow in their abilities. Although he had received both informal and 360-degree feedback that consistently said he had to step back and allow his reports to develop, the need to compete and win and show everyone that he was still the smartest person in the room continued to prevent him from following through on the needed change.

The gathering of early family history data on this client helped us uncover the early roots of his behavior. As a child, he was much smaller than his classmates—markedly so, until high school. He certainly was not able to outrun them, or outfight them, but he learned that he could outsmart them. He proved himself by being the cleverest, getting the best grades, coming up with the most creative schemes—and this approach was very successful. That pattern, well reinforced over the years, lost its connection to his early need to overcome a physical challenge and simply became his winning formula: if you are the brightest and the best, you will win. This formula manifested as fierce intellectual competitiveness, even at those times when he should have been coaching his people. He viewed every interaction as a battle of wits.

Our work with him helped him make the connection to his past. As he began to understand the roots of his style, he came to see that the foundation underlying his behavior was no longer based on actuality. He wasn't being physically threatened anymore, and he did not need to prove himself. His ability to be the smartest one in the room was unchanged, but, now, he could choose to remind himself to apply his intelligence to developing the abilities of others.

Other Sources of Unconscious Motivators

Of course, negative events are not the only causes of unconscious drivers. Neutral and positive events in our past can also shape us profoundly. For example, achievement-orientation might be driven by childhood experiences that reinforced a fear of failure or might be rooted in years of positive reinforcement. It could even be a reaction to a parent's lack of achievement.

For every past event or emotion, there are many behavioral permutations. For example, if two adult siblings have behavioral patterns that can be traced to the breakup of their parents' marriage years before, one sibling's behavior may evidence an overwhelming need for stability while the other may experience difficulty trusting and committing. Both are understandable responses to the same event.

A number of defining childhood events that seem negative viewed through adult eyes can often be reclaimed as positives when given some in-depth consideration. For instance, one of our clients felt chronically inferior in the business world because, having arrived as a young refugee in the United States, he believed he had never fully learned the unwritten social rules. He was in some ways ashamed of his humble beginnings, and this affected his ability to step into the limelight, speak to groups, and be a visible leader. In the course of coaching, he regained pride in his heritage as he came to recognize that his success was built on the same strength of spirit that enabled his family to start afresh in a new country. This realization and his newfound confidence provided a solid foundation for his work on skills such as assertiveness and public speaking.

The Influence of Emotions

We form our emotional styles in a similar manner—through trial and error and the resulting positive and negative reinforcements—and the original reasons behind our emotional reactions often become as lost as the early life experiences that influence our behavior. In his best-seller *Emotional Intelligence,* Daniel Goleman (1995) wrote that "emotions that simmer beneath the threshold of awareness can have a powerful impact on how we perceive and react, even though we have no idea they are at work" (p. 55).

Unlike skills-based coaching programs, the in-depth executive coaching experience allows clients to explore their underlying emotional reactions and begin to deal with them as drivers of behavior. In addition to interviewing people in our clients' work and personal lives, we also have them complete several personality surveys that provide a glimpse into their motivational and emotional makeup. Although Goleman focused on the extensive amount of time and energy spent on controlling emotions, we believe that, in addition to controlling our emotions when necessary, it is very valuable to learn how to utilize them effectively.

For example, we had a client who, as a unit leader, had been a high-profile agent of change, working to transform the division's culture and process—a project of which he had been very proud. Soon afterward, the larger company reorganized, his division was dissolved, and he was transferred elsewhere. During a team coaching session about a year later, the executive, who was perceived by many on this relatively new team as detached and cold, made passing reference to his earlier experience. The coach-facilitator asked how he had felt when his division was dissolved. As he began to answer, the executive showed emotion, evidencing his passion and pride in the work he had done and the pain he was experiencing in the wake of the loss. This provided a real breakthrough moment for his new team, who for the first time were able to see their boss as human and approachable.

Awareness and Change

While we do believe that unconscious motivators can drive behavior, we also assume that self-awareness—an appreciation of the influence of the past and the power of underlying emotions—allows the individual to gain some conscious control over those behaviors. That is, once we understand our own personal default settings, we can begin to explore ways of changing them that are appropriate to the situation.

However, we do not really want our clients to get rid of specific behaviors altogether. It is our belief that an individual is most effective when he or she has the widest possible variety of behaviors from which to draw. In working with executives, our coaches do not seek to remove troublesome behaviors from the client's repertoire because, although those behaviors may not be effective in one setting, they could very well be needed and appropriate in another situation.

So, rather than try to eliminate behaviors, we work to facilitate the individual's freedom to choose the most effective response rather than the one that reflexively appears. An executive who adds warmth, empathy, and openness to an inventory of possible responses and has the ability to consciously choose between critical and empathetic modes will be able to select the most effective behavior for each situation. The behaviors that were previously viewed as ineffective are not extinguished but may be used only rarely.

The coach can also help the client make the connections that will keep personal land mines from being so easily triggered. A colleague offering constructive feedback may initially spark the same immediate reaction of anger as did the critical comments of a parent in the executive's childhood. Rather than reacting explosively to negative feedback, however, he or she can develop the objectivity to recognize that the current situation is not the same as the one that initially created the automatic response. The coach can help the client cultivate the ability to draw back, consider the attributes of the current situation, and disconnect it from past triggers. This process enables the executive to make a conscious choice of response. With the freedom of conscious choice, clients have the opportunity to align response with aspiration and become the people they want to be.

Basics of the In-Depth Process

Although in-depth coaching breaks the boundaries of skills-based coaching, it is not without its own set of boundaries and rules. Successful use of the in-depth approach requires that the coach establish a safe and trusting forum for looking beyond the workplace in order to understand the individual. Not every executive coaching program will involve in-depth personal life exploration, but, by taking care to establish safety and confidentiality, the coach can create an environment in which these discussions may take place, if and when they are appropriate.

Thach and Heinselman (1999) asserted that executives seek coaching in order to "receive direct one-on-one assistance from someone they respect" (p. 35). When client and coach embark on the kind of transformative coaching program we recommend—a rigorous one grounded in extensive, qualitative, verbatim feedback—trust and respect must be established early.

Before this type of coaching can be successful, the qualified coach must meet four specific requirements: (1) the interpersonal understanding and skills derived from extensive psychological training, (2) absence of conflicting interests that comes from being external to the client's organization, (3) a sense of clear new boundaries for this type of coaching relationship, and (4) the willingness to commit to the client's development for the long term. Together, these four elements create the base from which a strong coaching relationship can grow over time.

Psychological Training

Psychological training is central to the in-depth coaching process. Crossing the boundary into a client's personal life raises significant ethical issues, and coaches with a combination of clinical training and executive development experience are best suited to lead this deep-level work. Given such a psychological background, they will be able to understand the influence of early family life and will know how to use the information to help their clients achieve greater awareness and behavioral flexibility.

The value of a psychological approach is apparent in the story of one client who had long thought of himself as intellectually average. As he rose in his company, his intolerance for those who could not match his speed at grasping new ideas or procedures became more problematic. His frustration with others stemmed from his belief that since he, an average person, could figure things out in a certain amount of time, others should be able to do so as well. His direct reports complained and gave frequent feedback about how demotivating his impatience could be. A skills-based coaching program would likely have focused specifically on the negative behavior and perhaps suggested that he attend active-listening workshops or study the tactics of successful mentorship.

However, through the interviewing process and interactions with him, his psychologist-coach became convinced that the situation belied its surface simplicity. In interviews about his early family history, the client explained that he had never done particularly well in school and often felt inferior while growing up. Even as an adult, despite substantial positive feedback from his colleagues, the client simply did not believe that he was at all above average in intelligence; he just thought he worked hard. The in-depth consultant conducted intelligence testing that placed the client at an IQ of more than two standard deviations above the mean. With this information, and with interpretive help from his psychologist-coach, he was able to not only truly recognize his intellectual gift but also begin to set more realistic standards for his employees.

Absence of Conflicting Interests

We believe that a coach's externality is the second requirement for building the real connection and rapport that can result in lasting change. A coach who is not from within the organization provides a measure of objectivity and confidentiality that cannot be obtained from an internal source. Among other things, an external coach, according to Thach and Heinselman (1999), allows executives to "have an *objective third party* they can talk to confidentially about work-life balance issues" (p. 35), thereby reducing stress and burnout while increasing executive support networks.

Even when individuals within the organization have a high level of training, it would be inappropriate for them to delve into the personal lives of their own company's executives. Clients must not be concerned about their private information, feelings, or thoughts becoming known to co-workers or superiors or ending up in personnel files. Only a coach external to the company can truly allay this concern, assure confidentiality, and establish the level of trust necessary to do in-depth work.

Clear New Boundaries

As in-depth coaches, we believe it is essential to articulate and adhere to very clear boundaries in our relationships with clients. Most important, we follow strict rules of confidentiality to guarantee that information we gather belongs to the client and cannot be shared with others without his or her specific permission.

Interactions with clients are carefully defined as work relationships, not friendships, and consultants do not socialize with clients. This allows clients to be confident of the coach's objectivity and to regard the coach as a safe confidant and guide in the process of self-understanding and personal change.

Long-Term Commitment

The final requirement is commitment to a long-term ongoing relationship (typically eighteen to twenty-four months) that allows the necessary level of trust and understanding. Developing our expertise with each client by collecting interview data and conducting psychological surveys gives us the credibility to help the client transcend defenses and attain a richer self-understanding. However, developing this expertise is not an overnight task.

Long-term commitment enables us to explore issues at deeper levels than would be possible with a more time-limited approach. In addition, the lengthier relationship offers clients time for reflection, opportunities to plan and rehearse new approaches or experiment with new behaviors, real-time support and encouragement in actual work situations, and feedback on the effectiveness of these trial approaches.

Phases of In-Depth Coaching

While a coach may broach the subject of personal life and history in many ways, our approach of gathering qualitative verbatim data through formal interviews with both clients and significant people from their work and personal lives supplies invaluable perspective. Personal life interviewees are asked about dimensions of a client's behavior and character—strengths and weaknesses, interpersonal relationships, integrity, and emotional competence—as reflected in the client's personal life and early family history.

At a two-day insight session, the psychologist-coach reads aloud to the client all verbatim workplace and personal life interview responses, thus bringing many valued voices into the room. The power of this process alone to create a readiness for change cannot be overestimated. This experience is a gift few have the opportunity to experience—the wonder and revelation of seeing oneself through so many sets of eyes.

For one of our middle-aged clients, the words of his eighty-year-old father began a series of life-altering events. The father was a former military man who had never shown much warmth to his son. In the course of our interview with him, we asked what advice he would give our client. The father, sitting rigidly with full military bearing, replied, "Tell him to tell his children he loves them, because I was never able to do that with him."

When hearing these words read aloud, the client was overwhelmed with emotion. He disclosed that he had a detached relationship with his own son and that he had concealed an alcohol-dependence problem for years. The affirmation of love from his father impelled him to begin redirecting his life. He successfully completed an alcohol treatment program, renewed and deepened his relationship with his father, and began to cross the gulf he had created between himself and his son. The executive's development process was greatly facilitated by the opportunity to hear this much-needed and healing message.

Data collection and the insight session make up the initial phase of an in-depth coaching program and lay the foundation for a development planning stage, in which clients create their own visions of how they want to be and decide on behaviors they would like to add to their repertoires. Together, clients and coaches define their approach to meeting these challenges.

Coaching beyond the initial delivery of feedback may take a number of different tacks. With the knowledge gained through the in-depth process, the coach becomes an expert in facilitating the client's own problem-solving process and fostering what is usually a tremendous experience of personal discovery for the client. Skills-based coaching may then be appropriate for some goals, rehearsal or in vivo experiences with the coach observing the client might be another possibility, or the coach could simply provide structure through timelines to help the client maintain his or her forward momentum. Further in-depth exploration may be appropriate to understand the underlying reasons for the ways in which the client exercises influence, makes decisions, sets expectations, handles conflict, or expresses emotion.

Conclusion

A change in observable behavior is the goal of all coaching, but self-awareness, behavioral flexibility, and attempts at congruency are additional aims of the in-depth coaching process. Throughout the course of our program, we use the themes and lessons learned in the initial stages to help our clients create and reach their personal visions.

Successful outcomes include facility with self-examination, self-understanding, and the associated freedom-of-response choice. In this way, the executive has gained abilities that may be utilized in facing future situations and problems. A continued process of matching responses with personal vision and the ability to examine the belief systems that fuel behavior allow for ongoing growth and the pursuit of personal excellence.

References

Bargh, J. A., and T. L. Chartrand. (1999). The unbearable automaticity of being. *American Psychologist* 54: 462–79.

Charan, R., and G. Colvin. (June 21, 1999). Why CEOs fail. *Fortune,* 68–78.

Goleman, D. (1995). *Emotional intelligence.* New York: Bantam Books.

Park, D. C. (1999). Acts of will? *American Psychologist* 54: 461.

Thach, L., and T. Heinselman. (March 1999). Executive coaching defined. *Training & Development* 53 (3): 34.

[6]

COACHING SENIOR EXECUTIVES FOR EFFECTIVE BUSINESS LEADERSHIP

The Use of Adult Developmental Theory as a Basis for Transformative Change

ROBERT G. GOODMAN

My purpose in writing this chapter is to present the practical and transformative change model I developed for coaching senior executives. This model, the Developmental Coaching Dialogue, is based on twenty-five years of experience as a developmental psychologist and change agent in the fields of business, psychotherapy, and education. In addition, its theory draws on some of the basic concepts and processes of constructive-developmental psychology, a life-span theory of cognitive and personality development (Kohlberg, 1969; Piaget, 1954; Kegan, 1982, 1994). Although I make use of other models in my work, I consider constructive developmentalism to be the most powerful and useful framework within which to understand and promote development.[1]

The Developmental Coaching Dialogue facilitates the evolution of adult thinking capacities toward increasing complexity, which is defined as broader perspective taking. I believe perspective taking is a critical underlying cognitive and interpersonal capacity that directs how leaders define, approach, and implement their work. Increased perspective taking on the *self* and on *others* is linked to crucial business leadership competencies such as systemic thinking and the ability to develop collaboration among diverse constituents, create learning organizations, and question and evaluate existing systems and models in order to innovate and make long-range strategic decisions.

Constructive Developmentalism

This chapter presents only those theoretical concepts of constructive developmentalism that are necessary for understanding this coaching model. Readers are encouraged to consult *In over Our Heads* (Kegan, 1994) and *A Guide to the Subject-Object Interview* (Lahey, Souvaine, Kegan, and Felix, 1983) for a complete description of the theory along with a discussion of "orders of consciousness," or developmental stages. (See also Chapter 2.)

In its broadest sense, constructive-developmental psychology describes the sequential evolution of human thinking capacities, identifies these capacities, and suggests conditions for their development. Constructive-developmental psychology has spawned a family of theories, extensive research, and a variety of practical applications in the fields of adult learning, educational pedagogy, professional development, clinical psychology, and leadership development.

The *constructive* in constructive-developmental psychology expresses the idea that human beings actively build or make meaning out of their experiences. It means that we actively create—or, more accurately, cocreate in the context of our relationships with others—our own psychological realities. As we engage in this lifelong activity of making meaning, we give coherence and purpose to our lives; in fact, according to constructive development theory, this activity defines what it means to be human.

The *developmental* in constructive-developmental psychology posits that people and organic systems evolve through qualitatively different stages of complexity according to regular principles of stability and change. In the tradition of constructive-developmental psychology, these stages, or "orders of consciousness" (Kegan, 1994, p. 34), represent increasing mental or cognitive complexity. They fundamentally shape our actions and thoughts (Kegan and Lahey, 1983).

As a person progresses to increasingly complex orders of consciousness, each new order incorporates more complexity than the previous one. Each order is transformed (hence the reason for describing the model as "transformative") and enlarged, and that which was *subject* in the prior order becomes *object* in the next. This is what it means to be "objective": to be able to separate from the very thing to which we once belonged and to view it, or reflect on it, from a new, more distanced perspective.

It is important to understand that development is a dynamic, ongoing process and is not defined simply by movement from one order to the next. This latter type of movement is a macro movement that often takes many years. Development also occurs on the micro level. When we become more aware of a perception, feeling, motivation, or way of thinking and use this awareness to broaden our perspective, we are developing.

For example, let's say I have a client named Ruth, and she perceives her report, Jonathan, as incompetent. Through our dialogue, Ruth discovers that the set of criteria she uses to determine competence essentially reflects her own preferences, i.e., a data-based, analytical approach to solving problems. When she evaluates Jonathan by standards that include interpersonal intelligence, his ability to collaborate and inspire the team to achieve goals shows up as evidence of a different but equally valuable competence. Ruth was *subject* to a set of criteria that she had never clearly articulated; through directed conversation, she was able to reflect on these criteria, i.e., take them as *object*. She then decided to broaden her standards to include interpersonal intelligence. Ruth's perspective taking on herself increased as she altered her perspective on Jonathan. Ruth developed.

In my work, I use the concept of a "holding environment" (Winicott, 1965) to describe the milieu created by the coach to support the transformation of a client's thinking and behavior. The key features of the holding environment are an abiding presence and a mixture of support and challenge. *Presence* means that the coach must be committed to, and actively engaged with, the client. *Support* is vital if clients are to be willing—and able—to take the risks that real transformation requires, and *challenge* provides the push that encourages that change. Without a balanced blend of challenge and support, the holding environment will not be conducive to optimal development. In some cases, development will stall. The Developmental Coaching Dialogue that follows illustrates the four-step process for building and sustaining a holding environment.

The Developmental Coaching Dialogue

The Developmental Coaching Dialogue is an iterative process for creating sustainable change in thinking and behavior. It helps the client actively create his own solutions rather than suggests the substitution of one behavior for another. The process consists of four steps:

- Asking for meaning
- Building a new perspective
- Creating a bridge
- Developing action

The process is presented in terms of steps, but in actual practice, these steps interact dynamically and often overlap.

The following hypothetical case provides an example of dialogue informed by the constructive-developmental paradigm.[2] Explanations of my actions or formulations about the client's thinking are enclosed in brackets and appear in roman type. I suggest ignoring these supplemental asides on the first reading.

My client, Todd,[3] is a forty-two-year-old white male, the COO of United Health Systems (UHS), Inc., a national health care corporation. Todd has extensive experience internally as a senior human resources (HR) executive and marketing VP and externally as an organizational consultant. He is bright and insightful and is known as a mover and shaker who is committed to advancing UHS, Inc., and making it a more efficient and smarter organization.

Todd has worked with Louis, the CEO, for five years. Louis is extremely successful in his career and has moved quickly up the ladder. People feel both loyalty and affection toward him, and he knows how to conduct relationships to his and the company's benefit. Until recently, Todd and Louis had a good working relationship, but Todd has become increasingly frustrated because Louis doesn't see eye to eye with him on immediate and long-term strategic goals and the best means of implementing them. Todd contacted me when he was on the verge of leaving his job.

As I tried to help Todd find his place within this organization, I also worked with him to increase his perspective-taking ability. Using the four steps of the Developmental Coaching Dialogue, I endeavored to guide Todd away from being embedded in his own perspective—and ineffective in his relationship with Louis—toward taking a different and broader perspective on himself and his boss.

Step 1: Asking for Meaning

The goal of the first step is to ask questions that will enable you and the client to achieve a deeper understanding of the behavior, issue, or dilemma. It is a codiscovery process, which involves asking questions that shed light on the client's beliefs or the meanings underlying his or her behavior(s). Our purpose here is to discover and affirm the client's current way of constructing meaning. In this step, the coach utilizes inquiry, validation, and paraphrase to create understanding and focus.

Questions that facilitate this phase typically begin with *how* and *what,* rather than *why. How* and *what* questions are potentially developmental, i.e., they encourage clients to elaborate the present manner by which they are going about their work and may lead to the assumptions that underlie their thinking (Lahey et al., 1983). *Why* questions often direct the client back to the past, and while understanding history and biography is important, it can shift the focus away from current thinking. During questioning, the coach paraphrases so as to support the client, e.g., "So when you decided to give Samantha a raise, even though she didn't merit it, you did it because you felt there was no way to be honest *and* preserve your relationship?"

Such questions are important to ask throughout the dialogue process. Learning about the client's ways of creating meaning is similar to peeling away the layers of an onion; it takes time and becomes more essential as the dialogue deepens. It says to the client, "I really want to know about you and how you, at your core, think about this situation."

Once the client has presented a dilemma, it is explored in terms of how the client is making meaning out of it. To get at the central issues of the dilemma, I ask questions such as

- How do you understand this dilemma?
- What does it mean to you?
- How do you hear it?
- In what ways have you chosen to resolve the dilemma?

When the dilemma involves another person (e.g., a direct report, peer, or boss), I ask questions such as

- What do you think it means to ____?
- How do you understand what ____ said or did?
- What do you hear when ____ says "____"?
- What are you trying to accomplish in the interaction?

The example that follows illustrates the use of these and other questions as I lead Todd through Step 1 of the Developmental Coaching Dialogue. This section represents my attempt to help both of us arrive at a deeper understanding of his concerns.

1 Todd, the client (T): *I'm so frustrated, I don't know if I can stay at this job any longer. My boss is unbelievable; it keeps getting worse. And I'm starting to get paranoid. Is he just trying to get rid of me by frustrating me so much? The guy's insane.*

2 Bob, the coach (B): *What's he doing that's frustrating you so much?*

3 T: *He's always throwing problems at me and then telling me to fix them. He says we need to improve our corporate systems, payroll, financial services, HR, on and on, so I start thinking about how to tackle the problem. I talk to people about it—you know, collect data and come up with a plan. It's rational; it addresses the problem company wide.*

4 B: *Tell me about the plan.*

5 T: *I want him to take a leadership position, present to the staff, communicate the vision . . . you know, this is not rocket science. So I go into his office, and before I even get the whole plan out, before I even finish telling him about how it's going to work, he shoots me down. He wants me to take the lead.*

6 B: *What do you think is his reason for reacting that way?* [I'm trying to get an idea of how Todd understands Louis's behavior.]

7 T: *I don't know . . . it's how the guy operates. He doesn't like that way of solving problems. This is a guy who wants me, just me, to go out and fix it, without involving other people, without getting their input.* [I discover that Todd cannot reflect in very much depth on Louis's approach to leading the company; instead he describes Louis's behavior.]

8 B: *So he's not interested in a team approach . . .*

9 T: *I tried to talk to him about the new bonus plan. "Here's my proposal," I said, and he immediately shot me down. The amazing thing about this is that the plan is in place company wide, but he thinks it was the work of the new manager of payroll. It's like he's looking for a person who fixed it, a single person, not a team or group.*

10 B: *Then what?*

11 T: *Then we get into a fight. The other day we were screaming at the top of our lungs. I'm trying to tell him, look, here's a plan that will take care of the problem, but he won't listen to my ideas.*

12 B: *Well, hold on a minute, what's going on here? Why do you think he's rejecting your ideas outright, without even considering them?*

13 T: *The guy's irrational. He doesn't get it.*

14 B: *What doesn't he get?*

15 T: *He doesn't get how to do business. He can't see the big picture. Once his mind is made up, don't try to present the facts. He does business just like he did when he was in politics.* [Here, Todd is beginning to explicate his theory that Louis does business as a politician. I am very interested in finding out Todd's idea of how politicians do business.]

16 B: *How so?*

17 T: *Well, he'd make all these deals with people, cut deals with them. "Here, you do this, you take this." You know, back-alley stuff. I'll give you this, if you do this.*

18 B: *So, he deals with people on an individual basis. Does that tend to be his style?*

19 T: *Yeah.*

20 B: *And you go in there talking about systemwide changes.*

21 T: *Yeah. The way you should be doing it when you are running a company—right!*

A more complete picture of the dilemma is now on the table. Todd articulated a deeper source of his frustration: the two very different approaches to solving business problems. This enhanced understanding emerged primarily through repeated *what* and *how* questions that were designed to reveal Todd's underlying ways of thinking.

In line 5, Todd describes his own approach to the problem, i.e., ". . . [my boss should] take a leadership position, present to the staff, communicate the vision," but he is unable to articulate his boss's approach. Todd can say things like "the guy's irrational . . . won't listen to my ideas . . . wants me to take the lead," but his anger and frustration have built up until these reactions are primarily what he can and must talk about. At this point, my client has very little ability to reflect, so my first coaching task is to support his framing of the issue, keeping my own reactions, feelings, and advice to myself.

It is important that Todd eventually understand Louis's approach to his work so that he can begin to understand the differences between them and take effective action. Even though Todd has begun to identify Louis's way of doing business, he displays little evidence of understanding Louis, and less evidence of any appreciation for Louis's point of view. Todd is still embedded in his own perspective, which is "this is how I do business, and it's better than Louis's approach."

Step 2: Building a New Perspective

Step 2 focuses on helping the client to see himself or herself and the current issue from another perspective, not the one in which he or she is presently embedded. This "disembedding" creates psychological distance—what some people call *objectivity*—from which we may view others, ourselves, and/or our behaviors and ways of thinking.

Helping a client build a new perspective begins with a clear understanding of his or her current way of thinking. The coach must first validate the client's current construction of the situation, because it is often dearly held. Essentially, this construction is the client's way of organizing meaning and is an integral part of a person's identity. The coach then introduces the idea that there may be another way of viewing the issue. In seeking to build a new perspective, the coach must proceed with patience and delicacy, constantly aware of the importance of the client's need to maintain his or her point of view. Step 2 utilizes the processes of inquiry, reframing, validation, and paraphrasing.

The technique of reframing is very useful in this regard. The coach can reframe the client's behavior to demonstrate that it was productive and useful at other times in the client's life, or the coach can show how someone else's (infuriating) behavior might be understood differently. Besides promoting understanding, it often helps the client to avoid feeling judged. In our example case, I would reframe Louis's behavior (characterized by Todd as "let's cut a deal") as a desire to work with people individually. In my continued conversation with Todd, we begin building a new perspective.

22 B: *Sounds like you're speaking different languages.*

23 T: *What do you mean?*

24 B: *Well, he seems to see business transactions in terms of this template he developed in politics, which is individual based, or maybe more relationship based . . .*

25 T: *You mean, let's cut a deal!*

26 B: *Yes, and you're thinking of these organization-wide interventions, considering multiple perspectives and developing an action plan.*

27 T: *Yes, and we're struggling more and more. It's getting worse.*

28 B: *I got that! But what about what I just said? Is this a way to describe how the two of you go about your work?* [I'm communicating to him that it may be time to stop focusing on the struggle. Can he take in what I said about their different ways of operating?]

29 T: *Hmmm. Well, I never thought of it that way.*

30 B: *Do you think he knows how you feel about his way of doing things? That it frustrates you?* [I am trying to test the idea that Todd may be explicitly or implicitly judging his boss's way of doing things as less adequate than his.]

31 T: *Oh yes, he can sense it. He knows he's making me angry.*

32 B: *So do you think he feels that you don't value his approach?*

33 T: *I guess so.*

34 B: *So one thing you're dealing with here is his feeling that you are judging him, like that's the subtext of your conversation, do you know what I mean?*

35 T: *Yeah. He probably knows that I don't respect his way of going about things.*

36 B: *So that might be getting in the way of having a conversation, too. Not just the different ways that you two have of thinking about the situation . . . Is there any way for you to see his way of operating as useful in business, in his role as CEO?* [I am trying to see if Todd can begin to view Louis's approach in a positive light. This type of "challenge" asks the client to consider another perspective.]

37 T: *Well, yes, it's very effective in external politics. He knows how to cut deals with people. He can get around difficult situations; he's smooth, you know, very political. Loyalty is everything!*

38 B: *What do you mean by "loyalty"?* [This question interests me because it has the potential to reveal more about another important meaning system for Louis, and knowing about it could help Todd better understand Louis.]

39 T: *Well, like in politics, you do something for someone, and then that person is forever loyal to you as you are to them. You stand by the person, no matter what.*

40 B: *How has Louis used this approach effectively?*

41 T: *Well . . . [hesitation] . . . because he inspires loyalty in certain key people, they do things for him that they might not do otherwise.*

42 B: *So it has some value. Do you think it might help if you can in some way validate his way of operating before presenting him with your way* *of going about tackling these initiatives? Letting him know that there is value in making sure individual people are taken care of first?*

43 T: *I could try that.*

In this dialogue, Todd has moved away from the idea that Louis has a different—and wrong—approach to business. Now Todd is beginning to understand what the two approaches are. He is beginning to think that it might be advantageous, from a business perspective, for him to be less judgmental of his boss's approach.

Line 24 illustrates the method of reframing by describing Louis's (frustrating, irrational) behavior in a different and more positive frame, i.e., as a mental model or approach that Louis uses in work. I suggest a new frame for Louis's behavior by considering this "let's make a deal" model as a way of doing business, one oriented to relationships first. Line 23 is significant because, in it, Todd is now asking me a question. This indicates that he has cooled down enough to inquire about the meaning of my statement.

By line 27, Todd has returned to the emotional fallout of his struggle with Louis. While it is normal to regress and lose newly gained focus, I decide to push Todd—to balance my support with challenge—to see if my formulation makes any sense to him. I discover that it does interest him somewhat, but it also appears to be a new idea ("I never thought of it that way"), and new ideas cause a certain amount of disequilibrium or cognitive dissonance. This experience of disequilibrium is a normal part of the process of building a new perspective.

Step 3: Creating a Bridge

After introducing a different perspective, the coach focuses on helping the client to begin the process of changing his or her thinking and behavior in accordance with the new insights. At this stage, the coaching discussion revolves around exploring the potential risks and threats attached to making the change. Every change entails loss, and this phase requires preparation, both for the process itself and in order to minimize the client's sense of loss by identifying and retaining for support some aspects of the old behavior, thereby enabling the client to "move forward" or "progress."

In this step, one of our objectives is to honor the human need to preserve order and stability. With this in mind, the coach explores the normal threats of making a change. To understand Step 3, the reader is encouraged to think back to a situation in which you were asked to change or when you initiated change. You might remember your own fears (sometimes seen by others as resistance) about giving up your old way of acting or thinking, or, in essence, surrendering an important source of identity and self-esteem. These fears can have an effect in spite of an expressed desire to change. As coaches, reflecting on our own past fears may lead us to remember that it is easier to make changes when we are able to hold on to some of our well-worn ways even as we're trying out new ones.

Naming a client's fears brings them out into the open, reducing their potency and making public something that was stored in the privacy of the client's mind. Private fears are much more powerful than those that can be examined in the light of day. In addition, knowing about the potential risks that give rise to the fears can help the client plan for success.

I use the following questions to help my clients name what might be left behind and to identify the risks of change:

- What would it be like to be more ____?
- What would happen if you weren't so ____?
- How does it change the way you think about yourself when you do things this new way?
- How is this a challenge for you? Tell me the ways.
- What aspects of your current thinking/behaving do you want to retain while you're trying out this new way?
- What are you giving up by doing it in this new way?
- Why would you want to hold on to your current way of behaving if you're getting feedback that it isn't working?

The following are supportive statements to use in Step 3:

- It's hard to give up something you know for something you haven't tried out.
- I can imagine how that would be risky for you.
- I bet it won't feel as threatening once we figure it out together.
- Change is hard!
- You don't have to give up ____ all at once; we'll take it a step at a time.

- It's hard not knowing where you are exactly.
- It's tough to feel like you're not in charge (competent, etc.).
- Let's build on your strengths first.

It is sometimes necessary to help a client slow down the rate of change. Guiding your clients toward building on their strengths (as suggested in the last supportive statement above) can be a paradoxical intervention; i.e., when people are told that they *don't* have to do something, they often feel more comfortable about trying it out.

The following segment of my conversation with Todd illustrates Step 3:

44 B: *What would be difficult about validating your boss's behavior in this way?*

45 T: *Well . . . I think I'd have to feel like it's a good way to go about solving the problem . . . better than my way.*

46 B: *Why does it have to be better than your way?*

47 T: *Because I do think my way is more systematic and fair to more people.*

48 B: *Within your system of thinking and operating, is there room for your boss? Can you see how this more personal approach could be fair?*

49 T: *I guess so . . . yes.*

50 B: *How so?*

51 T: *Well, he's looking after the one person he's dealing with; he wants to make sure he's taken care of that person first.*

52 B: *So could you imagine how to make a bridge between your approach and his?*

53 T: *This is a whole different way of thinking about it. . . . You mean like with the payroll situation—forget the flowcharts, talking about the root causes, doing the trials, just try and deal with it, but not system wide.*

54 B: *Well, do you think that would work? You know better than I.*

55 T: *I do. You know, when I first started working for him, he'd just say, "Here, there's this problem, fix it." His theory is that you hire the right* *person and let him run with the ball and take care of things. But now I'm going in to see him with proposals about how to look at these organizational issues, and he . . .*

56 B: *So you are wanting him to be a collaborator or coconsultant on these issues.* [I am trying to name Todd's expectations for Louis and to suggest that Todd wants Louis to act and think in the same way he does.]

57 T: *I want to exchange ideas with him and have him think about the whole reward system and then come to a decision.*

58 B: *Did he ever do that?*

59 T: *You know, it looks like he's collaborating, but now I see that he truly isn't. It's very different because there's no real exchange of ideas going on.*

60 B: *Is that hard to let go of, your wanting to be a business partner?*

61 T: *I don't think I realized it, but yes, it's true, and I feel relieved that I can stop chasing after something that won't happen.*

62 B: *So why do you think he can't truly collaborate? Why do you think it would be hard for him to do that?*

63 T: *I don't know . . . I don't know. I think he doesn't want to.* [This statement exemplifies the common conclusion that when another person does not behave as we want him to behave, it's by choice—in this case, perhaps because he's withholding or stubborn.] *Maybe it's not what he's used to.* [However, Todd then adds that maybe Louis isn't used to this way of thinking.]

64 B: *And maybe he isn't able to, and you are inadvertently becoming an irritant to him by continually asking him to see these issues in this systemwide way.*

65 T: *It's a different way of looking at it, like turning it on its head, flipping it around.*

66 B: *Yes, and you don't have to abandon your strategy. What would it be like if you tried talking to him in his language first, using his way of doing business? Then you can work your approach after you've established a common footing.*

In this phase of our dialogue (lines 44–45), I discover that one of Todd's risks in thinking about validating his boss's behavior is that he would have to think of Louis's approach as better than his. When I probe further (line 46), I find that this risk derives from Todd's notion of fairness and his view of his approach as more adequate. In a later dialogue not represented here, Todd and I learn that Louis actually can consider the fairness issue in a systemwide way, but only after he has taken care of key relationships.

Because Todd tends to think systemically and is a quick study, he is able to generate possible ways to create a bridge to Louis (line 53). Part of Todd's loss here comes from having to give up his need/desire for a collaborator, in the way he has defined collaboration. The model of two cocaptains at the ship's helm, speaking the same language and agreeing on the same course, is difficult to surrender.

In lines 63–66, Todd is beginning to have an important insight, namely that Louis may not be purposefully trying to frustrate him but instead is going about his work in the way he knows best. It clearly is not Todd's approach, but it is not without purpose.

Step 4: Developing Action

A plan developed from a constructive-developmental perspective requires that proposed changes represent a challenge appropriate to the client's developmental level. In other words, change should cause some disequilibrium in the client's thinking but not so much that it creates fear or confusion and/or undercuts motivation. In Step 4, the coach helps the client to imagine and then mentally rehearse the change. Again, inquiry continues to play an important role.

Challenge, one of the critical elements of a holding environment, is necessary in order to facilitate development. My goal as a coach is to help my clients craft developmentally appropriate challenges. By this, I mean challenges to current thinking or behavior that are incremental and stretch the client's existing meaning system.

If the client experiences too much disequilibrium, responses may include resistance, freezing up, and denial. Our task is to create a good match between the necessary change and the client's capacity to accomplish it. Whether or not the client is able to manage change and is prepared to tolerate the ensuing risks and business imperatives—as well as the scope and difficulty of the proposed change itself—are determining factors.

The coach can help the client mentally rehearse proposed changes by questioning, brainstorming, and imagining. Asking the client to envision the change before implementing it can increase his or her sense of control. The coach's task is to provide a holding environment in which the client can safely make mistakes and express developing ideas.

I ask questions like these to help prepare for change:

- Let's imagine doing it this way. What would that require of you?

- How could you imagine saying that? What words would you use?

- How do you think ____ will respond?

- How will you react if ____ responds (x) way?
  (y) way?
  (z) way?

- Why would you react that way?

- What kind of support do you need? Resources?

The action plan turns on a collaboration between client and coach and is customized to the client and his or her business objectives. Both parties should agree on an appropriate time line, and the coach provides assistance in assessing the client's work. The cycle of goal setting, practice, observation, and reassessment continues in the context of the iterative developmental coaching dialogue.

Here are the final lines of dialogue between Todd and me:

67 T: *So, it's like he's not taking all these perspectives that I'm gathering when I talk to people about trying to streamline corporate services. I'm looking to integrate services organization wide, and he sees it as interference . . .*

68 B: *I think that's how you experience his approach, too, as interference . . .*

69 T: *Hmm . . . OK, I could say, "Great, let's figure out how to take care of the finance people." Then I'd say, "You know what, there are a couple of people I'm worried about here who haven't gotten any money, and they worked very hard," but instead of presenting him with the solution, I'll just present him with the problem: "What should we do?"*

70 B: *So why would that work better?*

71 T: *Because I overwhelm him. I've been trying to convince him that it was inherently unfair because I was thinking about all the people in the system who deserved bonuses, too. So I was trying to lay out a plan that included all these people.*

72 B: *So if you went in and did it this way, how would that be for you?*

73 T: *Part of me says I'd feel too compromised, so hell no. But part of me also says, hell, whatever it takes. I think I can still get across all the essentials of my plan.*

74 B: *Can you see yourself actually doing this? When and where would you do it?*

75 T: *Let's see . . . I have a meeting alone with him next week. Maybe I'll suggest lunch—he likes that, yeah, that's what I'll do.*

In line 71, we see further evidence of Todd's growing awareness of the effect his actions have on Louis. This awareness is the hallmark of true perspective taking. Whereas Todd had the capacity to see the situation through Louis's eyes earlier, but clearly was not doing so, he is doing it now, in large part because he is no longer embedded in his own perspective. Todd is viewing both himself and Louis objectively; he is no longer subject to his perceptions of Louis and can evaluate them critically. He is able to imagine himself talking with Louis (lines 74–75) and developing a specific plan. In follow-up sessions, Todd enacted this plan and went on to successfully develop others.

Postscript

Todd was able to change some of his communication patterns in several subsequent conversations with Louis. Todd says he now understands that his boss's words and actions are rooted in Louis's meaning systems and are not intended to frustrate him.

He still has questions about his own role in the organization. How much influence can he have? Can he continue to adapt his own style to that of his boss? Should he seek a position in another organization where his perspective would be more appreciated and better utilized? How will he develop professionally in his present setting? These questions are part of our ongoing dialogue.

Todd's questions bring into perspective many of the developmental ideas discussed in this chapter, especially the need for organizations to provide developmentally appropriate holding environments within which leaders can exercise and develop more complex thinking, which includes capacities for increased perspective taking, systemic thought, and self-authorship, the ability to see interdependencies among systems, and critical reflection.

Conclusion

Coaching from a constructive-developmental perspective requires that we understand clearly and specifically how best to support our leaders as they undergo their own unique processes of developing these capacities. Such an approach requires careful attention to the quality of the holding environments or milieus in which leaders learn. As many organizational development practitioners and theoreticians argue (e.g., Senge, 1990), today's leading-edge organizations must dedicate themselves to transformational learning—learning that addresses not only knowledge (i.e., content and information) but the critical processes that underlie the continuous development and acquisition of knowledge.

The emergent practice of executive coaching, while showing promise as an effective vehicle for executive development, is in its toddlerhood, giddy with its newly acquired freedom to move and explore but lacking a consistent, future-oriented goal. As a theory of adult development, constructive developmentalism can map out processes and pathways for change that focus on the capacities for complex thought— which is essential for effective leadership. The long-standing theoretical, research, and practice bases of constructive-developmental psychology can help direct our young practice toward its next developmental stage.

Notes

[1] I have been deeply influenced by the ideas of Robert Kegan, Lisa Lahey, and Emily Souvaine. I appreciate the many forms of our collaboration and colleagueship over the years. The breadth and richness of their ideas and the generosity with which they

offer their thinking have provided me with fertile ground in which to develop my own.

2 This dialogue represents a condensation of three consecutive coaching conversations, each one lasting approximately two hours and taking place over six weeks. I have tried to remain true to the flow and tone of the real dialogue. Please note that I had worked with this client before this coaching engagement and a good deal of trust had already been established.

3 The names of my client and his organization are pseudonyms.

References

Kegan, R. (1982). *The evolving self: Problem and process in human development.* Cambridge, Mass: Harvard University Press.

————. (1994). *In over our heads: The mental demands of modern life.* Cambridge: Harvard University Press.

Kegan, R., and L. Lahey. (1983). Adult leadership and adult development. In B. Kellerman (ed.), *Leadership: Multidisciplinary perspectives.* New York: Prentice-Hall.

————. (2001). *How the way we talk can change the way we work: Seven languages for transformation.* San Francisco: Jossey-Bass.

Kohlberg, L. (1969). Stage and sequence: The cognitive developmental approach to socialization. In D. Goslin (ed.), *Handbook of socialization: Theory and research.* New York: Rand-McNally.

Lahey, L., E. Souvaine, R. Kegan, R. Goodman, and S. Felix. (1983). *A guide to the subject-object interview: Its administration and analysis.* Cambridge, Mass: Harvard Graduate School of Education.

Piaget, J. (1954). *The construction of reality in the child.* New York: Basic Books. (Original work published 1937).

Senge, P. (1990). *The fifth discipline: The art and practice of the learning organization.* New York: Doubleday.

Winicott, D. W. (1965). *The maturational processes and the facilitating environment.*

PART III

MANAGING EXECUTIVE
COACHING IN
ORGANIZATIONS

[7]

INITIATING EXECUTIVE COACHING IN YOUR ORGANIZATION

SUSAN ENNIS

This chapter is directed specifically to human resources (HR) executives who are responsible for successfully implementing executive coaching within organizations. I also hope this chapter will be useful to those in other roles, including other HR managers and staff and internal and external executive coaches.

The learning reflected in this chapter is based on three significant experiences. First, as executive development manager for a large U.S.-based bank, I set up an extensive executive coaching program that was recognized by my peers for its comprehensiveness (Hall, Otazo, and Hollenbeck, 1999). Second, my ideas were supported, critiqued, and improved on by my colleagues in the Boston Coaching Group, an informal learning community made up of executive development managers from six large high-tech and financial service companies, which serves as a catalyst and a reality check on my thinking. Third, I have drawn from my mistakes and successes as an executive development manager at two companies, my own experiences as a coach, and my recent consulting with clients who are establishing executive coaching efforts.

Ensuring the Success of Your Executive Coaching Program

As the senior HR manager, executive development manager, or manager responsible for executive coaching, your job is to ensure the success of executive coaching in your organization.[1] The forethought and planning that go into creating a successful program are time-consuming, but a rigorous process of selecting coaches and matching them to executives will more than repay your efforts by greatly increasing your chances of success. Coaching is about transferring skills, enabling learning, and empowering people to succeed. At the beginning of a coaching program, convincing executives to accept help is a key challenge. By the end, if you have done your job right, your executives will have learned to help themselves.

Executive coaching typically begins in one of two ways. The first involves a programmatic approach—a planned effort designed to meet the needs of multiple executives in the context of business requirements. Usually linked to leadership development initiatives and managed by HR, programmatic coaching can include 360-degree-feedback debriefings or a limited number of coaching sessions to supplement a training program. The coaching process is generally short and standardized, with preselected coaches and a set number of meetings. Executives usually realize how engaging and helpful coaching can be and often contract individually for more. Otherwise, executive coaching may start in an ad hoc way, when an executive requests a coach or informs HR of an existing coaching contract.

For either the programmatic or ad hoc approach to work well, you must analyze the role you want executive coaches to play in your organization. Carefully consider their fit with your leadership development strategy and also the business practices you want to establish for managing both coaching and the coaches themselves. It is important to develop in advance such components as fee structure, confidentiality agreements, and learning contracts. Inefficiency, ineffectiveness, or, worse, failure of the coaching process itself may result from reactive decisions made in response to ad hoc requests for coaching or because of performance problems. (For a comprehensive overview of potential problems, see Chapter 9). To ensure success, follow the seven-step process for establishing executive coaching:

Step 1: Link executive coaching to business strategy
Step 2: Identify a pool of potential coaches
Step 3: Screen potential coaches
Step 4: Bring the coach up to speed
Step 5: Match the executive to the coach
Step 6: Keep the coaching engagement on track
Step 7: Measure results

Step 1: Link Executive Coaching to Business Strategy

There are many issues to consider before introducing executive coaching in your company. Begin by assessing the organization's culture, financial resources, and priorities. Ask yourself the following questions:

- Does the culture encourage people to ask for help, or is seeking help seen as a sign of weakness or failure?

- How are consultants viewed—with suspicion, as scapegoats, as white knights, or as a source of expertise and support?

- What are the normative business practices and funding models in this organization?

- Does the business demonstrate its commitment to learning efforts for executives and other employees by offering strong financial support, or are these the first funds to be cut?

- Can executive coaching be aligned with other HR systems or successful initiatives, such as an implemented succession plan, a high-potential program, or a 360-degree-feedback and development planning process?

I believe executive coaching should not be a stand-alone intervention that meets the needs and enhances the prestige of an individual executive without supporting organizational business goals. For maximum success, executive coaching should be aligned with an executive development strategy that is firmly grounded in your company's business strategy. Solid links between executive coaching, executive development, and business strategy can form a strong foundation on which to develop executive coaching business practices. (For a full discussion on how to link coaching strategy with the business strategy, see Chapter 8). Consider the following examples.

Designing Strategies to Meet Specific Organizational Needs

In a start-up company, the business strategy may be to issue an IPO or seek a buyout. To respond to that strategy, the executive development plan would probably focus on retention of key talent and on-the-job development. Programmatic coaching would thus become something of an entitlement for select executives, designed to build their commitment to the organization. These select executives might be coached on a broad range of development issues, including career and life planning, leadership development, and skills enhancement. Rather than using discretionary business-unit funding, the company could fund coaching through HR as a corporate-retention initiative. Part of HR's task would be to develop clear criteria for determining who is eligible for coaching. HR would focus less on who needs coaching from a skills-development perspective and more on whom the organization wants to keep. In such a situation, the coaches selected must be loyal to the organization, with broad backgrounds in career, leadership, and organizational development. They should also be willing to work in short bursts, most likely at unusual times in order to accommodate executives whose schedules are demanding and unpredictable. The coaching itself is likely to be short term, intense, and tactical. In order to support the goal of executive retention, HR should establish clear ground rules about job search counseling.

The needs of the company described above are quite different from those of a company whose business strategy aims for growth over time, with an executive development strategy focusing on building leadership bench strength. Unlike the start-up situation, executive coaching in this context focuses on those who would benefit from the coaching. Eligibility would be linked to the succession plan or to high-potential criteria, with coaching formulated to support the long-term development of senior leaders and to prevent derailments. HR may want to package the coaching program with other approaches (such as 360-degree feedback or leadership training) and might expect the individual executive's business unit to fund longer-term coaching beyond the allotted sessions. The executive coaches, drawn from multiple sources with varied backgrounds and skill sets, should be familiar and comfortable with the company's culture, norms, strategic direction, development philosophy, and leadership profile. A critical element in this scenario involves making sure that the diverse coaches address individual needs in the context of the organization's overall executive development strategy and business requirements.

Examples of the Strategic Use of Coaching

Executive coaching programs can be tailored to a wide variety of business situations.

In a global investment bank, for example, the CEO wanted his senior team and their successors to be fully aware of their strengths and development needs as individuals and as team members. They had to be strong general managers for the entire enterprise, not just for their business units. The CEO used a small team of external coaches who worked collaboratively to meet both individual and team needs. This cadre of coaches aligned individual development needs with business issues and organizational strategies. Because the coaches were kept well informed and linked to the chairman's office, they provided their clients with consistent messages about individual expectations and organizational priorities. The CEO funded the coaching, conferring prestige on the selected executives and validating the process of becoming a senior executive.

Another financial services organization used coaching as a major element in its executive development strategy because group programs did not have the required impact or cachet. Coaching was funded by the line managers and provided executives with real-time, private learning on their own terms. This gave them the psychological safety net they needed to exhibit vulnerability and learn without peer competition.

In order to move decision making closer to the customer base and prepare its younger managers for this increased responsibility, another company used internal coaches to target the learning needs of high-potential managers. The positive implications of coaching were evident because no derailment cases were included.

A company seeking to acculturate senior new hires and increase the effectiveness of recently promoted executives established coaching as a normative activity during a major transition. This provided the needed organization-wide support for new employees and senior managers.

These are only some of the ways in which to introduce and implement executive coaching within an organization. But no matter what its form, it is imperative to link coaching with business strategy early in the planning process. An executive coaching program must support business requirements—and to be most effective, it must align with executive development strategy while meeting individual needs.

HR executives should be aware that, once executive coaching gains a foothold in an organization, executives usually continue to seek it out. HR executives should prepare not only for the introduction but also for the expansion of the coaching program by carefully thinking through goals, strategy, and implementation. Table 7 lists the critical questions to consider during the planning stages of a programmatic coaching effort.

Step 2: Identify a Pool of Potential Coaches

In domestic business hubs, the supply of available executive coaches often outstrips the demand, so finding local coaches is not a difficult task. Securing highly experienced, skilled coaches who want to work in partnership with you and your organization may be more difficult, and availability varies in some parts of the United States, most of Asia, and some areas of Europe. Added travel costs and complicated logistics may hinder responsiveness and deflect funds for coaching into travel per diems.

There are two major sources of executive coaches: large consulting firms and independent practitioners.

Most major human resources consulting companies, and now business management consulting firms, have recently formed executive coaching practices. The quality, experience, and perspectives of consulting company coaches vary widely. A person identified as a coach is often a consultant who will broaden an existing advisory role but does not coach on a regular basis.

There are advantages and disadvantages to using a large firm. On the plus side, the company may be known and viewed as reliable, with a management structure in place to which you may appeal for issue resolution. Consulting companies typically use a stated methodology and often provide a broad range of consulting services, which means that coaching costs can sometimes be subsumed within the larger consulting effort. Conversely, you are paying for the company's overhead, and you may find the methodology restrictive. Coaches from consulting companies schedule their time in

Table 7

What to Consider When Establishing
an Executive Coaching Strategy

Roles and Responsibilities

- Who is responsible for managing the company-wide investment in coaching?

- Who decides whether executive coaching is the best solution?

- How many coaches does our organization need?

- Who is responsible for vetting coaches?

- Who is responsible for firing a coach?

Strategy Considerations

- Are we sending consistent messages about the purpose of executive development?

- How do we determine who receives coaching?

- Which segments of the population, and at which levels, are eligible for coaching?

- Which coaching activities and practices will work for our organization, and how do they link with organizational needs and business strategy?

Learning Contract Issues

- Which aspects of the coaching process must be documented?

- What is a viable learning contract?

- What should be in the learning contract? Who has access to the contract?

- Who owns which type of data from an executive who is being coached?

Program Considerations

- Who pays for the coaching?

- What are acceptable rates?

- How do we determine organizational trends or needs based on executive coaching assignments?

- Who declares success or deems the intervention worthwhile?

- How will executive coaching be evaluated with regard to its impact on individual executives and the organization?

advance and may not be as flexible as independents. Your executives may not connect with the company's coaches, which could be problematic if they are your sole resource. And coaches from consulting firms are often measured by aggressive revenue goals and may actively seek noncoaching consulting projects during their coaching engagements. In addition, managing the vendor relationship will become your responsibility.

The marketplace is filled with myriad independent executive coaches drawn from many walks of life, and the best among them have often followed eclectic or unusual career paths. To begin a search for independents, tap into your network. As you interview prospects, ask them about their competition and their collaborators, and your list of potential coaches will quickly expand. Because independent coaches have an inherent capacity limit, they usually work in concert with other consultants and therefore can provide referrals. An experienced and effective coach often has a network of equally experienced colleagues.

As with consulting companies, there are positive and negative aspects to utilizing independent executive coaches. On the plus side, the independents can be less expensive, more responsive, uniquely experienced, willing to tailor their approach to your company's needs, extremely flexible, and easier to integrate into your coaching strategy and staffing. On the minus side, independent coaches may be mavericks who will require management by knowledgeable and experienced individuals responsible for the executive coaching. You can find candidates of substantial strength and experience, but you will need to prescreen, conduct qualifying interviews, and check references. The approaches and methodologies of independents vary dramatically, and you will have recourse only to the individuals—and not to a management structure—for problem resolution. Nevertheless, in my experience, the payoff is worth it. You will have a broad range of coaches handpicked for your organization, loyal to your client base, and committed to maintaining a specialized practice that includes your company.

Your route to executive coaching—consulting firms or independent coaches—should be based on your business needs, organizational culture, development strategy, and financial resources. Either option requires that you assess coaches for skills, organizational fit, and perspective. It is vital to ensure that each coach has the range and experience to represent you and your function and to competently address business and individual needs.

Step 3: Screen Potential Coaches

Assessing each candidate's suitability for your organization is much more difficult than finding a coach. Your decision should be based on coaching range and style. A coach's range includes training, career history, personal history and characteristics, adaptability, learning experiences, successes, and failures—plus the ability to reflect on these issues, integrate learning, and use that learning to help others. Who the coaches are as people, what they do, and how they interact with clients are critical factors in determining if their style will fit your organization and its executives.

Great coaches follow various career paths. Comparing their knowledge and industry experience is the easiest part of your assessment. It is decidedly more difficult to evaluate their coaching skills and personal characteristics, but a rigorous qualifying process will pay off. The following series of steps will help you screen potential coaches.

Prescreen

There are four recommended prescreening steps. The first involves gathering information about a coach. Begin with your colleagues in HR and business networks. Their experiences with, impressions of, and referrals for coaches can be invaluable. This information will help you decide if a coach is a potential fit with your organization and its culture.

Second, review marketing materials and samples of prior work. These materials not only reflect coaches' views of their practice, they also illustrate perspectives and tools and provide an indication of their coaching range. Bear in mind that independents may have simpler materials compared to the more elaborate packages of large consulting firms.

If you want to establish a larger pool of coaches or prefer to compare candidates, you may want to take the third prescreening step (see Table 8), a skills/experience inventory. Inventories completed and submitted before interviews simplify prescreening and eventually create a database. Some coaches dislike inventories or refuse to complete them, so decide beforehand how you might handle this reaction.

The fourth and final step is to provide prospective coaches with written guidelines on coaching in your company. Describe your executive coaching philosophy, purpose, and practices. Coaches who find your company's approach complementary to their own will be eager to work with you.

> **Table 8**
>
> ## Typical Topics for the Executive Coach Skills/Experience Inventory
>
> - Assessment instruments used in your practice
> - Certifications held
> - Coaching and consulting experience
>   - Managerial levels you've worked with
>   - Number of clients
>   - Years of coaching/consulting in each organization
>   - Types of industries
>   - Types of companies
>   - Sizes of companies
>   - Countries worked in
>   - International, global, and cross-cultural experience
> - Languages spoken; level of proficiency
> - Entrepreneurial experiences
> - Experience as an internal employee in corporations or organizations
> - Types of coaching experience or areas of interest
>   - Coaching for specific skills (list)
>   - Debriefing consultations (e.g., 360-degree, personality inventories)
>   - Coaching potentially derailing executives
>   - Coaching for development
>   - Coaching high-potential executives
>   - Coaching new hires or for newly promoted acculturation or orientation
>   - Career coaching/consulting
>   - Outplacement counseling
>   - Other
> - Special skill areas
> - Areas of interest (e.g., diversity, work/life balance, midlife issues)
> - Focus and philosophy of your practice

Regardless of their excellence or reputations, not all coaches will fit with your organization's purposes, values, culture, and norms, and it's best to eliminate the possibility of a mismatch before the coaching process begins. Your reputation as well as that of your program will be affected by the presence and behavior of every coach you select.

Conduct Phone Interviews

Once you feel a coach has the potential to work well in your organization, assess fit and competence through a phone interview. If you start the discussion by asking how the candidate became an executive coach, the response often clarifies coaching range and perspectives and may reveal philosophy, values, and cultural fit. After discussing career history, ask the coach to describe his or her approach. What would the candidate do and *not* do during an executive coaching session? Experienced and thoughtful coaches are usually quite clear on this issue. They typically are eager to share war stories and are adept at pointing out what they've learned.

Ask coaches explicit questions about the types of clients with whom they do and do not work effectively. Their answers will give you a solid indication of their experience, ability, self-assessment skills, candor, and willingness to reflect on their work. Capable coaches want to build long-term relationships and understand the situations, problems, and personalities with which they excel and those with which they are less effective.

Responses to the best-fit question should be specific, as in the following examples:

- "I connect well with technical folks who don't like, value, or want to engage in influence activities or politics, but who must do so to be successful."

- "My strength is in helping women confronting work-life balance, career, and success challenges."

- "I feel I have been most effective with people in midlife who realize they want to rethink their futures."

- "I'm definitely drawn to executives who are working within the context of mergers and acquisitions."

The opposite question, about the types of clients with whom they do not work effectively, can be even more revealing. Beware of the "I can coach anyone" response—a coach who expresses such a view may lack experience, self-awareness, or candor. Like best-fit responses, worst-fit scenarios should be specific:

- "It's harder for me to work closely with people who are derailed or derailing."
- "My area of weakness involves arrogant and demanding people, especially men."
- "Fragile, psychologically needy people are somewhat difficult for me."
- "I'm usually at a loss with executives who measure all worth by money."
- "I don't connect well with fast-track Gen Xers."

By the end of the phone interview, you should have a good sense of the coach's abilities and philosophy and can decide whether to meet face-to-face. You should also know how well the coach connects and communicates by phone—a skill essential not only to the ongoing coaching relationship but also to your interactions with the coach. Much of your coach-management activity is likely to take place over the phone.

Conduct Face-to-Face Interviews

If you are satisfied with the results of your phone interview, you are ready to assess the coach as a candidate. During the interview, you may want to talk further about coaching approach or clarify areas of expertise mentioned in the skills/experience inventory, résumé, and marketing materials. The interview should focus on the coach. Discuss in detail actual coaching engagements, both successful and problematic. Your object is to gather behavioral data on the coach's past performance, not to obtain opinions on hypothetical situations. This approach is based on the premise that past behavior predicts future behavior in similar circumstances.

Try to obtain an overview and a time line for each coaching situation you discuss. Probe for details such as

- What happened?
- Who said what?
- What did the client do and say? How did this executive react?
- What was the coach's actual response, including thoughts and feelings, as well as actions?
- What did the coach learn from this situation?

Another critical topic is the coach's approach to partnering with the HR staff who are overseeing the coaching program and with the HR business partner of the coached executive. Ask for specific examples of the coach's collaboration with internal and external resources.

During the face-to-face interview, you will have to assess a number of complex and subtle characteristics. Keep in mind your main goal: whether the coach's competence and expertise will fit your organization. Your overall assessment should answer the following questions:

- Is the candidate a quick study?
- Does the candidate's executive presence fit your company's values and norms?
- Will this coach be able to develop "comfortably uncomfortable" relationships with executives?
- Has the coach resolved personal issues, so that they won't be triggered during the coaching engagement?
- Is this person capable of improving both individual and organizational performance?

Worksheet 1 contains a checklist of specific characteristics that are important for coaching.

Check References

The candidate's HR clients and executive clients are the two most valuable sources of information for you. HR clients can reveal a great deal about coaching ability and willingness to partner. They can also help you assess the success of coaching from an organizational point of view. For a complete picture, however, you will also need to speak with coached executives, and I recommend talking to at least two clients per coach. When you call these executives, inform them that you will take no more than fifteen minutes of their time and briefly explain the purpose of your company's coaching program, your role as executive coaching manager, and the confidential nature of the conversation. You might introduce yourself to the executive by saying, "An executive at my company is considering selecting [coach's name] and wants to know what it's like to be on the other side of the table from him [or her]." Probe for details and examples. The answers will probably corroborate your own assessment, but the views of executive clients will carry extra weight with the executives in your organization when they are making their final selections.

Worksheet 1

Coach Assessment Checklist

CHARACTERISTICS	HIGH	MEDIUM	LOW	NO DATA
Professional demeanor				
Cultural fit				
Business judgment				
Toughness				
Practicality				
Aggressiveness				
Genuineness				
Empathy				
Interpersonal awareness				
Organizational savvy				
Learning ability				
Flexibility/adaptability				
Centeredness				
Trust/integrity				
Maturity				
Self-awareness/thoughtfulness				
Use of metaphor/imagery				
Clarity of explanations				
Responsiveness				
Availability				

Overall Assessment

_____

_____

Next Steps

_____

_____

Step 4: Bring the Coach Up to Speed

After selecting a pool of executive coaches, make sure that each one is familiar with your organization and its key individuals. As highly visible representatives of the executive development function and HR organization, coaches must act in accordance with your company's development strategy, HR philosophy, and organizational aims. This is your responsibility and not the responsibility of the executives who are being coached—they will be busy enough orienting their coaches to their areas of the organization.

Prepare and conduct a standard orientation for your coaches. If a number of coaches are beginning together, organize a group orientation. It is more efficient for you and allows coaches to meet one another and begin establishing working relationships. It also gives them the opportunity to discuss organizational issues, a frequent topic at coaches' meetings. As an added bonus, you will be able to observe the coaches in a group setting as part of your ongoing assessment of their capabilities.

Putting together a good orientation session means striking a balance between what to include and what to leave out. Focus on the key messages and provide documentation on other topics to which coaches can refer later. Develop an orientation guide and use it as a reference tool. A great resource to help build this content is *The Executive Coaching Handbook* (Executive Coaching Forum, 2001).

Initial Orientation

Topics for an initial orientation session and guide could include

- Company overview: Include history, culture, values, norms, initiatives, and strategy. Draw on existing resources, such as videos and handouts from your company's employee orientation program, annual report, public relations materials, Web site, and intranet.

- HR philosophy: Include the executive development and coaching strategy, so that coaches understand the positioning and uses of executive coaching in your company.

- Definition of leadership: Discuss your company's definition of leadership, the model that executives and coaches should follow, and examples of leadership behavior that your company wants to change.

- Expectations of coaches: Explain what you are looking for in a coach, your success criteria, what you expect, and what you *don't* want them to do. Clarify your company's business practices.

- Learning contracts: Explicitly state the intended outcomes and norms of the executive coaching engagement. Include purpose and objectives, time lines, scope and types of assessment, measures of success, identification and roles of stakeholders, confidentiality agreements, use of personal and coaching information, and communication and distribution of information.

- Measurements of success: Focus coaching and assure your ability to measure its impact on the individual and the business by communicating specific results and metrics (e.g., retention of key talent, employee or customer satisfaction, and productivity gains resulting from the coaching).

- Problem resolution and ethical dilemmas: Discuss how to identify and resolve problems. List guidelines for confidentiality to protect the executive, coach, and organization.

- Proprietary and confidentiality agreements: These documents will protect your company and allow coaches to access the people and information they need.

- Who's who: Include helpful names, numbers, and organizational information.

- Purchasing and contracting process: Provide specifics on contracting, billing, and payment. Include the names and phone numbers of necessary contacts in Purchasing, Accounts Payable, and other organizations, so that coaches can resolve any future billing problems.

- Glossary of terms: Give your coaches the key terms, acronyms, and essential tidbits of information they need to function in your company.

Orientation to a Specific Executive

Coaches also need specific orientation on their executive clients. Include input from the succession planning process, background files on each executive, press clippings, upcoming reorganization information, organizational perceptions of each executive, your own impressions, and so on. This broad organizational context will give the coach a good perspective on the executive's issues and feedback data.

Ongoing Orientation

This type of orientation stresses dialogue between you and your coaches. Ongoing orientations may take the form of coaches' meetings, held quarterly or in conjunction with other organizational events. Since coaches are in a position to spot organizational issues and trends, these meetings will enable you to receive feedback about the organization itself. As partners in executive development strategies, coaches are invaluable resources because they apply their energies to benefiting both the individual and the organization. They often work together to help individuals or departments develop solutions or opportunities for collaboration.

Step 5: Match the Executive to the Coach

Finding coaches is easy; matching executive to coach is more difficult. The in-depth process described here is useful when an executive is looking for a longer-term coaching engagement—one in which the coach will go beyond 360-degree data debriefing and a development plan to explore more ingrained characteristics and performance questions.

Construct an Effective Matching Process

There are three key components to the matching process.

First, know your coaches. In-depth knowledge of the backgrounds, perspectives, skills, strengths, personalities, and niches of prospective coaches will guide the matching process.

Second, know your executives and your organization. Consider cultural and normative organizational issues when you select potential coaches. By knowing the organizational code words and the buzz about people and situations, you can more accurately assess their needs and constraints. Include in your assessment the complexity of the issues on which executives want—and need—to work. Determine which coaches will create "comfortably uncomfortable" relationships. Executives must trust, confide in, and feel a bond with their coaches. Coaches, on the other hand, need to control the "uncomfortable" element in the relationships, convincingly deliver candid and constructive feedback, confront clients empathically during sessions, and help executives examine issues from new and different perspectives.

Third, it is critical to include executives in the selection process. Ideally, they should also participate in the decision to begin the coaching process. Make sure executives understand that it is their responsibility to orient their coaches to the organization: its goals and initiatives, people, and norms. Use the executive's checklist for coaching (Worksheet 2).

Evaluate the Request for Coaching

A request for coaching is a brief but telling event in terms of organizational and individual data. Did the request come from the HR manager, the executive's manager, or the executive? Who is seeing what needs? Pay attention to subtleties of language and organizational code words. In addition, by keeping your ear attuned to the rumor mill—without contributing to it—you may be able to anticipate an executive's needs and make an appropriate coaching match.

For example, an organization with strong conflict-avoidance norms requested coaching for a newly hired executive who was having difficulty integrating with the corporate culture and was, according to some people, derailing. The HR manager described the executive as "prematurely focused on outcomes" and "more junior than we anticipated." According to the executive's manager, the new hire "thinks the job is broader in scope than it is." Key stakeholders indicated that their expectations were not being met, yet they failed to provide the new hire with clear, practicable feedback. The executive in question felt that "people have feedback for me, but I can't access it." A closer look revealed that there was no consensus on role clarity and goals.

Meet with the Executive

Whether the coaching is ad hoc or programmatic, begin the matching process by scheduling a one-on-one meeting with the executive. Your goal should be to penetrate below surface issues and identify pressing needs as well as tangible and intangible criteria. Candor, incisiveness, and a willingness to ask tough and sometimes taboo questions are crucial qualities. Criteria for coaches should include, but are not limited to, industry experience, education, special skills, cognitive abilities, languages, experience in your company, and cultural, geographic, and coaching experience. You may also need to consider demographic characteristics such as age, race, gender, and personal interests. Candid needs-analysis discussions with executives should give you enough information to produce a coach profile. Your goal is to position both executive and coach for success.

I begin these meetings by providing executives with some brief context setting based on my knowledge of the particular situation, the people

---

Worksheet 2

Executive's Checklist for Coaching

✔ Meet with the Executive Coaching Manager and Human Resources Manager to discuss coaching. Source and select the coach.

✔ Prepare business/purchasing contract based on coach's proposal, executive coaching manager and HR review, and consultation.

✔ Gather key documents and materials the coach will need:

- Organizational charts
- Business plan and strategy documents, if relevant
- Job description
- Performance objectives
- Performance appraisals
- Development plans
- Prior feedback results (e.g., upward appraisals, 360-degree survey results, *Myers-Briggs Type Indicator* instrument)
- Key documents, articles, and videos written for or about your company
- Contact information: e-mail, phone, and addresses for key stakeholders (e.g., manager, direct reports, peers, colleagues, key interfaces)

✔ Generate a list of major stakeholders from whom the coach should gather feedback or input, including direct reports, key interfaces, manager, internal and external customers, and peers.

✔ Contact the stakeholders you want the coach to interview. Include

- Purpose of data gathering
- Time required
- Deadline for input
- Statements of confidentiality, anonymity, and applicability

✔ After receiving feedback, thank those who participated in the feedback process and give them a general summary of feedback results. Explain how you intend to use the information and request their support through the coaching process.

✔ Participate in an ongoing evaluation of executive coaching.

Worksheet 2

Executive's Checklist for Coaching (cont'd)

✔ Provide feedback on your coach and your experience with the coaching process to the executive coaching manager or HR manager.

✔ Give your coach feedback on what did and did not help.

✔ Give your coach ongoing information about you, your organization, or the company that will assist in the coaching process. Include reorganization memos, company newsletters, and feedback from others.

✔ Use the executive coaching manager and HR as needed to answer questions and provide advice. Their role is to ensure that coaching is an investment of value to you and the company.

involved, and comparative information about other companies and best practices. My intent is build a relationship, establish my credibility as a person who is able to find and manage the best coaches, and relieve any underlying trepidation. I then quickly ask, "What characteristics do you want in a coach? What don't you want? What is critical versus what is nice to have? What will it take to make you comfortably uncomfortable?" I listen intently on many levels to their answers, probing extensively, asking about feedback they may have heard, situations that forced them to rethink an issue, incidents that triggered their own behavioral changes, approaches that made them more recalcitrant, and similar occurrences.

My goal is to determine the executive's idea of the most important thing a coach can do to establish credibility and jump-start the learning process. I have found that there is often a visceral need on the executive's part to have some "common experience" around which to bond. This may include being downsized, working in a changing industry, facing difficult career decisions of a similar nature, or even something as sensitive as sharing race or gender. Determining which background element is most critical to the executive, while making sure that the coach is appropriate for short- as well as long-term needs (e.g., does the executive need a coach with skills in team building or organizational redesign?), is important in selecting potential coaches. This activity is for me a highly intuitive process that utilizes my own experience and judgment.

The range of skills required of a coach can be broad and the combinations unique. You may not always be able to find exact matches, and perhaps you shouldn't even try. The important task is to identify potential coaches who meet the executive's critical perceived needs—and who are skilled and flexible enough to discover and meet the needs that are as yet unseen.

Select Potential Coaches

Gathering a set of potential coaches is a highly intuitive step. It should be based on extensive knowledge of and feel for the coaches in your pool. This is where your organization benefits from the rigorous selection process applied earlier. Assemble a list of three to five potential coaches, basing your selections on results from the executive interview, coach assessments and skills/experience inventories, reference information, and your own gut feelings. Not all the coaches on your short list will exactly match the executive's profile, but your judgment on the likely chemistry between coach and executive will be a crucial factor in determining fit.

Provide Coach Bios

Now that you have a short list of potential coaches, send the executive an overview of each candidate. Ask for brief written reactions to each potential coach and rank the bios according to preference. Supply the executive with information that is brief, comparable, and easy to read. It is your job, not the executive's, to sift through marketing materials, so a one-page biographical sketch of each coach will suffice. Include coaching and consulting specialties and history, specific industry experience, client list, education, and contact information. If you prefer, you may provide the coaches with a format and ask them to write their own bios themselves, but do not include résumés. Because the coach's role is fundamentally different from that of a direct report or colleague, you must avoid giving the impression that the executive is interviewing a potential employee.

Help the Executive Select a Coach

As the executive coaching manager, your responsibility is to guarantee competent and committed coaches who are prepared and available. The executive will make the final selection based on chemistry and connection. Working together, discuss your reasons for sending each bio and then whittle the list down to two or three candidates for the executive to interview. In my experience, companies did not pay coaches for participating in these interviews, but coaches were willing to take part for three key reasons. First, this business practice was stipulated early in the screening process and did not come as a surprise to the coaches. Second, I asked coaches to make themselves available for interviews only if there was a likely fit. Third, I provided them with timely and specific feedback about why they were or were not selected.

After the interviews, conduct a follow-up discussion with the executive. Help the executive compare and contrast each coach and try to tease out reactions. Remember that the coach's presence, behavior, and demeanor should add to the executive's credibility. For example, in one company, an executive whose manager questioned his leadership strengths required a respected and seasoned coach who had worked successfully with other senior executives in the same organization. Some of the executive's initial choices were not considered challenging enough by his manager. The most appropriate coach's profile emerged through a series of discussions between the HR partner and the executive, with support from the executive development manager, and a person was selected according to those criteria. Had one of the less demanding coaches been chosen, the manager would have not have taken the executive's efforts seriously.

Executives may get stalled with their final decisions if they feel conflict between the coach they *should* select and they one they *want* to select. If you have provided capable but diverse candidates, then allowing executives to choose their own coaches should produce the desired outcome.

Contact the Coaches Who Were Not Selected

Because you helped the executive through the selection process, you will be able to provide feedback to coaches who were not chosen. Coaches value this feedback; they know selection sometimes boils down to chemistry or personality. Your feedback will help them refine their practice and their own sense of self, and it will benefit you by strengthening your relationships with coaches and providing you with more data.

Work with the Selected Coach

Schedule a meeting with the selected coach to discuss additional organizational or individual information, provide in-depth context, and introduce the HR manager who will be involved in the coaching. If the coach is new to your organization, set up a learning contract and stakeholder review. Finally, establish how you, as the executive coaching manager, will work with the coach during this particular engagement.

Fees are often determined at this point. It is best to establish the funding model(s), rates, and business practices related to coaching fees at an earlier stage in the process. Approaches vary based on whether your arrangements are programmatic or ad hoc, how purchasing and contracting are done in your organization, and by what means coaching is funded (by the executive's own business unit or as part of a program budget funded by the company). I have seen coaching contracts that establish a fixed price for all coaching activity completed within a specified time period, others that stipulate fees and hours for each coaching engagement, and some that negotiate varied fees for individual situations. It is extremely helpful to think through this issue before coaches are actually engaged.

Step 6: Keep the Coaching Engagement on Track

Once a learning contract has been finalized and coaching begins, you should be able to step into the background. You've briefed the coach and prepared the executive. It is now up to the coach to establish trust and establish an initial footing with the executive's HR manager. In fact, the coach and the HR manager will interact with increasing frequency. You will, of course, be available to meet with the HR manager, coach, or executive and may check in with them occasionally via informal conversations, voice mail, or e-mail. Do not overmanage the coaching relationship—let it generate its own bonds.

When to Check In

Throughout the course of the coaching process, there are a few key events that represent optimum check-in times: after the first coaching session, after feedback sessions, midway or late in the coaching engagement, and after the closing session. Table 9 reviews these milestones.

Some situations demand speedy intervention and more active management on your part. These include breaches of confidentiality (e.g., a coach sharing information about an executive or the organization with someone outside your company), violations of ethical guidelines (e.g., gift giving), and lack of responsiveness or inappropriate actions on the part of the coach, executive, or HR manager (e.g., calls not returned promptly, multiple cancellations).

Act as a contact point for coaches by giving them opportunities to air their multiple perspectives if they are concerned about overlapping or

Table 9

Check-in Points during the Coaching Engagement

When	Who	What
After first coaching session and before feedback sessions	Executive	• General satisfaction • Expectations met • Questions
	Coach	• General questions • Information needs
	HR manager	• Key stakeholders for feedback • Partnering with coach • General questions • Information needs
After feedback sessions	Executive	• Reactions • Questions • Reducing potential resistance
	Coach	• Reactions • Need for more information or context
	HR manager	• Discuss common phenomena of executive resistance and surprise • Validate feedback findings when appropriate • Offer support
Midpoint or late in coaching engagement	Executive	• General satisfaction • Meeting goals • Feedback for coach and others
	Coach	• General needs • Feedback • Meeting goals
	HR manager	• Quality partnering with coach • Transition plan

After closing session	Executive	• Goals met
		• Expectations met
		• Satisfaction
		• Next steps
	Coach	• Goals met
		• Feedback
		• Next steps, if any
	HR manager	• Follow-up role
		• Feedback

conflicting roles and objectives. For example, two different coaches were working with two executives, one of whom was the direct report of the other. Both coaches were confused about how to handle the relationship between their two executives, and both separately raised their concerns. The coaches and the executive development manager met to explore the problem, generated potential solutions, and together planned the coaches' next steps.

Do not hesitate to mediate conflicts between coaches and HR. For example, a vice president of HR requested a performance report comparing and contrasting two executives from a coach who had worked with both. The coach felt that this would violate confidentiality norms and the established learning contract, but the vice president insisted. The coach and the executive coaching manager jointly resolved the conflict by having the coach discuss the request with the executives in question. The executives then generated a list of their strengths. With these lists in hand, the coach responded verbally to the HR vice president by enumerating the strengths of each executive.

Because coaching is a highly visible form of intervention, problems can quickly take on suprising significance. Successful partnering among all parties—executive coaching manager, coach, HR manager, the executive's manager, and the executive—is the key to keeping a coaching engagement on track.

Step 7: Measure Results

Measuring the success of executive coaching is a notoriously difficult task. In a recent evaluation study at a midsize financial services institution, more than 57 percent of the executives who had been coached felt it was "difficult to impossible" to measure the business impact of the coaching. Yet 81 percent of these executives were personally "very satisfied" with their coaching, and 92 percent felt that the organization had received "high value" from the coaching investment. The managers of the coached executives had a similar, though less dramatic, reaction. While 43 percent said it was "difficult to impossible" to measure business impact, almost every manager saw positive behavioral changes in direct reports who had undergone coaching. Fully 88 percent of these managers felt that the organization received "high value" from the coaching.

Interestingly, few executives or their managers felt that annual performance appraisal ratings reflected coaching results, although the appraisal content may have done so. The performance appraisal process was not sensitive enough to capture positive changes in the numeric rating, making this tool unreliable in assessing behavioral change via coaching.

What and How to Measure

Most often, if the executive's manager feels there is improvement on an issue of concern to the manager, then the coaching is deemed worthwhile. This applies to other key stakeholders as well. It is possible, however, to measure success by more objective means. On a continuous improvement basis, you may apply simple standard measures to customer satisfaction, coach responsiveness, coaching quality, the perceived value of the coaching, and management of the process. A phone or e-mail survey asking for responses on a high-medium-low scale, plus commentary, would suffice.

Measuring the business impact of coaching is a much harder task. In my view, it is important to track, on an individual basis, the identification and attainment of coaching goals—without violating confidentiality agreements. Organizational metrics such as retention of key employees, unit performance, and individual and group rewards may be used to measure the impact of coaching.

In addition, 360-degree assessment results and measures of organizational climate before and after coaching often reveal improvement over time. Skills attainment, such as presentations and media relations, are relatively easy to ascertain with observational techniques. Although more subtle behavioral changes are harder to demonstrate, they can be calibrated through qualitative assessments based on personal interactions.

If you want to measure coaching effectiveness and value, you must set and document clear, measurable goals from the beginning and then establish business-impact measures and track results for each individual over an extended period of time. For example, if an executive is being coached because his leadership style has resulted in poor employee retention, the assessment could focus on retention improvement and accompanying cost savings.

A critical goal of executive coaching is to increase self-reliance by improving the executive's capabilities in the areas of leadership, management, and business issues. A well-designed and executed coaching program also builds the ability of the HR manager to support the executive and the organization in confronting the challenges that lie ahead.

Conclusion

Your executive coaching initiative, whether programmatic or ad hoc, has a better chance of succeeding if you begin by linking it to executive development and business strategy. The best coaches have unique characteristics that may be hard to assess, and, no matter how competent, not all coaches will meet the needs of your company and your executives. By establishing a rigorous and thorough process of selecting, qualifying, and orienting coaches, you will build a database of prospects who fit your company and its culture. Devoting care to the coach–executive match and involving the executive in the decision increases the chances of successful coaching engagements. Remember, coaching is a four-way partnership that involves the coach, the executive, the HR manager, and you. As the contact point between the various stakeholders in the coaching process, it is up to you to make it work.

Note

[1] Most of my experience has been working with external coaches, and therefore this chapter focuses primarily on issues involving external coaches. Internal staff are also a potential pool of coaches. For an in-depth discussion on using internal coaches, see Chapter 10.

EXECUTIVE COACHING AND BUSINESS STRATEGY

MARY JANE KNUDSON

This chapter analyzes the intersection of strategy and executive coaching in two different ways. In the first section, we examine how executive coaches can work with senior leaders to support and enhance the development and implementation of a company's business strategy. Next, we explore ways of designing and implementing executive coaching programs that are linked to business strategy.

This exploration of the link between strategy and executive coaching is directed primarily to the human resources (HR) practitioner whose role relates to the use of executive coaching in an organizational setting. The information may also be useful for the practicing executive coach who strives for the maximum effect on both an individual and the organization in which the individual is a critical player.

I based this chapter on a combination of ongoing learning acquired from generous and insightful colleagues in executive development and executive coaching, the literature, and my own experience of more than twenty years in the fields of executive development, organizational development, training, and career counseling. Since 1997, I have learned much from my colleagues as a member of the Boston Coaching Group. Relative to executive coaching, I have performed this function as an internal HR professional, overseen the sourcing and utilization of coaches, initiated the use of executive coaches by designing executive coaching programs as part of larger development efforts, and trained executive coaches.

Executive Coaching and the Formulation and Execution of Business Strategy

Successful executive coaching requires sophisticated understanding of organizations as well as of individuals. Nowhere is that more apparent than in the intersection of business strategy and the executive coaching that supports it. Senior leaders play a critical role in setting direction, defining strategic positions, and providing focus for the business operations needed for successful execution. Through executive coaching, a leader can be more effective, as an individual, in guiding the *execution* of the strategy. Furthermore, given the positions these individuals occupy in their organizations, coaching can also affect the *formation* of strategy.

An essential HR responsibility is to support the business strategy with initiatives, programs, processes, and business partner consulting that may help the organization achieve its business goals. Executive coaching is one area in which HR has the potential to support not only the execution of the strategy but its development as well. Involvement of HR in executive coaching may take a variety of forms that include supporting an ad hoc request for coaching, developing a coaching program as part of a larger HR or executive development strategy, or providing executive coaching directly as an internal coach.

A few qualifiers are in order regarding strategy. First, strategy involves many people and could be examined in terms of teams, groups, businesses, or the entire organization. However, since an executive coach generally works with one person at a time, this chapter will begin with the individual leader and the effect of coaching on his or her role in the strategy process. Second, although this section focuses primarily on executives and their role in strategy, they are clearly not the only ones involved in this complex subject nor are they involved in all decisions with strategic implications. Finally, while this section will often differentiate development of strategy from its execution, strategy management is not a strictly linear process; it is iterative as it evolves. The content of strategy is typically deliberate at some level, but much of it emerges as a firm pursues its goals.

The Nature of Strategy in Organizations

In the broadest sense, strategy is about the directions, decisions, and actions that enable an organization to adapt to change. Fahey (2000) argued that the first work of strategy is leveraging change by identifying its inherent opportunities and determining how a firm can capitalize on those opportunities. The next task of strategy is an intelligence challenge: understanding current change, finding emerging trends, and then defining potential possibilities and their implications for the organization, thereby in effect learning from the future before it happens. Finally, but not insignificantly, there are strategic choices regarding the challenge of execution. The resulting strategy has three core elements:

- Scope: What products and/or services to offer customers
- Posture: How the organization will compete to gain customers (product features, functionality, service, availability, image and reputation, price)
- Goals: What the organization wants to achieve (improved market share, image, revenue, shareholder value, ROI, cash flow)

By considering these elements, a firm will be able to determine its long-term goals and identify the means and approaches it will use to attain them. It can then select business objectives that will advance it midway toward those goals and formulate specific short-term tasks that will become the operating goals.

Perspectives on strategy differ, with some seeing it as *deliberate*—that is, relatively linear, rational, and prescriptive (e.g., Porter, 1998)—and others seeing it as a more *emergent* process that unfolds as a firm implements its strategic plan over time. A recent integrative book on strategy (Mintzberg, Ahlstrand, and Lampel, 1998) argued that few strategies are purely deliberate or emergent. Furthermore, the authors asserted that high-performing organizations allow for several simultaneous perspectives both planful and incremental at once.

The crafting of strategy as described by Fahey and by Mintzberg et al. implicitly demands a great deal of leaders. Leaders must be both directive and participative. They must be sufficiently confident and decisive to provide a sense of direction, yet able to empower others so that they can contribute to emergent learning as they act on the firm's strategic direction. Leaders must have at their disposal the relevant details (regarding customer requirements and behavior and the strategies of competitors) and at the same time be able to step back and see the big picture—the subtle emerging patterns and connections that suggest potential market opportunities not yet apparent to others. They must be analytic while they are conceptual; in the terms of the *Myers-Briggs Type Indicator* (MBTI) instrument, they must use Sensing as well as Intuition. Additionally, they must be driven and urgent builders who have the courage and capability to break down what they have just built or to reconfigure and adjust as conditions change.

In a recent study reported in *Fortune* (Charan and Colvin, 1999), few of the recent CEO failures involved flawed strategies. Rather, it was failed *execution* of strategy that led to the downfall of otherwise highly successful CEOs. The study asserted that the number one reason for failure of execution was what Charan and Colvin called "people problems." The biggest people mistakes are failing to put the right people in the right place and not fixing people problems quickly enough. The authors found that most CEOs they studied knew they had problems but either denied the facts or delayed taking action.

It is an enormous challenge to craft a strategy that responds effectively to a complex and fast-changing environment, but it is as great a challenge to mobilize an organization to make the strategy real. Since strategy development and implementation are challenging and pivotal to a company's success, executive coaching programs that support both are likely to have the greatest impact on business results.

Coaching That Supports Strategy Formulation and Execution

Executive coaching has proved to be an effective tool, with strong potential impact on an executive's development and learning and ultimately on business strategy and results. Not surprisingly, given the complexity of individuals and the strategic work of organizations, there is no single way of describing how the executive coaching of individuals affects the development and implementation of strategy. The most fundamental requirement is ensuring that coaching begins with a substantive contracting process in which coaching goals are explicitly related to real business objectives, thereby ensuring that the coaching is not of a purely personal nature (see Chapter 9 for more details on the contracting and alignment processes). Beyond that requirement, which applies to all good executive coaching, the following sections explore how executive coaching facilitates learning that is critical to an individual's effectiveness in the work of strategy. The topics include

- Two frameworks that can be used to specify ways in which coaching results in the learning of executives
- Some common mistakes regarding strategy made by executives and how coaching can help avoid them
- Identification of the secondary, usually implicit, consequences of coaching that affect strategy formulation and implementation
- Implications of these issues for HR

Two Coaching Frameworks

These frameworks for executive coaching illustrate the variety of ways in which coaching an individual can support business strategy.

Four Different Coaching Roles This approach (Witherspoon and White, 1996) defines each coaching role according to its purpose:

- Coaching for *skills*, which focuses on specific skills required for a current job
- Coaching for *performance*, which focuses more broadly on a present job
- Coaching for *development*, which is directed toward learning for a future job

- Coaching for the *executive's agenda,* which focuses on learning that is related to an executive's agenda in the broadest sense

The last role, coaching for the executive's agenda, is the most directly relevant to strategy. Building on Witherspoon and White's model, in this role, a coach might

- Be a sounding board for an executive who needs to explore the feasibility of several potential strategy scenarios

- Help test an executive's assumptions regarding marketplace realities and the opportunities they present

- Point out blind spots on the part of the executive that are impeding implementation

- Enhance creativity

- Support the efforts required to pursue a given strategic direction by helping an executive lay out a change strategy that supports the business strategy

The role of coaching for the executive's agenda seems to have the greatest relevance for strategy; however, any of the roles could help focus learning that relates to business strategy. For example, when coaching for skills, an executive may need to address some of the following areas:

- Acquiring more knowledge about the new Internet economy in order to fully understand emerging strategic options

- Honing negotiation skills for new partnerships with customers who simultaneously become partners, suppliers, and competitors

- Further refining expert communication skills with the goal of implementing and providing leadership through major organizational change

The other two roles, coaching for performance and coaching for development, may also be appropriate for specific situations involving strategy formation or execution.

Five Levels of Coaching Dynamics This framework sheds light on how coaching an individual can have an effect on business strategy. Adapting the work of Reddy (1994) to executive coaching, Yahanda (1998) outlined five levels of coaching dynamics.

Level 1 refers to *cognitive* and *task-* or *skill-related learning,* with the focus primarily on work to be done.

Level 2 relates to describing and naming *behavior;* coaching is targeted toward directly observable behaviors such as self-presentation, approach to conflict, problem solving, decision making, and methods of exerting influence on others.

At Level 3, coaching is conducted at the *emotional/reflective* level, and the issues are more often covert as compared to the presenting issue. Level 3 concerns, primarily inferred from Level 2 behaviors, are made up of core personal issues of inclusion, control, power, competence, and affiliation.

Level 4, entitled *interpretive/reframing,* addresses values, beliefs, and assumptions about reality. Coaching work at Level 4 illuminates how the executive's assumptions about people and the world determine behavior and results.

Level 5, which deals with the *unconscious,* is not appropriate for business coaching situations and is more appropriately explored in personal psychotherapy.

According to Yahanda, although the presenting or contracted issue may appear at one level, the real issue often emerges eventually at another level. The executive coach decides, after evaluating various sources of information, at which level to focus the learning work and also when to move from one level to another. The examples below, based on my work as an executive coach, illustrate common mistakes and how these different levels of coaching intervention can enhance effective formulation and implementation of strategy by executives.

Common Errors in Strategy and How Coaching Can Help
Because developing and implementing strategy is a challenging and complex process, many missteps are possible. The following examples of some common mistakes include suggestions for applying the two coaching frameworks described above.

First, if strategic direction has been set at too high a level, people will have difficulty seeing how their work aligns with the strategy and may not even realize that a direction has been set. Coaching at Level 1 would provide the framework and tools for helping the executive design communication processes and structures for translating strategy into action. Or, using the Witherspoon and White framework, an executive could enter coaching at the skills or performance level, to address current communication issues.

Second, strategy may be clear and somewhat fleshed out but only for senior management. Communication to the rest of the organization is incorrectly assumed, ineffective, or lacks context. Executives who were fully immersed in the information and who took part in discussions that evolved into business decisions may lose sight of the fact that exposure to the same information and exchanges is not organization wide. Again, coaching at Level 1 or Level 2 could address some of the issues by providing information, developing communication skills, and helping executives understand the effects of their behavior. In the Witherspoon and White framework, coaching would likely begin at the level of skills or performance.

Third, an organization's leaders may be ineffective at building shared mind-set regarding competitive threats, market opportunities, customer requirements, and resulting business decisions. Among the coaching options are Level 1 interventions aimed at providing executives with more information on other points of view that will help them understand the valid, rational reasons behind dissent. Level 2 interventions might help executives see how their own behavior is interfering with building a shared outlook. A Level 3 approach could identify an underlying mechanism of conflict avoidance, which suppresses the free exchange of opposing views that leads to genuine consensus. At Level 4, the coach and an executive might explore the executive's unexamined assumptions about how to handle conflict in a group setting or whether the process that produces shared mind-set is worth undergoing. In the Witherspoon and White framework, the coaching role would likely address skill, performance, or the executive's agenda. Additionally, learning how to build shared mind-set could be the coaching-for-development goal of an emerging leader.

Fourth, an organization might continue to pursue a strategy long after inertia has set in or there is widespread belief that the strategy is no longer right. Any intervention level would be appropriate in such a case. For example, a coach might help the leader search out the right data, listen to the views of other constituencies, or learn about new fields (e.g., developments in e-commerce or emergence of new competitors). Coaching could lead the executive to see how his or her own behavior, and perhaps Level 3 emotional issues, are blocking the necessary learning in an attempt to fend off bad news or contrary views. Especially at Levels 3 and 4, a host of reasons could be behind the executive's denial of the need for major change.

Fifth, perhaps an organization prematurely selects a strategic direction. Several of the same coaching issues involved in the previous example could be at work here. Perhaps the executive is relying too much on his or her intuition and experience instead of paying attention to market and customer intelligence or working out a viable business model that can actually yield acceptable profits. Again, any of the interventions described in Levels 1 through 4 could be appropriate.

Secondary Consequences and Their Impact on Strategy
In addition to achieving the specific agreed-on goals, a rich and successful coaching experience inevitably yields secondary consequences, or what could be called meta-learnings, for the individual being coached. These are the "learning how to learn" outcomes, which can have both short- and long-term effects on strategy formation and implementation. These objectives are usually implicit and include the following:

- Accepting and learning from feedback
- Identifying and solving self-generated problems
- Improving the executive's ability to observe and process personal data within his or her role and in real time
- Developing the capacity for identifying and reflecting on implicit assumptions that may be compromising the executive's ability to discern existing business opportunities or to accurately assess the firm's progress and success in executing its strategy
- Valuing and seeking out opposing views and challenges to the executive's position

The last two abilities in particular enable executives to challenge conventional wisdom, thereby moving from making incremental changes to seeing the opportunities that could enable their firms to redefine the rules of the game. Some of the other implicit objectives help executives improve their ability to reflect and learn from their experiences in the moment and thus monitor their deployment for themselves. In addition, coaching can show executives the part they play in shielding themselves from bad news or opposing viewpoints on customer, market, and organizational realities, which can greatly limit collective understanding of the environment and choice of strategic direction.

Achieving both the primary coaching goals and these secondary learning objectives can have a long-term effect on the individual executive and on subsequent strategy work in the organization. Such coaching may help a leader attain an understanding and mastery of both the deliberate side of strategic planning and the emerging nature of the strategy process. In today's fast-paced marketplace, critical assumptions regarding industries, competitors, and strategy could easily change overnight. The coach can help the executive learn from experience—while also pointing out that the lessons of experience may *not* always be a guide to the future.

In the coach, an executive finds a safe, private sounding board for examining alternative directions and exploring new ideas about strategy itself. The executive may gain insight into the need to create an organizational context that facilitates learning at all levels; this could improve the effectiveness of the emerging strategy as well. As the coached executive receives honest, trustworthy feedback, he or she can explore the intended as well as unintended outcomes of certain behaviors. By analogy, executing strategy may have similar results: any given direction leads to intended as well as unintended consequences. This awareness may encourage an organization to prepare for contingencies and thus become more nimble.

Implications for HR

Executive coaching can be extremely effective if used appropriately; however, successful outcomes do not generally happen by accident. HR is in the best position to provide the stewardship necessary to ensure effectiveness, integrity, and accountability in the use of executive coaching. (See also Chapters 7, 9, and 10.)

HR professionals involved in the introduction and utilization of executive coaching require sophisticated knowledge and skills. They should have outstanding observational and analytical abilities with which to frame the coaching objectives (including determining whether coaching is appropriate at all). They must be fully immersed in the strategic concerns of the business in order to envision the positive effects of coaching a particular individual or set of individuals. Keen diagnostic skills must be applied to both individual and organizational dynamics. They need the courage to confront those issues others might prefer to ignore and the seasoned judgment to select coaches wisely. Strong contracting skills will produce the clearest possible agreements at the beginning of the coaching process. In addition, the HR professional must be fully versed in the business—its current position and its problem areas. Understanding the connection between coaching and business results is critical.

HR engagement means overseeing the whole coaching process, consulting with all parties involved regarding the requirements for a successful outcome, ensuring alignment with business needs, communicating logistic requirements, ensuring explicit contracting and clarity regarding roles, keeping track of goals and expenses incurred, and managing the coaches.

Linking Executive Coaching Programs to Business Strategy

Whenever a firm uses executive coaching, the link to business is a major part of accountability. When HR introduces executive coaching, it is important to articulate this linkage for two reasons. First, coaching is expensive. Second, when people have not been exposed to executive coaching, the connection to strategic success is a persuasive means of gaining support from senior executives who are busy and must constantly make difficult decisions regarding the most effective use of their scarce time. Some leaders may even see their career success as evidence of their effectiveness and may believe they do not need coaching.

In some cases, the link between strategy and executive coaching is fairly straightforward; in others, it may be more difficult to discern. As noted earlier, companies vary in their approaches—deliberate versus emergent—and in the clarity of their strategies. In addition, the current context will often require midcourse correction or even complete overhaul. As a result, making a case for executive coaching that supports business strategy requires careful analysis of both the current strategy and the potential contributions of executive coaching.

Any strategy suggests the capabilities necessary for execution—and consequently the kind of leadership the situation requires. Strategies also contain substrategies that address objectives such as financial, product and operational, and human resources, which in their turn contribute toward the goals of the strategy. All strategic decisions, whether related to overall competitive positioning or the resulting operational requirements, are potentially relevant to executive coaching. For this reason, there are usually several options for linking executive coaching to business strategy. All options require translating strategy into actions that enable people and their organizations to contribute to successful outcomes, which was not done by the failed leaders studied in Charan and Colvin (1999).

The HR agenda must be an integral part of any given strategy, however explicit or implicit it may be. Ensuring the organization's capacity to achieve the business strategy is a critical aspect of such an agenda. As derived from that strategy, the required capability comprises both organizational structures and processes and the talent of the individuals within the enterprise— their knowledge, experience, skills, and behaviors. Organizational capability requirements, along with financial, market, and organizational realities, form the basis for HR strategies that include talent acquisition, development, retention, reward, and motivation.

The executive coaching program must be designed within the context of the overall HR agenda. Business strategy drives the HR agenda, which in turn drives the executive development strategy, of which executive coaching is one key element.

One powerful way to link executive coaching to strategy is to articulate the critical competencies required of senior leaders. For example, a strategy built on continuous innovation calls for leadership competencies that would not serve a strategy based on growth through merger and acquisition. Crucial leadership competencies must be derived directly from the strategy, which means avoiding the use of generic competency models or lists of general characteristics. In addition, to ensure maximum effectiveness, a company's leaders should be directly involved in identifying and confirming the competencies or requirements for their own strategy.

Once critical competencies have been identified, a business case can be made for how executive coaching will support their development and use, thereby contributing to the company's strategic momentum. The following example demonstrates one approach to linking executive coaching to business strategy.

A small financial services firm was implementing a strategy designed to improve service quality. Considerable research and experience had led the company to conclude that outstanding service quality represented a competitive advantage that would enable them to achieve their growth objectives vis-à-vis competitors. The business was based on building long-term, value-added relationships with customers; such an arrangement resembled a consultative business partnership rather than a situation in which product sales were paramount. Furthermore, the leader believed that superior service quality depends on a focus on employee satisfaction. The leadership team realized that the company's new direction demanded different competencies at all levels, including their own. They delineated the necessary leadership competencies, and each participated in a process of executive coaching and 360-degree assessment. In this way, executive coaching, designed to build the required leadership competencies, was introduced as an integral part of the overall initiative to execute the strategy, while the 360-degree assessment pinpointed areas for development, which resulted in further ongoing coaching for many executives.

Implementing Coaching Programs That Support Business Strategy

Implementing an executive coaching effort requires assembling such elements as sponsorship, supporting data, first clients, and coaches. The following suggestions may be helpful in initiating the process. (See also Chapters 7 and 9.)

Select the Right Coaches

Effective executive coaching requires a complex view and experience of both individual and organizational dynamics. Coaches who are not oriented sufficiently to business outcomes, lack adequate knowledge of organizational complexities, or overemphasize personal enlightenment will ultimately undermine a coaching program.

Collect Quantitative and Qualitative Data to Support the Use of Coaching

Once the business priorities of senior leadership are clear to you, collect data (hard and soft) that connect your program with these priorities. Obvious sources include any existing strategic or business plans, as well as an organizational diagnosis that emerges from key executive interviews. The interviews may bring the stated plans and directions to life and disclose the identity and source of the organization's real energy. These interviews also provide an opportunity to build personal credibility, which will be of vital importance as coaching proceeds.

Other supporting information can be very compelling. Gather data about attrition, the cost of talent replacement, organizational climate, promotion rates of successful leaders, and anything else that may capture the attention of the affected executives. One company, for example, discovered that each member of the executive team accounted for about $30 million in profits a year. Due to the stressful nature of the industry, the company justified providing a coach for each executive with the goal of keeping them all "in the game" for as many quarters as possible, thus connecting additional quarters of tenure to profitability streams.

For many company leaders, information regarding the War for Talent (the fiercely competitive market for executives and other key talents) provides persuasive reasons for investing in coaching that may help minimize the disruption and costs associated with continually losing and acquiring executive talent.

Link Coaching to Strategy Formulation and Execution

There are many ways to link executive coaching to strategic success. For example, you could position the coaching program around themes that concern most senior leaders. Such themes might include alignment of organization and direction (shared mind-set), adequate accountability, or development of a legacy of durable change that will continue to guide the organization even after the leader moves on.

Another approach is to direct executive coaching at those areas of the organization that are urgently in need of new learning. An unforeseen business opportunity, a shift in strategy, or a possible failure often motivate firms to seek help with initiating and implementing change. For an individual, occurrences such as a new area of responsibility, a promotion, or a missed opportunity may generate a receptive attitude toward executive coaching. Market or competitive realities, potential or existing business crises, and newly recognized business and personal opportunities demand enhanced effort, which executive coaching supports.

Finally, appeal to the desire of key leaders to be good managers. Dialogue with executives about their organizations' development needs often provides the right context for discussing development for the executives themselves.

Use Executive Coaching to Retain Key Leaders

Executive coaching can be a significant factor in retention because it offers increased opportunities to continue to learn, grow, and increase capability. Executives who have received coaching often express appreciation to their companies for investing in their growth and success.

Obtain the Right Organizational Sponsorship and Support

Identifying and securing the right sponsorship and support can have an enormous impact on the success of executive coaching. Several possible approaches are presented below.

Try building a coalition by *not* going with the expected sponsor or usual first user of new HR initiatives. Most executive teams have at least one member who is the most HR oriented or from whom the HR leader first seeks support. Gaining vocal approval, or even sponsorship, from the least likely supporter will have a powerful effect on the other executives.

Verify that this work has a high priority on the HR agenda. Executive sponsorship may be hard to come by without HR's support.

Directly involve the board of directors by linking leadership development to their responsibility to assure succession.

Use Care in Selecting the First Coaching Candidates

If possible, the first participants should be informal influence leaders and/or those executives who are most widely recognized as rising stars. Understanding them—their goals and aspirations, strengths and weaknesses, and business challenges—and developing personal relationships with them (or their most trusted advisers) increases the likelihood that they will consider coaching an option when the need arises. The executive's ability to influence opinions is more important than mere position, although the two are not necessarily mutually exclusive.

Ideally, the first few coaching situations should lend themselves to the development of well-defined and observable goals. If possible, select individuals who are highly motivated to learn. Take extra care to ensure that executive coaching is clearly the appropriate response to the needs identified in early candidates and that the executives involved are *not* seen as failing or on their way out.

Publicize Success

Make sure to connect coaching success with progress toward the program's targeted business goals. One means of doing so requires laying out the relevant metrics ahead of time. Provide the board of directors, the leader, the sponsor, or the executive team with program outcome data that examines the effect of the coaching program. Anecdotes (carefully worded to protect confidentiality) can also be extremely powerful.

In addition, some leaders might be willing to speak publicly or go on the record in some manner regarding the personal and organizational effects of their coaching experiences. For example, a leader who was general manager of a large geographic area saw revenues increased by 10 percent in the quarters after he participated in a coaching program. In his public statements, he explicitly noted the link between coaching and performance. Another executive, whose company was concerned about executive retention, indicated that the coaching his firm provided for him was worth more than his bonus. An executive in a large organization reported that going through 360-degree assessment and executive coaching with his senior team resulted in his ability to reorganize his direct reports overnight without a snag. He indicated that the time saved was an indispensable part of his subsequent success.

Conclusion

Executive coaching can be an extremely effective development tool if it is designed and managed with business strategy in mind. When coaching outcomes are effectively tied to strategy and performance, coaching becomes a highly visible example of how executive development and/or HR can support the company's business goals. With time and attention, executive coaching may serve as a positive lever for enhancing strategy implementation for executives and enabling achievement of business objectives for the firm. Indeed, executive coaching often has an influence on strategy formation itself.

References

Charan, R., and G. Colvin. (June 21, 1999). Why CEOs fail. *Fortune*, 69–82.
Fahey, L. (2000). Unpublished seminar notes.
Mintzberg, H., B. Ahlstrand, and J. Lampel. (1998). *Strategy safari*. New York: Free Press.

Porter, M. (1998). *On competition.* Boston: Harvard Business School Press.

Reddy, W. B. (1994). *Intervention skills.* San Diego, Calif.: Pfeiffer.

Ulrich, D. (1997). *Human resource champions.* Boston: Harvard Business School Press.

Witherspoon, R., and R. P. White. (1996). Executive coaching: A continuum of roles. *Consulting Psychology Journal* 48 (2): 124–33.

Yahanda, N. (1998). Unpublished seminar notes.

[9]

USING EXECUTIVE COACHING IN ORGANIZATIONS

What Can Go Wrong (and How to Prevent It)

WILLIAM H. HODGETTS

During the past few years, the use of executive coaching has grown exponentially as organizations have discovered the benefits of providing key executives with individual coaching to address specific skill deficits, enhance performance, or help them grow into expanded leadership roles. When undertaken for the right reasons and with competent practitioners, executive coaching can yield significant and lasting benefits for both individuals and organizations. Like many other organizational innovations, however, executive coaching is in danger of becoming—if it has not already become—the latest in a long line of business fads. When not managed well, it is worse than ineffective; it can cause real harm to individuals and organizations and waste untold amounts of dollars.

Perhaps not surprisingly, as coaching has grown in popularity over the past few years, so has the number of books and magazine articles devoted to this topic. Yet few authors have written about the process of *managing* coaching in organizations—the procedures and steps that organizations must put in place to ensure that coaching is well utilized—and none has written extensively about what can happen when coaching is badly managed. This chapter explores some common organizational errors that sometimes occur in the early stages of executive coaching. By studying what can go wrong, we can learn how to get it right.

Like most practical knowledge, the lessons outlined in this chapter were gained through my work in executive development with companies that implemented a variety of executive coaching programs—with different levels of success. These lessons should be useful for individuals concerned with improving the practice of executive development in organizations as well as for executive coaches who are interested in maximizing their own effectiveness. The following cases and lessons are representative of those I have experienced or have drawn from communications with executive development professionals at many other companies.

The chapter is divided into two parts. The first discusses common errors that organizations may make in using executive coaching. The second explores the implications of these errors and suggests some general guidelines for effectively managing the coaching process.

What Can Go Wrong

When human resources (HR) managers or others who are responsible for executive development in organizations first discover the potential benefits of executive coaching, they may not understand that the process has organizational implications beyond the immediate relationship between coach and executive. To be optimally effective, coaching must be well managed and aligned with other organizational goals and processes. (See Chapter 8.) Many of the errors recounted in this section stem from a failure to recognize this fact.

Errors in Assessment, Diagnosis, and Strategy

There are many useful approaches to executive development other than executive coaching. A partial list includes action learning, developmental job rotations, external seminars, and leadership development programs. Companies that make effective use of executive coaching first utilize a disciplined assessment process to identify coaching as the right intervention. The common errors in assessment and diagnosis listed below may lead organizations to choose executive coaching when it is not the best response.

Failure to Align Coaching with Business Strategy

Because coaching is essentially a private activity that occurs behind closed doors, it is easy to view it as separate and distinct from a company's overall business strategy. Yet doing so is a mistake; unless coaching is clearly linked to business strategy, goals, and outcomes, there is the real risk that the hard work of both coach and executive will be directed toward goals that are irrelevant to organizational success, however personally important they may be to the person being coached.

It is best always to confirm the desired outcome of a proposed coaching engagement and, more important, how this change will solve a business problem or further business strategy. Unless a good answer is forthcoming, coaching should not be recommended.

John, a computer programmer and technical analyst in a commercial insurance company, was referred for coaching by his boss, who felt that John needed help with presentation skills and dressing appropriately in a business environment. When the HR specialist responsible for coaching talked at greater length with the boss and others in the work group, she learned that John, an ex-hippie, had long hair and wore unusual ties and shirts. His appearance fell within the guidelines of the company dress code, however, and no one seemed bothered by his hair and somewhat unusual fashion sense except his boss. John's job did not require customer contact, and his performance was excellent. The company hired an executive presentation coach, with whom John initially agreed to meet and work. At this point, John also secretly began looking for employment outside the firm. Because he was technically very competent and his expertise was in demand, he easily found a position at a rival firm. The company lost in at least two ways. First, it incurred the considerable expense of coaching to change a behavior that was not interfering with the productivity or performance of the work group. Second, by making John's dress a focus of coaching, the company confirmed to John (and to others in the group) that it was more interested in outward appearances than in actual results. Ultimately, the company lost John's considerable technical talent and skills as a result of trying to fix something that, from a business strategy perspective, wasn't broken.

Failure to Identify an Organizational Problem Masquerading as an Individual Issue

Things are not always what they seem in organizational life. What at first appears to be an individual issue sometimes turns out, on closer examination, to have significant organizational antecedents. If this fact is not recognized, a great deal of money and effort may be wasted in attempting to fix a problem at the wrong level. Several typical variations of this pattern occur in coaching.

One common situation involves singling out a subordinate when the boss is a major contributor to the problem. If the boss's contribution is not addressed and acknowledged, the issue will recur with other subordinates, as illustrated in the following example.

In a department of a medical products company, every direct report of the department head was receiving individual executive coaching at great expense to the organization and with mixed results. The only manager who was not being coached was the head of the department, who was widely known to be the real problem. Yet, because of her political position in the organization, no one was willing to suggest that she needed coaching as much as or more than the others.

In another common scenario, a subordinate or other individual is singled out as the problem when serious unresolved organizational conflicts are contributing to the person's difficulties with meeting organizational goals. For example, an executive may be hampered by interdepartmental rivalries that limit allocation of resources and are beyond his or her power to control. Or a job may be so impossibly designed that no one could possibly succeed in the role.

This was the situation at one large, decentralized high-tech company, where the corporate head of HR was identified as ineffective and in need of executive coaching. Historically, the role itself was seen as a revolving door—the company had been through ten heads of HR in the past twelve years. When interviewed privately, many HR staff members admitted that the position was a nearly impossible one, because the head of their department was held accountable for change but had no authority to influence the heads of business units who ultimately held the real power in the organization.

Failure to Assess Openness to Feedback and Coaching

Even if there is no real business need for executive coaching, and even if the problem is primarily individual and not organizational, the coaching candidate must be open to feedback and change, or coaching will not be effective. This sounds obvious, but many organizations do not test for individual readiness before suggesting coaching. They risk wasting a great deal of time and money on individuals who are only going through the motions and will accomplish little in the way of behavioral change for the effort.

For example, a department manager was suggested as a good candidate for coaching because he intimidated his subordinates and contributed to poor morale in the group. This manager was also viewed as narrow, defensive, and generally closed to receiving feedback about himself. The executive development specialist in charge of coaching decided to begin by testing his readiness for change through 360-degree feedback on his management style and perceived effectiveness. The manager agreed to participate in the feedback process and also expressed willingness to work with an executive coach. One strong theme that emerged in the data was his lack of openness to receiving feedback. When the executive development specialist tried to give the manager this feedback, he indeed became defensive and blamed others for misperceiving him. The manager was unwilling or unable to acknowledge his part in creating these negative perceptions. The executive development specialist took this as strong confirmation that he was not open enough to benefit from coaching at that time and recommended against it.

Errors in Selecting the Right Coach

Selecting executive coaches and matching them to individuals is a high art and a critical one. With so many practitioners now referring to themselves as executive coaches, it is more important than ever to exercise care when selecting a coach. (See Chapter 7.) Competent and effective executive coaches possess at least three sets of related skills.

First, they must be *interpersonally skilled* at coaching and influencing others. Good coaches make this part seem effortless, but, in fact, successful coaching demands a high level of interpersonal skills. Good coaches must be extremely self-aware, good at listening and responding with empathy, yet also able to deliver difficult feedback in a direct, even tough, but nonjudgmental way. They must also be sufficiently mature in psychological terms so that their own needs for approval, affection, or control do not interfere with their coaching work and they will be able to accurately diagnose complex situations and interactions.

Second, good coaches must be perceived by their clients as both *competent* and *trustworthy.* These two qualities encourage executives to feel that a coach is truly on their side.

Third, executive coaches must have *sufficient understanding of business and organizational politics* to help their clients decipher, understand, and respond appropriately to situations and dilemmas that arise during the coaching process. For coaching at a senior level, this skill set is especially critical because, as Schein (1997) and others have noted, the organizational culture and political realities at the CEO level are different from those at the middle and lower levels of many organizations. Most errors in coach selection involve individuals who lack skills in one or more of the three broad areas listed above. Without clear guidelines, those responsible for selecting coaches are apt to hire the first coach who walks through the door.

In addition to these skill sets, personal chemistry between coaches and executives and such factors as gender, socioeconomic background, and life experiences are also important considerations in making effective coaching matches. Personal chemistry is difficult to define but seems to involve any number of characteristics in the coach that create a feeling of "Yes, this coach has something to teach me" (competence) and "Yes, this coach is enough like me that I can work effectively with her" (trustworthiness). Some other intangibles have to do with the extent to which a coach seems to fit the executive's model of a coach. For some executives, the most effective coaches will be from shared racial, socioeconomic, or geographic backgrounds; other executives might prefer the perspectives of coaches from different backgrounds or who have had different life experiences. Such issues are complex—and may be taboo to discuss—but they play important roles in the match between coach and executive. One helpful approach is to offer executives their choice of two or three prescreened coaches. This allows executives to pick the coaches with whom they feel most comfortable, which in turn helps establish their sense of ownership of the process.

The following examples illustrate some of the factors discussed above.

Failure to Attend to Business and Organizational Dimensions

Another executive coach, Mary, had a doctorate in psychology and practiced as a psychotherapist for many years. When managed care began to erode her private practice, she decided to become an executive coach. Mary displayed fine interpersonal skills and was adept at coaching individuals whose concerns were primarily personal in nature. But, because she had never worked in a business organization, she was unable to fully grasp the complexities of organizational politics and tended to view all issues at the personal level. In a critical coaching engagement, she failed to help an executive make sense of the changing organizational environment and formulate a strategy for surviving under those highly politicized conditions. As a result, the executive was blindsided by an organizational power play that led to his demotion; soon after, he left the company, taking with him invaluable technical and organizational knowledge.

Coach Lacking in Interpersonal Skills

Harold, an executive coach, was a Harvard MBA and had worked for many years at a prestigious strategy consulting firm. His background, experience, and understanding of business strategy made him extremely credible as an executive coach, and he was hired by a large technology company to serve as coach for the CEO and his team. However, after a few sessions, it was clear that Harold had been the wrong choice. He was still operating as a consultant/expert and not as a facilitator/coach. The CEO and others complained that Harold did not listen well and mostly told everyone what he thought they should do. By not giving others space to talk and come to their own conclusions, Harold hastened his own exit. Although he was extremely knowledgeable about business strategy, he lacked an interpersonal skill that is vital for an effective coach: the ability to listen and respond empathetically.

Failure to Select a Coach Who Will Appear Credible to the Client

Bob, a hard-driving senior executive, was responsible for significant growth in his business unit during the previous year but also had a reputation for being abusive and disrespectful to subordinates, especially women. Turnover on his senior team was extremely high, and the organization decided to bring in an executive coach to soften his style. They chose a well-regarded female coach with a strong business background to work with him. Bob initially agreed to meet with her but soon began rescheduling and canceling his coaching sessions. He confided to a colleague that he could not respect the coach's competence because she was a woman, and he did not think he could learn anything from her.

Errors in Creating and Maintaining Effective Coaching Roles and Processes

As noted earlier, organizations new to coaching are often unaware of the need to manage this activity and, consequently, do not assign oversight to someone in the organization. Much can go wrong with the unmanaged process, as the examples below illustrate.

The Case of the Missing Manager:
Failure to Hold Coachees Accountable for Change

Managers often struggle with and avoid giving difficult feedback to subordinates who are not performing well or need to improve some aspect of their work. As executive coaching has grown in popularity, some managers have come to view coaching as an easy way to avoid uncomfortable conversations with their direct reports. They think, "Why not just let the coach give the individual the feedback? After all, isn't the coach the expert in feedback and behavioral change?"

This approach is a mistake for several reasons. First, coaching is only successful if someone in the organization (other than the coach) holds executives accountable for specific behavioral changes. Without such accountability, only the most self-motivated individuals will benefit from coaching. Second, without the direct feedback of a boss or manager, people are much less likely to believe that they really have serious problems. Coaches cannot be the ones to hold their clients accountable for change because they would then be seen not as allies but as authority figures who control positive or negative consequences.

A senior manager in a large financial services organization was having trouble with Gail, a subordinate who, while very competent technically, was disrespectful to her staff and co-workers and was generating a serious morale problem in her group. At the suggestion of the vice president of HR, the senior manager gladly hired an executive coach to assess and work with Gail. The senior manager traveled extensively, making it easy to avoid discussing his coaching goals with Gail. Because her manager did not explicitly state the reasons for coaching, which of her behaviors required intervention, and what the consequences would be if she didn't change, Gail did not take the engagement seriously. The coaching work accomplished little, and the morale problems in Gail's group intensified.

Failure to Identify All Stakeholders

Coaching is often viewed as a simple activity that occurs between executives and their coaches and does not involve anyone else in the organization. Yet there are often others in the organization who also have some interest in the outcomes. These interested parties are usually the executive's manager, the HR manager, an executive development specialist, and the manager's manager; others could be included as well depending on the organization and situation. It is therefore important to identify all the stakeholders and their expectations at the beginning of the coaching engagement. As a next step, all stakeholders must reach some agreement on realistic goals for the coaching.

An example involves Arnold, the head of a division of a recently acquired consumer products company. Arnold was identified as a candidate for executive coaching by Janet, the company's vice president for HR. Arnold and Jason, the company's CEO, fought often and did not see eye to eye on many issues. Jason felt that, although Arnold brought crucial product and industry knowledge to his role, he was often inflexible and unwilling to consider other ways of doing things. Janet hoped executive coaching might help Arnold become more flexible and cooperative. Arnold was agreeable to the idea of coaching. A suitable executive coach was found, and Jason, Janet, Arnold, and the executive coach attended a contracting meeting to define and clarify the goals of the coaching work.

In an effective coaching process, coachees are ultimately responsible for their own changes, and coaches act as their allies or as resources toward achieving those changes. The executives' managers hold them accountable by clarifying objectives, measuring progress, and providing periodic feedback. In larger organizations, an HR manager is generally best positioned to manage the coaching process; in smaller ones, the executive's manager may also assume this role. Sometimes, an executive development specialist conducts an initial assessment of the situation, makes recommendations about the suitability of coaching, and, if appropriate, makes referrals.

Failure to Agree on Clear Objectives and Time Frames
In coaching, as in many other organizational activities, it is vital to establish clear contractual agreement on objectives among all interested parties. Otherwise, it will be nearly impossible later to measure progress, gauge effectiveness, or know when the need for coaching has ended.

Consider the case of a large manufacturing firm that had been paying an executive coach to work with one person in one of its departments for three and a half years. The director of HR who had originally initiated the coaching left the organization, and Tom was hired to take her place. He was shocked to discover that the company had paid the executive coach more than $100,000 without ever specifying goals or objectives. Without a clear contract, Tom had no way of gauging the effectiveness of the process or even whether coaching was still necessary.

Making Coaching Mandatory

Organizations use coaching for both remedial and developmental purposes. In remedial situations, coaching focuses on bringing some aspect of an individual's performance up to acceptable standards. In contrast, developmental coaching emphasizes preparation for a new or expanded role or job that requires additional skills and competencies. Developmental coaching is almost always offered as an optional, voluntary activity. Remedial coaching, however, is sometimes a mandatory condition of employment. In that situation, the employee is often held accountable for participating in the *process* of coaching but is not necessarily held accountable for behavioral *outcomes*.

In my view, it is a mistake to make any kind of coaching mandatory because an employee may comply with the request to work with a coach but will not take the process seriously or change problematic behavior. It is much more effective to hold an individual accountable for behavioral change, so that the changed behavior, not the coaching, becomes the condition for continued employment. After explicitly stating this expectation, coaching can be offered as a resource supplied by the organization to help the employee through the process of change.

For example, Ellen, a difficult manager with a reputation for alienating both clients and co-workers, was told she would have to work with an executive coach to address this problem in order to keep her position at the firm. At first, she strongly defended her behavior and resisted the notion that she needed coaching. But when she realized that the organization intended to make coaching a condition of continued employment, she consented and dutifully met with her coach as directed. The coach, however, soon came to feel that Ellen was not taking the process seriously and was only saying what she felt he wanted to hear. At the end of the coaching period, Ellen's behavior had changed little. Yet, because she had complied outwardly, the company found it difficult to remove her from her position without risking a costly and difficult legal suit.

Failure to Distinguish between Coaching and Therapy

Coaching and therapy share certain features. Both aim at behavioral change, both help individuals understand that their cognitive and emotional reactions may interfere with personal effectiveness, and both are conducted by skilled practitioners who establish strong alliances of trust with their clients. Yet in certain important and essential ways, coaching and therapy are different and should not be confused.

The goal of coaching is to improve a person's effectiveness at work in ways that are linked to overall business strategy. To this end, a coach will sometimes guide individuals toward increased awareness of how their thoughts and emotional reactions lead to problematic behaviors in the workplace. Therapy may share coaching's goals of improved personal effectiveness and increased awareness of problematic thoughts and emotional reactions that may impede work effectiveness. But therapy also addresses nonwork aspects of an individual's life and could involve in-depth explorations of the client's early history, including relationships with parents and other family members—issues that may be only tangentially related to business effectiveness. Therapy may also lead to deep and sometimes intense emotional experiences that demand skillful guidance from an experienced practitioner. Due to the differences in these two approaches, what is acceptable for one intervention may be inappropriate for the other. For example, while a therapist may legitimately explore the early-childhood and familial roots of difficult behaviors, it is less appropriate for an executive coach to do so. If a coach feels there is important unfinished emotional business hampering an executive's performance in the workplace, he or she should refer the executive to a competent therapist.

When organizations fail to draw the line between therapy and coaching, they leave the door open for coaches, especially those with clinical training and backgrounds, to practice therapy at the company's expense, with potentially negative consequences. First, coaching that becomes too clinical and therapeutic can unduly lengthen the coaching process and increase the overall cost to the organization. Second, therapeutic coaching may leave coachees emotionally vulnerable in ways that are not always helpful and might interfere with their professional efficiency and effectiveness. Third, if coaching focuses on deeply rooted emotional issues, it diverts attention away from important work-related problems that could be dealt with in simpler, behavioral terms. Fourth, therapeutic coaching leaves a company vulnerable to legal risks if it ends badly. Because coaches have been selected for their coaching expertise and not their clinical ability, there is no guarantee that a good coach will also be a competent therapist.

Failure to Manage the Coach's Selling Behavior

Because the nature of coaching work involves building trust, a competent coach who has worked with one or several members of a department or group will eventually build up a reserve of trust in the organization. Ethical coaches do not misuse this trust and understand that they must defer to the HR generalist or designated coaching gatekeeper when they are seeking additional work. Such coaches will educate organizations that have not yet assigned such a position by explaining which situations are and are not suitable for coaching; they must also be extremely careful not to accept coaching assignments for which they are not qualified or that are better addressed through other interventions. Ethical coaches will also try not to oversell their services because they know that, in doing so, they ultimately diminish their apparent integrity and trustworthiness.

Sometimes, however, a coach tries to exclude the HR generalist or organizational gatekeeper and will approach a new internal client directly. From the organization's perspective, it is a mistake to allow this kind of behavior because the coach will be operating virtually unmanaged within the organization. In such a situation, even executive coaches with the best of intentions may be tempted to prolong relationships beyond their usefulness or to collude in ways that are detrimental to the organization with powerful individuals with whom they have worked.

Violations of Confidentiality

Coaching cannot succeed without a relationship of trust between the coach and the executive. Clear guidelines, including boundaries defining confidentiality and the kinds of information that can and cannot be shared, are critical to the establishment and maintenance of trust.

In general, all parties involved—such as the boss or manager, the executive, the coach, and whoever is managing the coaching process—should clearly understand and agree on the goals of the coaching engagement. Coaches should periodically inform organizations of the times and dates of coaching sessions and, in general terms, how coaching is progressing. A coach might report, for example, that the executive appears to be actively engaged in the process and motivated to change; conversely, the organization may learn from the coach that the executive has rescheduled the last four appointments and frequently arrives late or leaves early, perhaps indicating a lack of commitment to the process. Under all circumstances, however, the actual content of specific coaching sessions should remain confidential information that is known only to coaches and exetives.

Organizations should also have on file signed confidentiality agreements from their coaches, to limit the risk that sensitive organizational information could be inappropriately revealed to others.

Sharing Confidences within the Organization

Most coaches realize that honoring confidences is their ethical obligation as well as in their enlightened self-interest because it maintains their reputation for honesty and integrity. However, if a coach has multiple allegiances and/or plays multiple roles within an organization, preserving confidentiality for all parties is not always an easy task.

For example, if an executive coach is engaged with both a boss and his or her subordinates, knowing what information to share and what to keep secret is sometimes unclear. For this reason, some coaches will not work with bosses and their direct reports at the same time. Occasionally, coaches who are also primary business or account representatives for coaching firms may be tempted to share sensitive personal information with their client organizations in an effort to ingratiate themselves and secure additional business. A different kind of confidentiality violation occurs when an organization asks a coach to assess an executive's potential for promotion. In this case, the coach is being asked to make a judgment that is based in part on information gleaned during coaching sessions, which were defined as strictly confidential.

Violations of confidentiality usually lead to major breaches of trust, which can severely damage or end the coaching process, as the following example suggests.

Bill, the head of an assessment, coaching, and consulting firm, was coaching five senior executives. In addition, he was consulting with the head of HR about creating a coaching program for all senior managers in the firm. In the course of discussing the prospective program, Bill talked freely about the five individuals he was coaching, revealing personal details he had learned in his coaching sessions. He did this to please the head of HR and also to demonstrate his knowledge of the organization, hoping to win additional business. However, his willingness to violate confidences raised serious questions about his integrity in the eyes of the head of HR, and when Bill's coaching engagements ended, he did not get more work from the firm.

Sharing Confidences outside the Organization
Executive coaches who have worked at senior levels soon come to know a great deal about their particular organizations. Most are discreet and careful not to reveal confidences or share potentially damaging information with the press or other outsiders. Organizations can limit this threat—it can never be fully eliminated—by insisting on written confidentiality agreements with coaches before engagements begin.

Errors in Ending and Assessing the Value of Coaching

Well-managed endings are just as essential to coaching success as clearly defined and explicit beginnings are. Good endings help maintain the changes begun in coaching, whereas a poorly managed ending (or no ending) can perpetuate a firm's dependency on the coach, thus increasing overall costs with little or no additional benefits. Organizations also err when they attempt to assess a coach's effectiveness on the basis of one or two assignments alone or solely on the basis of their coachees' opinions of the coach.

The Never-Ending Coaching Engagement

Executive coaching is similar to therapy in the sense that it, too, can go on indefinitely. This is not necessarily a bad thing because we have the potential to continue growing and there is always more to learn about ourselves and others. However, in the context of organizational coaching tied to clear business strategies and their related objectives, coaching should end once these objectives have been met—unless other business-related objectives are identified for further work. A well-managed ending happens gradually, with the time between coaching sessions increasing until the final session is scheduled. During this period, the coach should be working with the executive to identify other resources in the organization (and beyond it) that will continue to support the changed behaviors. The following example illustrates this process.

Don, an executive vice president for a major consumer products company, had been engaged in executive coaching with Jim for almost seven years. When he joined the firm three years earlier, Don had specified coaching as part of the initial employment agreement and had refused to sign on unless he could continue working with Jim. Over many years, Don came to trust his coach implicitly and, as a result, never made a decision, even a minor one, without first consulting him. Although Don had learned a great deal from Jim, he had not learned to operate as an autonomous individual. Instead, and at significant expense to the organization, Don grew extremely dependent on Jim's counsel. Jim, in turn, encouraged this dependency by not ending his coaching relationship with Don.

Blaming the Coach When Goals Are Not Met

When coaching does not lead to the expected results, it is easy to blame the coach. However, coaches can only be responsible for the quality of their coaching work and not for actual changed behavior. Only those who are being coached can choose to change and act differently. The best coach in the world would produce lackluster results with an executive who was closed to learning and unwilling to change. Conversely, some individuals are so ready to change that almost any coach will do. Such variations in readiness make it difficult, but not impossible, to assess a coach's skills and track record. It would be a mistake, however, to make such assessments on the basis of one or two coaching engagements.

It is also a mistake to judge the quality of a coach by whether or not an executive enjoys the relationship. Of course, there is always the possibility that an executive likes working with a coach because that coach is effective and facilitates change and growth. Conversely, however, an executive may like the coach because their relationship is comfortable and not challenging. There is also a difference between enjoying a coach and enjoying the results the coach helps one achieve.

Errors in Assessing Organizational Readiness for Change

Avoiding the errors noted above does not automatically guarantee successful coaching experiences. In their zeal to create change, coaches and others inside an organization sometimes overestimate the readiness of key individuals and of the organization itself and conversely underestimate the resistance that may surface as a result of their work. People do not always mean it when they say they want a certain individual or situation to change. Senior leaders, like the rest of us, are often ambivalent and may both want and fear change. In this context, coaching could actually be too successful, as when its very success causes fear in the leaders who originally sponsored it. This in turn may lead them to bring the process to a premature end, as explained in the following examples.

Sarah, a vice president of a major medical institution, was referred for coaching by the CEO, Elaine, who thought Sarah was too nice. Elaine said she needed Sarah to be tougher and more assertive both with her and with others in the organization. Sarah also wanted to become more forceful in her private life, so she actively embraced the coaching and quickly became a dominant presence in her work environment. It was almost as if a new Sarah had emerged, self-confident, demanding, and unwilling to accept unfair treatment from others. Sarah began to stand up to Elaine and was no longer willing to accept treatment that she considered abusive or unfair. This change in attitude was Elaine's stated goal, and Sarah worked hard to achieve it, but when the reality of the new Sarah sank in, Elaine felt fearful and ambivalent about the results. It turned out she had really wanted Sarah to push back with others but not with her. Elaine ended the coaching after just two months, declaring it a great success. In doing so, she deprived Sarah of the opportunity to fully consolidate her gains and build support for continued change into her daily work environment. She was also sending mixed signals about Sarah's newfound assertiveness. Sarah, however, did not want to return to her old submissive role. She ultimately concluded that Elaine was unable to adjust to her changed behavior and therefore left the organization.

In another example, the leadership at a large bank in Cincinnati decided to provide 360-degree feedback and follow-up coaching for all senior managers who were within two levels of the chairman. By many measures, the program was a great success, and a number of participants established initiative action teams to tackle serious long-standing organizational issues. Their plans called for fundamental changes to established ways of doing business and therefore indirectly challenged the firm's leadership. On learning of these positive, almost revolutionary results, the CEO and chairman lauded the program as a great success and then abruptly ended it. The company made no attempt to continue the coaching and feedback processes at lower levels or repeat it for senior management.

Implications: Getting It Right the First Time

In the sections above, we discussed some (but certainly not all) of the ways in which coaching can fail or lead to negative consequences for individuals and organizations. What are the positive implications and lessons that have emerged from these common errors? How can we apply these lessons so that we do not repeat the same mistakes?

Most of the errors outlined in this chapter stem from failure to effectively manage the process of coaching. I summarize them below for the benefit of those who are performing this function in their organizations.

Lesson 1

Accurately assess and diagnose each potential coaching situation. Be sure that executive coaching, and not some other approach to executive development, is the correct intervention. Proceed with coaching only if you are reasonably certain that the issues involved are primarily individual, not organizational, and only if the desired behavioral changes can be linked to business goals and strategy and will improve business effectiveness. Even if these initial conditions are met, proceed with coaching only if the individual to be coached seems relatively open to feedback and change and if others in the organization are likely to support these changes.

Lesson 2

Select the right coach for the situation. Define the goals and objectives of coaching work as clearly as possible, and choose a coach with the competencies and skills to address these issues. If possible, give executives the opportunity to choose between two or more prescreened potential coaches. (See also Chapter 7.)

Lesson 3

Clearly define the roles of coach, coachee, boss or manager, HR generalist, and HR organization development or executive development specialist. Assign responsibility for managing the coaching process to someone in the organization, and inform the boss or manager that the executive is to be held accountable for whatever changes are targeted by the coaching.

Lesson 4

Identify key stakeholders with an interest in the outcome of a coaching situation. Verify that they all understand and agree on critical items such as objectives of the coaching process, how the coaching will proceed, and when and how to assess progress.

Lesson 5

Never make coaching a mandatory condition of employment. Instead, hold employees accountable for changing problematic behavior or performing at acceptable levels. Then offer coaching as a voluntary activity or resource that the employee may or may not use to help achieve these changes.

Lesson 6

Carefully monitor the activity of external coaches who are working in your organization to ensure that they understand and respect the boundary between coaching and therapy and that they are not engaged in inappropriate selling activity. You may do this by periodically gathering feedback from executives, their managers, HR managers, and others in the organization who have interacted with the coach.

Lesson 7

Carefully manage confidential information. Make sure that everyone understands what information can and cannot be shared and with whom. Require legally binding confidentiality agreements from external coaches before they begin working in your organization. Respond quickly to violations of confidentiality in order to head off major breaches of trust. When possible, avoid situations in which coaches or others with access to sensitive information are asked to play dual and potentially conflicting roles. Do not ask coaches to act as executive assessors after their coaching engagements have begun, unless this role was part of an explicit agreement among all parties from the outset.

Lesson 8

Assess progress periodically against agreed-on objectives. Ask managers to provide as much directly observed data as possible that will document and support claims of changed behavior. If necessary, adjust or change the coaching objectives as the process unfolds, but make sure all key stakeholders are aware of any changes.

Lesson 9

Manage endings well. Do not allow coaching to continue indefinitely. It is probably time to end formal coaching if the objectives seem to be permanently out of reach, if there is general agreement that the original objectives have been met, or if the objectives themselves are no longer relevant to the situation. Well-managed endings happen gradually, as the frequency of coaching sessions decreases, and leave executives with resources and supports inside the organization that will help them maintain their new behaviors after formal coaching ends.

Lesson 10

Do not determine a coach's competence based on one or two coaching engagements. Instead, track performance with multiple clients across multiple settings whenever possible. In addition, do not assume competence simply because an executive likes working with a coach. Enjoyable relationships are one thing, but results are what matter.

Lesson 11

Be realistic about whether the organization and key individuals in it are ready for change. People sometimes say they favor change but don't really mean it. It's better to assume that most people are ambivalent about change. If possible, design coaching and other interventions to match the readiness of the organization.

Conclusion

These lessons are not exhaustive, and they are offered as guidelines rather than as inflexible rules. Their applicability varies according to situations and organizations, but the general principles behind them have held true in my experience. Following these guidelines will help you avoid the kinds of costly errors and negative consequences described throughout this chapter. In doing so, all involved should have a greater opportunity to realize the tremendous organizational potential of executive coaching.

Reference

Schein, E. H. (1997). *Organizational culture and leadership*. San Francisco: Jossey-Bass.

COACHING FROM THE INSIDE

When, Why, and How?

CASEY STRUMPF

Increasing numbers of organizations have discovered executive coaching as a highly effective means of helping individuals develop skills, achieve business goals, prepare for future challenges, and clarify their strategic vision. However, after making the decision to introduce executive coaching into an organization, a key question quickly arises: which is the better choice, an internal or an external coach? While many of the chapters in this book focus specifically on the potential of *external* coaching, this chapter will question the assumption that it is better to bring in coaches from the outside. Instead, this chapter suggests that there are a wide variety of considerations to take into account as human resources (HR) managers and others begin to implement executive coaching programs.

Every coaching strategy needs to be evaluated for best fit in terms of the needs of the organization: the use of internal coaches, external coaches, or a combination of internal and external coaches. This chapter focuses on the potential for internal staff to take on the role of executive coach, either solo or in partnership with external experts. It is divided into six parts:

- Choosing internal or external coaching
- Strengthening internal coaching
- Supporting the development of internal coaches
- Responding to particular challenges for internal coaches
- Maximizing resources
- Linking coaching with other HR functions

My experience with executive coaching stretches back over twenty-five years of work in the fields of training, organization development, continuous improvement, and executive development. Much of that work, both as an external consultant and as an internal staff member, provided opportunities for experimentation, practice, and learning in the field of executive coaching. While I have coached executives as an internal coach, I have also headed internal and external coaching initiatives. I have been responsible for hiring external coaches, assigning coaches to executives, and assisting with the professional development of internal coaches. In addition, I have worked to develop and refine organizational policies and practices regarding the use of both internal and external coaches.

Choosing Internal or External Coaching

The first question to be decided at the outset of an executive coaching program is whether to use external or internal coaches, or a combination of both. On the one hand, an internal coach knows the culture; on the other, an external coach may be more comfortable with handling politically charged situations. An internal coach can tap into other HR systems; an external coach can offer highly specialized skills coaching. In short, the answer depends. Although the skills and guidelines required for effective executive coaching practice are virtually identical for internal and external coaches, circumstances will typically dictate the advantage of one over the other.

Many situations demand external coaches. These include existence of a strong cultural bias for external coaches, an HR function that is perceived as more tactical than strategic, a very senior executive coachee, a highly political situation, and/or a need for specialized coaching that internal coaches are not qualified to provide.

Conversely, internal coaches are the best choice in other situations. They can offer in-depth knowledge of both the industry and the specific corporate culture as well as an understanding of the immediate system in which the executive operates. They may be more cost effective than external coaches and, if effective, may strengthen HR's reputation. In addition, they may optimize the coaching experience by linking it with other HR functions, particularly training, organization development, and employee relations. Lastly, the internal coaching role provides an exciting development opportunity for HR staff.

There are five main factors to consider in determining whether to recommend an internal or external coach. Each is discussed below.

Cultural Bias and Readiness

Some corporate cultures have a distinct leaning toward the familiar "not invented here," or NIH, syndrome. These firms gravitate to homegrown solutions versus those generated by consultants. It may be difficult to introduce an external executive coach into this type of environment. However, this type of culture can be a mecca for internal coaching and may perhaps enable its use as a means of paving the way for partnership coaching (which is discussed later). A quick scan of an organization's track record will probably indicate its cultural bias: if it welcomes external help, the footprints of past work by outside individuals will be evident.

If, in fact, external help is de rigueur, internal coaches will have a more difficult time being effective. External coaches may carry the critical advantage of instant credibility. One solution for internal coaches could be to partner with any existing external coaches; they might even share expertise, and eventually the work, as part of their contractual agreements.

If an organization has a bias for external expertise, another possible approach to integrating internal coaching is to hire an individual from outside the organization whose prescribed role will be to provide internal executive coaching. This solution might seem somewhat paradoxical, but it could effect a successful melding of the best of both worlds. The newcomer to the organization, if correctly positioned and mentored, might more easily establish a credible identity as a coach than could a veteran who carries the baggage of previous roles or history. Over time, this individual will also acquire an insider's advantages.

In addition, a newcomer whose sole or principal responsibility is that of coach may be less pressured to juggle a variety of roles compared to a veteran who continues to have significant noncoaching responsibilities. Finally, the newcomer can more easily ask the kinds of naive but provocative questions that elicit fresh thinking and self-awareness. Unless veterans have already played a quasi-coaching role or don't know the particular executive well, they may have a more difficult time doing this.

The organization's stage of evolution is another consideration when evaluating cultural readiness for internal coaching. A young, fast-moving, or entrepreneurial culture in high-growth mode may be more open to internal coaching than would an older, more staid culture, unless external coaching is already an organizational norm. Likewise, an organization in the downward spiral that sometimes follows a stable period might be more open to internal coaching, compared to one whose stock is literally or figuratively up, if only for economic reasons. (See Chapter 8.)

Credibility of the HR Function

An organization may be predisposed to internal coaching as a result of a strong, strategically positioned head of HR who acts as an informal coach to the CEO and other senior managers. Once a powerful role model has been established, it is more easily emulated by others in the organization.

An internal coach's credibility will be in direct proportion to the overall credibility of the HR function, assuming HR manages or provides coaching for the organization. A highly respected HR department with a strong reputation for contributing to the organization's strategic agenda and working with senior management on an equal footing (as described in Ulrich, 1998) can more effectively support both the concept of coaching and the individuals who provide or manage it. Also, the addition of coaching as an HR service, if successful, will generally enhance the function's credibility.

Executive Level and Political Environment

Internal coaches should pose this simple but critical question to themselves before undertaking a coaching engagement: "Can I tell the truth and still keep my job?" Implicit in this question are two of the key criteria to consider when deciding between an internal and external coach: the executive's level and the political environment. Where level is concerned, the general rules of thumb are, first, the more senior the executive, the more likely it is that an external coach is a better choice; and second, the wider the gap in level between the executive and the proposed internal coach, the more advisable it is to engage an external coach. These guidelines are based on two interdependent factors: credibility and the relatively small pool of individuals at the top levels of corporate hierarchies, which makes it difficult to identify an internal coach who doesn't "live in the executive's neighborhood" but occupies an equal or proximate position.

For example, the CEO of a large organization is unlikely to pay much attention to the coaching efforts of a person who is lower in the organization than his or her direct reports. Direct reports will also have a hard time coaching their managers. At the less senior levels, however, the pool of individuals of the same or slightly lower rank than a given executive is larger, thus facilitating the identification of an internal coach.

A highly political scenario is often best handled by an external coach. An example of such a situation might be an individual who is highly regarded and rewarded by senior management but is a poor manager of people, as demonstrated by high turnover and employee relations complaints. An external coach is especially recommended if the internal coach has a vested interest in the outcome of the situation, might become a political pawn in a turf or other type of battle, or might not be trusted with sensitive information. In such situations, even the HR individual who is managing the coaching process must be of a sufficiently high level that it affords protection from possible repercussions.

Type of Coaching Needed

In addition to level and politics, type of coaching is another relevant criterion. Witherspoon and White (1998) identified these four coaching areas: skills, performance, development, and leadership agenda. *Skills* coaching, such as presentation skills coaching, may be provided by internal coaches with the particular required expertise but is more often the purview of highly specialized external coaches. *Performance* coaching, which concentrates on improving present job performance, and *development* coaching, which applies to a future job, can both be provided by internal coaches.

Internal or external coaches can work in the area of *leadership agenda*, i.e., clarifying strategic vision, although the factors of level and politics discussed above must also be considered.

Type of Coachee

There are five general types of coachee, and each one warrants consideration when deciding whether to hire an internal or external coach. Most executives fall into one of the following categories:

- High potential
- Valuable but at risk of derailing
- Newly hired or newly promoted
- Expatriate
- Diamond in the rough

High potentials are the dream of every internal coach. Typically bright, ambitious, and motivated, they are highly responsive to coaching, given the right context. One of the best contexts is a CEO-sanctioned initiative, in which coaching is one of many targeted development components for a pool of highly talented individuals who are moving up the succession ladder. Individual work with high potentials outside the context of a program may also be successful; the lack of programmatic panache can be counterbalanced by development work driven by more immediate needs, such as expansion of responsibility. The only downside to coaching high potentials is their rare tendency to believe they have nothing to learn, but early, thorough assessment usually reduces the occurrence of that problem.

Coaching individuals who are at risk of derailing may be more complicated. In many situations and for a number of reasons, such coaching is best left to external coaches. First, this policy protects the internal coach from developing the reputation of a corporate "grim reaper," which could contaminate work with other individuals. Second, such work may sometimes be less a genuine coaching effort than a last-ditch effort—and paper trail—prior to firing an executive. However, helping a person with real potential who has been poorly managed or placed can be tremendously rewarding. Additionally, the internal coach who works with a potentially derailing executive may have better access to the executive's manager, a critical link in helping the client get back on track.

Coaching newly hired or newly promoted managers is clearly the territory of internal coaches of long standing, who can share their knowledge of organizational culture and structure, key players, etc. The coach can help integrate new hires into the organization and relay feedback from others. The coaching of newly promoted individuals may focus on topics such as difficulties in managing direct reports who were recently peers and the challenge of moving from an operational focus to a more strategic one.

Internal coaches are also well suited to working with newly returned expatriates, who may need guidance as they relinquish some of their former autonomy and acculturate themselves to home office practices. They sometimes also need help reintegrating their families.

Diamond-in-the rough individuals are those who could be high potentials but whose advancement is impeded by such factors as personal style and self-presentation. These individuals are typically young or inexperienced; their naïveté may simply reflect poor management or lack of guidance. An internal coach is probably preferable for these executives because mentoring could be an important part of the development plan, and an internal coach can more easily identify and broker a mentoring relationship.

Strengthening Internal Coaching

Once internal coaching has been identified as a worthwhile approach, HR managers should increase capacity for internal coaching within their departments. There are several key issues to keep in mind at this point.

The Politics of Human Resources

Ideally, the head of HR consciously parlays his or her role by coaching senior executives while positioning and mentoring other internal coaches to work with second- and third-tier managers. The HR head may also partner with external coaches as needed and actively encourages partnering of the more junior internal coaches with external ones. Such actions can, over time, exert significant influence on the corporate culture, giving internal coaches the credibility usually ascribed to external coaches and optimizing the potential of partnership coaching.

Developing an Explicit Confidentiality Policy

An explicit, written policy regarding confidentiality should be developed, provided to, and discussed with all coachees during the contracting process. It is critical that identical messages be communicated to their managers. For example,

> Confidentiality is essential to successful coaching. Our policy is "zero tolerance"—anything shared by the coachee within the parameters of the coaching relationship is shared in confidence. If coaches seek help from their colleagues to enhance their coaching ability, it is their responsibility to protect the anonymity of the coachee. The only exceptions are violations of the organization's code of ethics; violations of the law (e.g., harassment); and indications of functionally incapacitating or self-destructive mental/emotional instability.

The policy could be communicated in this way: "Everything we discuss in these sessions is confidential, unless I believe you are doing or are thinking of doing something that might be harmful to yourself, violates our organization's code of ethics, or is illegal."

Getting and Using Feedback

Credibility for internal coaches hinges in large measure on their consistently practicing what they preach, and for this reason, continuously examining and improving coaching performance is key. Coaches may do this by periodically asking clients for feedback on the coaching process itself. Feedback is likely to be most candid if it is collected confidentially, either by written survey or with the help of a shadow coach (an external coach who is working with the internal coach) who interviews coachees and reports the feedback to the coach. Such feedback can provide internal coaches with valuable information about their strengths as well as areas in need of development. Credibility is likely to increase simply as a result of asking for feedback and should increase even more when coaches act on the feedback they receive.

In addition to gathering input on the coach's effectiveness as discussed above, it is valuable to gather input on *results*, which is probably the final word on determining credibility. Although coachees' perceptions are important, their managers are likely to be seen as more objective. Periodic updates on managers' perceptions of progress will inform coaches and add to their credibility. This might also lead to opportunities to coach more senior individuals.

Conducting 360-degree feedback at approximately eighteen-month intervals also quantifies results and builds credibility; in addition, this process serves to inform coaches, executives, and managers regarding progress. Actual feedback need not be shared with managers, but, with permission from coachees, improvement percentages in targeted areas may be used to demonstrate the effectiveness of coaching.

In summary, applying a continuous improvement model to the coaching process is a significant way to build capability. Collecting data about the process, analyzing it for success as well as for breakdowns, staying close to the client, and continuously seeking out enhancements are invaluable development tools for coaches. Internal coaches need to practice what they preach and show by example that development is an ongoing journey, not a destination.

Role Modeling

One of the most important means of developing credibility is through consistent role modeling. Internal coaches don't have the option of leaving the organization after conducting their coaching sessions; they live within it and are therefore always under the magnifying glass. Given these circumstances, internal coaches must live up to the values and practices they espouse, particularly that of acknowledging their own need for development. Acting as role models doesn't mean trying to appear perfect; however, it does mean always aspiring to perfection.

Supporting the Development of Internal Coaches

It is possible for organizations to create environments that favor the development of internal coaches. To do this, I recommend the following strategies: support self-development, select appropriate coaching assignments, partner with external experts, and create coaching networks. These four strategies all depend on nontraditional, self-driven learning opportunities. They are not mutually exclusive; in fact, a combination of the four may provide the most potent recipe for building capability.

Supporting Self-Development

Self-development tools include reading, conferences, and reflection. Targeted reading provides the novice with theoretical models, suggestions for structuring the coaching experience, and coaching techniques. Coaching-related conferences offer opportunities to acquire information and identify future contacts. Reflection is perhaps the most important self-development tool. Just as coachees are often asked to keep logs or journals of reflections regarding experiments with new behaviors, so coaches might keep notes on readings, conferences, and coaching experiences.

Selecting Appropriate Coaching Assignments

Novice coaches may be able to develop their coaching capability more easily by tackling lower-risk situations before advancing to highly visible individuals and situations. Lower-risk options include trusted colleagues in the organization, people who are already enthusiastic about the concept of coaching, or individuals of junior rather than senior levels.

Partnering with External Experts

This strategy is a highly interactive means of building internal capability. Partnering may take several possible forms.

For example, a novice internal coach in an organization that uses or intends to use external coaches might negotiate agreements with external coaches regarding the sharing of expertise. External coaches would then provide information on such topics as theoretical models and their application, specific coaching strategies, and coaching techniques.

Outsourcing specific parts of the coaching process is another way of partnering with external coaches. Outsourced items might include assessment, psychometric testing, and/or data debriefs. This type of arrangement fills the gaps in the internal coach's repertoire and could also serve as a springboard to sharing additional coaching-related expertise. For example, in the process of discussing psychometric test results, an external coach may offer ideas regarding possible ways of approaching the coachee. In addition, if the partnership continues, the external coach can continue to advise the internal coach, thus adding value to both the coaching process and the internal coach's developing expertise.

Another means of developing expertise is the shadow coach. Shadow coaches may be internal or external. They work behind the scenes and provide internal coaches with feedback and information. As mentioned earlier, shadow coaches may also assist by interviewing executives about their coaching experiences. They must be highly skilled people who are familiar with the corporate culture and have the trust of both internal coaches and their organizations. Some external coaches handle outsourced work and act as shadow coaches at the same time. Such a situation has its advantages, in that the shadow coach will be familiar with the executive and can thus make coaching suggestions that are better targeted to that individual.

Creating Coaching Networks

One type of coaching network consists of internal coaches from the same organization who meet to share their learnings, review cases, provide consultation to one another, and bring in external experts for development sessions. This type of group is an ideal forum for hammering out corporate policies regarding confidentiality, coach–coachee matching, contracting, referrals, and roles.

Alternatively, the network may be made up of internal coaches from a variety of organizations. This group represents a wider range of perspectives, since individuals represent different corporate cultures and perhaps even different industries. In general, group members should not come from organizations that are in direct competition, and they should not know the other members' clients. Under these conditions, they will feel more comfortable discussing their own obstacles and failures as well as their clients' situations.

The Boston Coaching Group[1] (BCG), of which I am a member, is an example of the second type of group. The BCG has been meeting since 1997. Several organizations have been represented, with technology and financial services dominating. The BCG sets an agenda for each meeting and has explored many of the issues discussed in this book, such as the sourcing of coaches, contracting, confidentiality issues, and specific coaching techniques. The group also brings in external experts to share their theoretical models and respond to cases. The open sharing of problems, materials, and experiences in combination with the intense camaraderie developed by this group has significantly enhanced the ability of its members to learn from one another and has created a true learning community.

Responding to Particular Challenges for Internal Coaches

Due to their position within an organization, internal coaches may face situations or conflicts that do not arise for external coaches. Two major challenges are discussed below.

Maintaining Confidentiality

Maintaining confidentiality is probably the biggest challenge for internal coaches. By "confidentiality," I mean trust, the most essential ingredient in any coaching relationship and one of the rarest commodities in the corporate world. The issue of confidentiality can be more challenging for internal coaches because internal coaches and their coachees belong to the same corporate world. Internal coaches also may play multiple roles, and there is often easier and more frequent access between coach and management. For example, the internal executive coach who also facilitates the succession planning or selection for promotion process is in a difficult position. And the internal coach who is working with a derailer may be asked for input on the executive's progress—input that could seriously affect that person's continued employment.

There are a number of ways to minimize these problems. First, internal coaches should avoid conflicting roles whenever possible. Illustrate the problem of balancing these roles by asking managers to put themselves in the shoes of the coachee who is openly discussing his or her problems with a coach; then ask them to imagine the difficulty of maintaining a relationship of trust when the same coach ends up evaluating the coachee for succession or ongoing employment.

Second, if conflicting roles are unavoidable, internal coaches should develop and secure agreement from management regarding a policy of disclosing only positive information about coachees. For example, when a manager calls and asks whether the coach thinks a certain executive is the right choice for a promotion, the coach might respond, "You're probably the better judge of whether Jill is ready for a promotion. But I can tell you that I believe Jill has made significant strides in the areas we identified for development several months ago. She's set up better communications within her team and improved her team's structure." A test of confidentiality also could occur more casually, for instance, while the internal coach is waiting in the lunch line. When asked to evaluate a coachee's progress, or, more specifically, to comment on how the coachee's peer ratings compare with the manager's on his 360, the coach must reply with tact and discretion. A suggested response might be "David is doing fine. I know you're aware that his 360 data is confidential. Are you concerned that there might be a discrepancy between how his peers and manager view him?" This example utilizes the well-tested tactic of throwing the ball back to the questioner.

For another illustration of a situation specific to internal coaches, imagine the coach is waiting for the elevator. The doors open to reveal a number of people, including the coachee, who only an hour ago had tearfully divulged her fear of managing staff members ten years her senior. The coach's and coachee's eyes meet. A flicker of embarrassment crosses the coachee's face. At that moment, the coach must quickly establish a normal, friendly, but professional tone, thereby reassuring her that whatever was discussed in the coaching session will stay there. A good approach might be "Hi, Sue. Have you heard we won the contract with the XYZ Corporation?"

Internal coaches may also face confidentiality-related issues when they coach their immediate peers. This generally is not a wise practice because conflicts of interest and other awkward situations may arise. As a rule of thumb, the greater the lateral organizational distance between internal coach and coachee, the better. If there is only one internal coach available, perhaps an external coach could be engaged or additional internal capability developed.

Two final notes on confidentiality. First, trust can only be gained over time, by example, and through reputation. Coaches who freely admit this early in the coaching relationship will gain at least an initial iota of trust from their executives. Second, a breach of confidentiality is far worse for an internal coach than for an external one. The internal coach's reputation is at stake within the organization, whereas an external coach who has lost the trust of an organization can move on to other clients.

Understanding the Culture while Providing an Oasis

To help executives change, coaches must understand an organization's culture but not reflect it literally in the coaching process itself. If, for example, the culture is fast paced or bottom-line oriented, internal coaches must understand that these are the conditions under which coachees operate, but they should not bring the culture into the coaching sessions. Successful coaching is rarely fast paced. Or if the culture is one in which people's motives are analyzed for primarily political purposes, the coach must reframe exploration of motive as a means of enhancing self-awareness and development.

As shown by these two examples, the miniculture created within the coaching process may counter the corporate culture to some extent. The coach's role is to create an oasis within which coachees can reflect, practice new behaviors, and disclose fears and concerns.

Differentiating—and Linking—Coaching and HR Advising

It is important to differentiate between executive coaching and HR advising. Advising provided by HR generalists focuses on improving effectiveness within a business context. It deals with day-to-day business and HR issues and helps executives solve ongoing tactical and strategic business problems. Executive coaching focuses on behavioral, management style, or personality issues that impede effectiveness.

At the outset of coaching, it is good practice for the coach and HR generalist to meet and discuss their roles in relation to the executive who will receive coaching. At this time, they should also agree on key ground rules, especially those regarding confidentiality. Ideally, the coach, HR generalist, and coachee should meet to discuss the development plan, so that the generalist may, over the course of the engagement, provide coach and coachee with feedback regarding progress on goals.

Maximizing Resources

Whenever possible, decisions regarding the resources to be devoted to coaching should include an evaluation of the proposed extent of the coaching and the role it will play in a larger corporate initiative (e.g., a high-potential development program). Coaching that is a carefully conceived component of an overall strategy will generally be more effective over a shorter period of time, and therefore more cost effective, than coaching done with little context on a case-by-case basis. When viewed as part of an overall strategy, the cost of coaching can be measured against other development options. For example, the organization could weigh the relative effectiveness of a multiday seminar, including travel costs, compared to several months of coaching sessions.

Making good resource decisions about whether to use internal or external coaches requires thorough knowledge of the relative costs involved. On an hourly basis, external coaches are generally more costly than internal coaches. However, internal coaches are paid full salary plus benefits. One possible option is to apportion a percentage of an internal's position to that of coach and to partner internal with external coaches as appropriate.

It is important to remember that when the situation calls for coaching, the most expensive coach is *no* coach. An executive who is allowed to operate at less than optimal levels, or who is dysfunctional and destructive of others, is a drain on the organization and may even cause respected, highly productive staff to leave. A decision on whether to provide an individual with a coach based primarily on resource restrictions instead of careful needs analysis may, in fact, cost the organization in lost time and money.

Linking Coaching with Other HR Functions

The internal coach is in a unique position to add value to the organization by linking the coaching process to other HR disciplines, including training, organizational development, employee relations, staffing, compensation, and benefits. Used to its fullest potential, internal coaching serves an informal triage-type function, thus optimizing HR's ability to respond to a variety of needs. Likewise, HR may enhance and supplement coaching, providing clients with well-rounded, integrated, and comprehensive support.

Training

Both internal and external coaches may be able to supply valuable needs assessment information, either through aggregation of 360-degree feedback or through informal feedback about developing needs. This information can enhance the training function's needs analysis process, guide the selection of seminar topics, or fine-tune existing training programs.

Organization Development

The collaboration between coaches and organization development experts offers powerful support to both new and seasoned managers. For example, a coach may see that an executive's problems are driven in part by poor organizational structure, inadequate ground rules, or unclear decision-making processes. An organization development expert could complement coaching work in all these areas.

Furthermore, a coach may be working with several individuals who are having difficulties communicating with one another, reaching consensus, and so forth. Again, the coach could collaborate with the organization development expert to help them find more productive ways of working together.

When engaged with a newly hired manager, the coach may suggest that an organization development expert conduct a structured assimilation process, which aids direct reports in asking questions and gathering information from and about their new manager and vice versa. The organization development expert may also facilitate start-up team-building sessions to establish ground rules, communication norms, and strategic directions.

Employee Relations

When should a coaching engagement become a case for an employee relations specialist? The coach needs to distinguish, for example, between a coachee who needs to refine his or her communication style and one who is harassing staff. Coaches must be particularly careful to guard against breaches of confidentiality in these types of delicate and potentially explosive situations. If, however, the coach suspects unlawful behavior, such as harassment, he or she should remind the executive that there are limitations to their confidentiality agreement and give notice that employee relations will be informed of the situation.

In another example, an organization may decide to "counsel out" an executive due to performance problems. Employee relations counseling is more appropriate than coaching in such a case. Coaches who suspect that they are unwittingly participating in terminating coachees should meet with the appropriate managers or employee relations managers. Disclosure and open discussion of the situation would be the purposes of the meeting.

If a coachee is planning to lay off or terminate an employee, the coach could offer guidance regarding the employee relations resources available and might invite the employee relations specialist to assist in the process. When in doubt, coaches should clarify the situation and coaching goals with their coachees' managers before discussing the matter with an employee relations specialist.

The distinctions in these situations are fine ones; therefore, the link between coach and employee relations manager must be close and ongoing.

Benefits

In the course of coaching, the coach may encounter individuals who are struggling with such issues as illness or death in the family, personal health problems, and substance abuse. The coach should direct these people to the company's employee assistance program, health care and mental health benefits departments, crisis counseling, and other services.

Compensation

Salary inequities, low morale, or turnover caused by noncompetitive salary ranges may create major problems for managers and damage an organization's reputation in the marketplace. During the course of their work, coaches may become aware of salary inequities within or among corporate functions or notice disparities between internal salaries and the marketplace. In some instances, coachees may not even know the reasons for their staffing problems. Coaches can serve as an important link to the compensation function, which may then conduct analyses to confirm or disprove the validity of the dissatisfactions. If confidentiality is a concern, the coach should encourage the executive to contact the organization's compensation function directly.

Conclusion

The role of internal coach can be exciting and rewarding and may expand the range of possibilities for HR staff who are interested in development. Focused one-on-one work can greatly enhance development and produce impressive results—when executed with rigor, intelligence, and integrity.

The coach's work often has a cumulative effect as executives begin to incorporate coaching into their own management styles. One of a coach's best moments may be when a coachee reports having successfully used a coaching approach with a direct report. In a corporate world in which risk taking, reflection, and confidentiality are rare, it is the internal coach's distinctive role to ask the important, provocative questions and be the person entrusted with a manager's thoughts, ideas, triumphs, and fears.

Note

[1] A note of appreciation to the members of the BCG—Victoria Brooks, Susan Ennis, William Hodgetts, Mary Jane Knudson, Catherine Lawrence, and David Montross—for their thoughtful insights regarding many of the topics discussed in this chapter.

References

Ulrich, D. (1998). *Delivering results: A new mandate for human resources professionals.* Boston: Harvard Business School Press.

Witherspoon, R., and R. P. White. (1998). *Four essential ways that coaching can help executives.* Greensboro, N.C.: Center for Creative Leadership.

PART IV

EXECUTIVE COACHING

ISSUES

ON SEEING THE FOREST WHILE AMONG THE TREES

Integrating Business Strategy Models and Concepts into Executive Coaching Practice

CATHERINE FITZGERALD

He who is number one in swordsmanship doesn't have to worry about the number two person, but rather about the person ignorant of swordsmanship but knowledgeable about gunpowder.

—Mark Twain

Executive coaches support their clients by recognizing, enhancing, and leveraging their strengths and by identifying and enhancing their knowledge and skills in relevant developmental arenas. A great deal of the work of executive coaching has taken place in two general topic areas. The first focuses on ensuring that executives have the interpersonal skills and style they need to develop and maintain the complex web of relationships that is essential to their effectiveness and success. The second area focuses on ensuring that executives have (and use) essential management skills (including self-management), such as goal and priority setting, decision making, communicating, and delegating.

Learning to be effective as an executive coach across the wide range of interpersonal and management skills and styles is challenging and takes considerable time. As a result, seasoned executive coaches have typically spent many years in related practice areas (such as leadership training, 360-degree instrument interpretation, and organization development) prior to entering the field of executive coaching.

Like that of most executive coaches, my work is often focused on interpersonal and management skills and style issues. However, in my work with executives at more senior levels in organizations, I have found another arena of knowledge to be increasingly important to the effectiveness of the coaching process: understanding business strategy formation and implementation.

A working knowledge of business strategy is important for a number of reasons. First, basic knowledge of the themes, dilemmas, and trends in business is essential to understanding the context within which clients operate. Second, business strategy considerations affect the requirements for effectiveness in other arenas of skill and style. And, third, whereas business strategy was once the concern of only a handful of the most senior executives, the fast-paced nature of today's marketplace demands an understanding of strategy by executives at lower and lower organizational levels.

In Search of an Understanding of Business Strategy

For the past five years, I have been trying to develop a working knowledge of business strategy that would increase my understanding of the context within which my clients work and enhance my ability to support their effectiveness and their development.[1] To this end, I searched widely for books and articles that would contribute to my understanding; I also spent time with experienced executive coaches and senior human resource practitioners, discussing the frameworks, experiences, and approaches that had helped them understand business strategy. I paid close attention to my clients' discussions of strategic concerns and tried not only to grasp the substance of the issues but also to identify the combinations of experience, training, and individual interests and aptitude that distinguished executives who were especially adept at dealing with strategic issues.

Learning about strategy turned out to be a challenging venture. The books and articles I read were initially more confusing than illuminating. Each one seemed somewhat convincing but incomplete—and some occasionally contradicted earlier books or articles I had read. I also found that I couldn't retain even the most persuasive perspective on strategy in my mind for very long. Moreover, the glimpses I was getting of the strategy process from talking to my clients suggested that the process was often idiosyncratic and haphazard and was strongly influenced by individual preferences, biases, and personal histories.

Over time, I encountered resources that provided extremely useful frameworks and concepts. And, through my coaching experience, I developed approaches to addressing business strategy issues to which my clients have responded well and which have increased their effectiveness in dealing with strategic issues.

The purpose of this chapter is to provide some guideposts for executive coaches who are interested in increasing their understanding of business strategy. The three key topics addressed in this chapter are

- Understanding the multidimensionality of strategy formation and implementation
- Identifying broad strategic patterns within and across industries
- Viewing marketplaces and companies as complex adaptive systems

Understanding the Multidimensionality of Strategy Formation and Implementation

How wonderful that we have met with a paradox.
Now we have some hope of making progress.
—Niels Bohr

As I mentioned earlier, although reading about, discussing, and observing strategy formation and implementation was interesting and absorbing, my early reaction was one of confusion rather than enlightenment. However, I was fortunate to find two resources that made me feel enlightened *in my confusion*.

The first resource, an article by Gary Hamel (1997), a distinguished professor, practitioner, and writer about business strategy, presented a contrarian view about strategy:

> Everyone knows a strategy when they see one—be it Microsoft's, Nucor's or Virgin Atlantic's. We all recognize a great strategy after the fact. . . . [But] anyone who claims to be a strategist should be intensely embarrassed by the fact that *the strategy industry doesn't have a theory of strategy creation.* (p. 74)

Hamel's perspective was reassuring, as a straightforward link between the theory and the practice of strategy had been difficult for me to find.

A second resource proved invaluable in providing a framework for the many different—and sometimes contradictory—perspectives on strategy I was encountering. In *Strategy Safari: A Guided Tour through the Wilds of Strategic Management,* Mintzberg, Ahlstrand, and Lampel (1998) argued that the word strategy has at least five different meanings and is used "freely and fondly" (p. 9) by managers to describe plans, patterns, positions, perspectives, and ploys. Not surprisingly, the multiplicity of meanings and the lack of precision of use can make discussions about strategy confusing. After alerting readers to the confusion in terminology, Mintzberg and his colleagues provide a valuable analysis of the vast literature on strategy and describe ten distinct schools of thought in strategy. (See Appendix A for a list of these ten schools of thought.)

What I learned from *Strategy Safari* that has been invaluable in my work as an executive coach is that the enterprise of strategy formation and implementation is a profoundly multidimensional one and that it is an inevitably messy process that involves a mix of planned and emergent components and that utilizes elements of all ten schools of thought. Another critical insight is that the greatest failures in strategy formation and implementation have occurred when leaders and/or organizations have heavily favored one point of view and have used it to the exclusion of others. As Mintzberg and his colleagues speculated, "pervasive strategic failure in many large corporations may well be attributed to the army of business school graduates who have been sent out with an incomplete tool kit" (p. 20).

As a result of reading (and rereading) *Strategy Safari,* when discussions of strategy come up in my coaching sessions, I am better at tracking the conversation and am also more able to ask clarifying questions about my client's strategy process or, perhaps more commonly, about his or her critique of the boss's (or company's or competitor's) strategy process. I also have a greater understanding of the tensions inherent in the strategy process (for example, planned versus emergent), which allows me to identify contending perspectives in my client's view versus the views of others and to be aware of what may be one-sided or narrow approaches. Although my job is never to make judgments about the content of strategy (and I'm always keenly aware of the limitations of my knowledge about my clients' businesses and industries!), I can sometimes raise helpful questions and concerns that may lead my clients to develop more intentional and complex approaches.

This awareness of the multidimensionality of business strategy hasn't discouraged me from attempting both to understand strategy and to support my clients in enhancing their strategic capacities. It has, however, made me abandon my search for *the* approach to strategy and has encouraged my interest in finding more complex frameworks of understanding.

Suggestions for Clients

Based on my understanding of the multidimensionality of business strategy, there are four suggestions that, when appropriate to their role and to the dilemmas they are facing, I make to clients:

- Regularly devote time to enhance your ability to contribute to strategy formation and implementation.
- Use a variety of different methods and approaches.
- Appreciate the focus and pace of work on strategic thinking.
- Recognize that different perspectives on strategy can lead to conflict within the company and learn how to integrate diverse perspectives.

Each of these is discussed below.

Regularly Devote Time to Enhance Strategic Ability

Executives typically are under enormous pressure from day-to-day demands and often have little time or attention to devote to broader strategic issues and the development of their strategic thinking. Research suggests that executives who are successful in high-velocity business environments pay "thin" attention to the future, devoting a small but consistent amount of time to future-oriented activities (Brown and Eisenhardt, 1998). I often recommend that clients try to allocate about 5 percent of their time to strategic development. To free up that time, I suggest that they identify tasks that could be delegated to others or that might serve as developmental assignments for direct reports.

Use a Variety of Different Methods

Executive coaches can help clients brainstorm about the actions that would contribute most to their strategic abilities. Depending on the executive's role, interests, and current strategic thinking, these actions might include

- Seeking out opportunities to participate in or observe high-level strategic conversations and decision making
- Periodically meeting with people in his or her company and industry who are known for having big-picture perspectives and/or are able to spot trends early
- Devoting time on a regular basis to getting close to customers from a different angle than usual, in order to keep his or her knowledge of the evolving needs, desires, and frustrations of customers updated and salient
- Attending courses on strategy, innovation, and related topics
- Attending an occasional conference or training event *outside* of his or her industry, to look for patterns in other industries that might provide new insight
- Reading targeted books and articles about strategic issues and approaches
- Visiting companies or sites that are doing things in new and promising ways
- Consciously developing a working knowledge of key strategic patterns within and across industries (see the next section), and identifying and tracking these patterns in his or her own industry

Another action involves periodically engaging staff, peers, and bosses in informal, unstructured discussions about emerging trends and patterns, using open-ended questions such as the following:

- "A year (or two years or five years or . . .) from now, how could you imagine our business being different?"

- "If you had 10 percent of your time, plus an adequate amount of seed money, to devote to the most promising new business development idea, what might you pursue?"

- "What would customers (or other key constituencies) love for us to do differently?"

- "What is the biggest potential opportunity we're not paying enough attention to? What is the biggest area of risk or threat?"

- "What are our competitors doing that we might consider doing?"

- "If we were bold, what might we do? What might we stop doing? If we were *five* times as bold, what might we do or stop doing?"

Appreciate the Focus and Pace of Work on Strategic Thinking

Many executives live fast-paced lives—they work fast, move fast, and decide fast. They tend to focus on efficiency and on solving problems quickly in order to keep moving full-steam ahead. This approach to work is often necessary and can be highly effective in many situations.

However, executives should understand that the focus and pace of strategic thinking are different. Strategic thinking is *not* something you can—or should—do efficiently (although you can and should use your time wisely). Strategic thinking is not accomplished in a short burst of activity or along a straight, linear path. It often takes time to incubate emerging patterns and ideas or consolidate confusing data and conflicting viewpoints. Executives will find it valuable to learn ways of intentionally slowing down and changing the nature of conversations, so that they become less formal and more open-ended.

Recognize That Different Perspectives Can Lead to Conflict

Successful strategy formation and implementation are the result of a complex and multidimensional process that requires, over time, both planned and emergent components, a focus on top-down as well as bottom-up efforts, and an emphasis on both the capacities of the organization and the needs of the marketplace. People in different parts of the organization, in different roles, and with different personality types, skills, and aspirations, may see value in different aspects of or approaches to strategy. Conflicts may arise as a result, and people may become polarized.

When executives recognize that different perspectives on strategy can lead to conflict, they often see more options for resolution and may take such conflicts less personally. In addition, by appreciating the inevitably multidimensional nature of effective strategy formulation and implementation, executives may be encouraged to search for integrative solutions that will satisfy all sides of what at first may appear to be opposing approaches (for instance, being planful and emergent, focusing on short-term versus long-term gain).

When appropriate, I work with clients to support both their understanding of the strategic differences that may underlie conflict and their search for integrative solutions. A first step toward crafting an integrative solution in polarized situations involves creating the conditions for useful and constructive conversations about each perspective or approach. At times, I suggest ways in which clients may inquire productively about the strategic perspectives or approaches of others. I may also brainstorm with clients on how they might effectively present their perspectives or approaches to those who hold other views.

Identifying Broad Strategic Patterns within and across Industries

In developing a framework for identifying the many different meanings of and approaches to strategy, Mintzberg and his colleagues provided one accessible way to get a meta-perspective on strategy. A different, although equally valuable, meta-perspective I sought involved the identification of broad strategic patterns across industries.

As I listened to clients talk about emerging industry trends, and as I read analyses about various companies and industries, I became intrigued by those executives and analysts who were able to identify emerging patterns within and across industries. It is clear that the stakes for identifying such patterns—and, in recent years, for discovering them earlier and earlier—are very high. Early identification can lend enormous competitive advantage;

delayed identification can place executives and their companies at great risk. Slywotsky, Morrison, Moser, Mundt, and Quella (1999) vividly describe both the frequency and the impact on executives of late identification of key trends:

> At least once in every executive's career, he or she experiences a "chilling moment" : an icy sensation of fear caused by the sudden, terrible realization that they have "gotten it"—the strategic pattern transforming their industry—*too late.* (p. 327)

As I became more interested in broad strategic trends, I found that I could discern certain primitive patterns across industries. For example, I noticed a pattern across a number of industries that involved the movement to either large firms or small firms, while midsize firms grew large, were acquired, or failed. Another noticeable pattern was the decline of middleman companies in some industries and the rise of such companies in other industries. Whenever I was able to detect a broad strategic pattern, I felt potentially better equipped to view business strategy from a meta-perspective. As a result, in my reading about strategy, I sought to learn about other broad patterns. Work by Adrian Slywotzky and his colleagues, which provides a broad and comprehensive view of strategic patterns across industries, is the most useful I have found.

Profit Patterns: 30 Ways to Anticipate and Profit from Strategic Forces Reshaping Your Business (Slywotzky, Morrison, Moser, Mundt, and Quella, 1999) identifies and provides detailed descriptions of thirty major strategic patterns, within seven categories. (See Appendix B for the seven categories and sample patterns within each category.) For example, one pattern (Profit Shift) involves situations in which in the past all customers were profitable and now most customers are *not* profitable. To be successful, companies must analyze their customers and identify and pursue the profitable ones. Another illustrative pattern (Product to Solution) involves a value shift from a product to a solution. In this pattern, great products are no longer enough to solve customers' problems; to be successful, companies need to assemble offerings of products, services, and financing.

Slywotzky and his colleagues make a compelling case for the importance of seeing broad patterns in an industry, suggesting that patterns are lenses through which we can see and understand a complex reality. Thus, patterns provide an organized way of understanding events and our environments, sensitize us to different aspects of current strategic challenges, enable us to see and analyze key movements in our industries, allow us to define more options, stimulate us to continuously expand our fields of vision, and enable us to respond to changes in the competitive marketplace with greater speed and success. The authors assert that, as change and complexity increase, patterns occur more frequently and pattern recognition becomes even more important.

Slywotzky and his coauthors (1999) believe that strategic pattern recognition is a skill that can be learned:

> The ability to anticipate how and why a company's strategic landscape is changing, connect symptoms to causes, and then create strategies that lead to significant, sustained profitability is an art and a skill everyone . . . can profitably cultivate. (p. ix)

They outline an approach executives can use to increase their ability to recognize strategic patterns.

Reading *Profit Patterns* increased my awareness and understanding of some of the key high-level patterns that are playing out within and across industries and has allowed me to develop hypotheses about some of the underlying competitive patterns that were challenging (and worrying) my clients. Having a sense of the broad patterns has also increased my interest in, and comprehension of, the business press (such as the *Wall Street Journal* and *Fortune*).

Suggestions for Clients

With regard to learning about and tracking broad strategic patterns, there are two suggestions that, when appropriate to their role and the dilemmas they are facing, I make to clients:

- Develop familiarity with common broad strategic patterns within and across industries.
- Search for and pay attention to early signals of shifts in the marketplace.

Each of these is discussed below.

Develop Familiarity with Common
Broad Strategic Patterns

I'm still experimenting with ways to best support clients in becoming more familiar with broad strategic patterns. Although clients often express a desire for increased strategic capacity (and sometimes their bosses have indicated that clients *should* become more "strategic" in their thinking), it can be difficult to make progress because clients tend to be busy with operational responsibilities and because there tends to be little support within their companies for discussion of strategic matters.

The best way I've found for clients to begin familiarizing themselves with strategic patterns is to read either *Profit Patterns* (Slywotzky et al., 1999, discussed above) or *The Profit Zone: How Strategic Business Design Will Lead You to Tomorrow's Profits* (Slywotzky and Morrison, 1997). Analyzing changing circumstances in their industries in terms of the thirty patterns can be instructive and can prompt valuable conversations with bosses, peers, direct reports, and/or customers.

Search for and Pay Attention to Early Signals
of Shifts in the Marketplace

Because executives typically need to justify their actions and intended actions in self-confident, tough-minded ways, they may be reluctant to pay attention to their hunches, inklings, and early concerns about emerging patterns and shifts in the marketplace. In the past, when business moved more slowly, waiting for certainty was a prudent course. However, in fast-changing environments, early identification of trends and potential opportunities and threats is important and "will become a survival trait as change becomes more and more unpredictable" (Slywotzky et al., 1999, p. xii).

In coaching sessions, clients often express their misgivings about how things are going in their business and/or their sense that their company is "missing the boat" with regard to some opportunities or threats. Supporting clients in articulating their early concerns, however preliminary and elusive, and in considering taking careful action (collecting more data, comparing notes with peers, or having informal discussions with their bosses) can yield positive results and reinforce their confidence in their early reading of the environment. There are times, of course, when clients decide not to act on their hunches or inklings and prefer to wait to see what unfolds.

Viewing Marketplaces and Companies as Complex Adaptive Systems

While I was pursuing the two meta-perspectives discussed earlier (the multidimensionality of strategy and broad strategic patterns at the industry level), I was also exploring a set of ideas that I believe have enormous implications for business strategy. These ideas involve the application to organizations of complexity theory—an emerging multidisciplinary attempt to understand the rules that underlie such varying systems as bacteria colonies, national economies, and galaxies. (See Waldrop, 1992, for an intriguing discussion of the origins and key questions of complexity theory.) In the last ten years, there has been increasing interest in viewing marketplaces and the companies that operate in them as *complex adaptive systems*—a notion that comes out of complexity theory. A complex adaptive system is an environment in which a large number of agents interact with—and react to—one another, creating an endlessly adapting and essentially unpredictable system.

Although the work on complex adaptive systems can be difficult to understand and absorb, it drew my continuing attention because it captured some important aspects of what I was both experiencing and reading about within many marketplaces. Chief among these was the rapid evolution of practices and players—an evolution influenced by the actions and reactions of both experienced businesses and newer entrants. The impacts of technological changes, changes (both actual and anticipated) in government policies, shifts in the economy, and changing boundaries within and across industries created a variety of fast-moving and unpredictable marketplaces. The unpredictability of such marketplaces had a profound impact on my clients, increasing the speed with which plans and approaches to their work had to be radically modified, and possibly even abandoned, and raising the level of pressure, stress, and sense of risk.

When I first began to explore complex adaptive systems, some writers were beginning to explore not just marketplaces but organizations themselves as complex adaptive systems. This view was at first not consistent with my experience in organizations, in which I still saw many fairly predictable, nonchaotic operations. However, as I worked with executives at higher organizational levels and as the speed of change accelerated, I encountered more parts of organizations that had the characteristics of complex adaptive systems.

A complex adaptive systems perspective views organizations as resembling living organisms—which evolve over time—more than machines. One of the most important aspects of complex adaptive systems is that they don't operate in linear ways. According to Lewin and Regine (2001), "In a linear world, things may exist independently of each other, and when they interact, they do so in simple, predictable ways. In a nonlinear, dynamic world, everything exists only in relationship to everything else, and the interactions among agents in the system lead to complex, unpredictable outcomes" (pp. 18–19).

The nonlinearity and unpredictability of complex adaptive systems create enormous challenges, as those who manage and lead them "cannot *control* their organization to the degree that the mechanistic perspective implies; but they can *influence* where their company is going and how it evolves" (p. 19). The implications for business strategy of viewing marketplaces and companies as complex adaptive systems seem enormous, and I believe many leadership and organizational perspectives and practices will be redefined and rethought as we gradually incorporate into our work an understanding of such systems.

Suggestions for Clients

Based on my understanding of complex adaptive systems, there are three suggestions that, when appropriate to their role and to the dilemmas they are facing, I make to clients:

- Increase your ability to work on the edge of chaos.
- Be intentional about interactions with others.
- Look for small changes that could have big impacts.

Each of these is discussed below.

Increase Your Ability to Work on the Edge of Chaos

There is compelling reason to believe that most companies need to operate *on the edge of chaos*, that is, at some remove from stable, orderly functioning, yet not in a place where things are entirely out of control. When discussing aspects of decision making such as structure, roles, and control mechanisms, my reference to the notion of operating on the edge of chaos in order to be competitive has been well received; indeed, it has often led to the development of practices and perspectives that have proven valuable to clients. I often accompany discussions about operating on the edge of chaos by referring to the view of Davis and Davidson (1991), which is that, because we are in the midst of a major, decades-long economic shift, our organizations will *never* quite catch up with our businesses and, if an organization does catch up, it probably is in decline.

No executive has ever disagreed with me about the need to be on the edge of chaos. And clients typically express rueful relief about the inevitability of their organizations trailing their businesses; the concept seems to describe their experiences well and relieves them of a sense of failure because their organizations are not orderly or settled enough.

In order to function on the edge of chaos, organizations must be sufficiently adaptable to move quickly in the marketplace, which means they must be less structured and hierarchical than many executives find comfortable. The ideal approach is a wise and careful mix of structure and flexibility—I think of it as the *minimal necessary structure*—and that mix needs to be continually and intentionally reexamined and adjusted to match changing conditions.

Personality characteristics often have a significant effect on the client's degree of comfort in working on the edge of chaos—in particular, a specific dichotomy of the MBTI personality inventory: Judging and Perceiving. Judging types are drawn to orderly, organized, planful environments, while Perceiving types favor those that are more flexible, adaptable, and spontaneous. Because most executives are Judging types (McCaulley, 1990), living at the edge of chaos is a substantial challenge. During coaching, my clients and I talk about ways of letting go of some control without allowing things to fall apart and/or experiencing great anxiety that things are going to fall apart. Small experiments are often helpful—and sometimes necessary—to move in the direction of less structure and control. Searching for models (that is, leaders and environments that produce excellent business results with less structure and control) can be illuminating and inspiring to clients.

Once clients accept the notion of operating on the edge of chaos, the metaphor may become a reference point for analyzing problems as well as possible solutions. As a result, clients may recognize that some of their planned solutions are too linear or too focused on control and will move toward more complex and sophisticated actions.

Be Intentional about Interactions with Others

I have often been impressed with the ability of those clients who have active interpersonal networks to receive valuable information, get out the word about a particular activity or issue, and adapt quickly to organizational shifts. Complexity theory highlights the value of this kind of interaction and may help refine our understanding of it. For example, complexity theory directs our attention to network nodes (people who are highly connected across different grapevines). When clients talk about how to gather or disseminate information quickly, I often ask them to think of which people are the first to hear the news or are most effective at passing it along.

Complexity theory also emphasizes the importance of *informal* interactions. In complex adaptive systems, the ability to sense trends and shifts in the system as early as possible is extremely important for successful adaptation. My experience with organizations suggests that information about what is worrisome, heretical, or outside a company's normal way of thinking (such as shifting customer interest, unhappy staff, competitor incursions) is slow to find its way into formal meetings or written material. I often suggest that clients cultivate and use as many informal settings and mechanisms as possible—to ask, for example, "How are things going for you?"—and pursue interests and concerns that are not yet clear-cut. If the situation permits, going for a walk with someone to talk about elusive matters or concerns can be valuable; in this more informal and out-of-the-ordinary setting, the rules of evidence tend to shift and people don't feel the need to be 100 percent sure of something, but can say, "I'm a little worried about . . . ," or "I've noticed . . . ," or "I'm wondering if we did this a little differently. . . ."

In addition, complexity theory recognizes the importance of some regular interaction *outside* your everyday contacts. Research suggests that agents in a system adapt most effectively when they "partially interact" (Brown and Eisenhardt, 1998, p. 75) with one another. For example, people usually find jobs through acquaintances, not through close friends, because friends tend to have the same contacts, whereas acquaintances, who participate in different networks, offer a much larger variety of contacts (Gladwell, 2000). I often encourage clients to set up periodic lunches with people in their companies or industries who are especially good at spotting industry trends or providing a big-picture or more objective perspective on an issue, concern, or strategy.

Look for Small Changes That Could Have Big Impacts

Even though a great deal of our experience in the world tells us differently, we can still assume that the level of a particular intervention or change in an organization will determine its degree of impact. In contrast, complexity theory maintains that, in a complex adaptive system, there is no linear relationship between an action and its impact. As a result, big actions may have small impacts and small actions may have big impacts.

In my coaching practice, discussing the phenomenon of nonlinearity with executives has been very useful to them. When a planned change is especially important to clients or to their businesses, they tend to want to take big steps. Rethinking the linearity of the relationship between big steps and big impacts—and most executives have had some experience with big steps that resulted in little impact, or even had the opposite of the intended effect—can lead to useful experimentation with smaller changes and can sometimes prevent overly elaborate changes that would have had limited payoff.

Other Resources for Exploring Complex Adaptive Systems

I have found four books especially useful in my efforts to understand complex adaptive systems as applied to organizations. *Harnessing Complexity: Organizational Implications of a Scientific Frontier* (Axelrod and Cohen, 1999) offers a rigorous model of complex adaptive systems, with clear definitions and analysis, as well as discussion of its implications for organizations. *Weaving Complexity and Business: Engaging the Soul at Work* (Lewin and Regine, 2001) provides a brief and lucid overview of complexity and its implications for business. In particular, it focuses on a needed shift in management style toward connections and relationships. *Competing on the Edge: Strategy as Structured Chaos* (Brown and Eisenhardt, 1998) analyzes the strategic challenges of thriving in fast-changing marketplaces and offers sophisticated and compelling guidance for succeeding in such environments. *The Tipping Point: How Little Things Can Make a Big Difference* (Gladwell, 2000) is an engaging best-seller. Although not framed in terms of complexity, it contains three intriguing rules that illustrate a critical aspect of complex adaptive systems: that small interventions can have big impacts.

Conclusion

My reading of strategy books, my discussions with colleagues, and, perhaps most important, my work with executives who are involved in crafting and implementing strategy have given me *some* sense of the business strategy process. However, I still feel that my understanding is incomplete. My hope is that those of us who are executive coaches can individually and collectively increase our understanding of business strategy so that we can support our clients—both the executives we coach and the organizations they lead—as they try to see *both* the forest and the trees. Perhaps then they will be able to face the challenge that Erwin Schrodinger proposes:

> The task is not so much to see what no one has yet seen, but to think what nobody has yet thought about that which everybody sees.

Appendix A

Ten Schools of Thought in Strategy School

Prescriptive (how strategy should be developed)	Addresses Strategy Formation As
The Design School	A process of conception
The Planning School	A formal process
The Positioning School	An analytical process

Descriptive (how strategies actually get made)	Addresses Strategy Formation As
The Entrepreneurial School	A visionary process
The Cognitive School	A mental process
The Learning School	An emergent process
The Power School	A process of negotiation
The Cultural School	A collective process
The Environmental School	A reactive process

Configurative (stages or episodes that organizations go through)	Addresses Strategy Formation As
The Configuration School	A process of transformation

Source: Adapted from Mintzberg, Ahlstrand, and Lampel, 1998.

Appendix B

Seven Categories of Strategic Patterns within and across Industries

Category	Examples of Patterns within the Category
Mega-patterns	Collapse of the middle, De facto standard
Value chain patterns	Reintegration, Value chain squeeze
Customer patterns	Profit shift, Micro-segmentation
Channel patterns	Multiplication, Channel concentration
Product patterns	Profit multiplier, Product to solution
Knowledge patterns	Operations to knowledge, Knowledge to product
Organizational patterns	Skills shift, Conventional to digital business design

Source: Adapted from Slywotzky, Morrison, Moser, Mundt, and Quella, 1999.

Note

[1] My search for an understanding of business strategy was no doubt influenced both by the characteristics of my clients and by my own cognitive style. My clients have largely been executives in private sector companies (mainly financial service companies) at the vice president level and above. My cognitive style leads me to seek broad conceptual frameworks of understanding in order to make sense of my experience. (For those familiar with the *Myers-Briggs Type Indicator* instrument, I am an Extraverted Intuitive Thinking Judging [ENTJ] type.) Executive coaches with different client bases and different cognitive styles may approach their understanding of strategy issues in very different ways.

References

Axelrod, R., and M. Cohen. (1999). *Harnessing complexity: Organizational implications of a scientific frontier.* New York: Free Press.

Brown, S., and K. Eisenhardt. (1998). *Competing on the edge: Strategy as structured chaos.* Boston: Harvard Business School Press.

Davis, S., and B. Davidson. (1991). *2020 vision: Transform your business today to succeed in tomorrow's economy.* New York: Simon & Schuster.

Gladwell, M. (2000). *The tipping point: How little things can make a big difference.* New York: Little, Brown.

Hamel, G. (1997, June 23). Killer strategies that make shareholders rich. *Fortune, 135,* 70–79.

Lewin, R., and B. Regine. (2001). *Weaving complexity and business: Engaging the soul at work.* New York: Texere.

McCaulley, M. H. (1990). The Myers-Briggs Type Indicator and leadership. In K. S. Clark and M. B. Clark (eds.), *Measures of leadership* (pp. 381–418). Greensboro, N.C.: Center for Creative Leadership.

Mintzberg, H., B. Ahlstrand, and J. Lampel. (1998). *Strategy safari: A guided tour through the wilds of strategic management.* New York: Free Press.

Slywotzky, A. (1999). Foreword. In S. H. Haeckel, *Adaptive enterprise: Creating and leading sense-and-respond organizations.* Boston: Harvard Business School Press.

Slywotzky, A., D. Morrison, T. Moser, K. Mundt, and J. Quella. (1999). *Profit patterns: 30 ways to anticipate and profit from strategic forces reshaping your business.* New York: Random House.

Slywotzky, A., and D. Morrison. (1997). *Profit zone: How strategic business design will lead you to tomorrow's profits.* New York: Random House.

Waldrop, M. (1992). *Complexity: The emerging science at the edge of order and chaos.* New York: Simon & Schuster.

[12]

LOVE AND FEAR
IN EXECUTIVE COACHING

SALLY CARR

There are only two feelings. Love and fear.
There are only two languages. Love and fear.
There are only two activities. Love and fear.
There are only two motives, two procedures,
two frameworks, two results. Love and fear.
Love and fear.

—M. Leunig, A Common Prayer[1]

It is such a privilege to be an executive coach. We have the opportunity to influence people who in turn influence the lives of many others. We have an unusual kind of authority, and it is important that we use it wisely. Wise authority offers guidance but also freedom, and will be supportive but also questioning. Its foundation is a deep interest and caring, rooted in something much like love—perhaps even identical to love in the broadest sense of the word. And yet it easily becomes warped into the need for control, often through the effect of fear.

The business world, with its accelerating pace of change, has plenty in it that promotes fear and the need to control. As coaches, we can provide a safe space in which people may recognize and look beyond their fears—a space in which they can grow. Our job is to release potential, helping others make the best use of their knowledge, wisdom, and experience. Fear, especially unrecognized fear, keeps people from expressing that which is best in themselves.

To create that safe space requires more than technical or professional skill. It requires that we look at ourselves and the quality of presence we bring to coaching. Our ways of being and interacting will have as much influence as our words. In this chapter, I invite you to consider the proposition that a fundamental aspect of our role is to help release fears and to promote action from a place of love. But to do this, we must try to recognize those times when our own actions stem from fear. Otherwise, we risk being driven by fears that we do not recognize, and, whether we want to or not, we will provide a model of authority stemming from fear. This may sound like a new burden, but I will argue that it is the exact opposite—that this responsibility is a call to freedom and joyous living.

The Chain of Fear and Why It Matters

I can see myself very close to being overwhelmed. I like taking on projects, and I've got a reputation for delivering, so my boss just keeps handing me more and more of them. Please don't talk to me about working smarter, not harder. I reckon I'm working just about as smart as anyone could. The time has come to say no to something. But it's not so easy. My boss is great, but she's made comments that scare me about people who have left. "He couldn't stand the pace—I really burned him out!" When you hear comments like that, you think twice about saying no.

Satish's story will sound familiar to anyone involved in executive coaching. Torn between what he wants to do and fear of the consequences, he feels out of control, his motivation undermined by resentment of demands he feels unable to refuse. His irritability and tension are passed on to his staff, so the whole department is on edge.

Unbeknownst to Satish, his boss is also subject to fear, although she would not initially have called it that. Patricia came into a failing department and achieved a spectacular turnaround in only two years. She received praise and respect for her achievements from top management and now feels enormous pressure to maintain the momentum. "I really want people to enjoy their work and have balanced lives," she says, "and I know that they can't go on forever, doing more with less. But we *must* keep on improving. We've *got* to show that we can go on delivering." Patricia has gone beyond wanting to achieve results; she now feels driven—by her fear of failure—to do so.

Why is the issue of love versus fear so important? If fear gets results, why worry? And it would seem that, at least to a certain point, fear does get results. For example, Christophe Dejours (1998) conducted extensive research in French manufacturing organizations, and he found that, as fear became an increasingly prevalent means of controlling employees over the past fifteen years or so, productivity soared. He argued that this increase in productivity would be impossible if workers were merely "doing their jobs" because organizations only function effectively when people put intelligence and ingenuity—*le zèle de travail*—into their work. His research led him to conclude, reluctantly, that fear could be used to mobilize this zeal, contrary to the received wisdom that says this level of engagement comes only through positive means of motivation. Unpalatable as I find this conclusion, it helps explain why fear may be such a popular tactic.

Nevertheless, I would argue that fear won't get results in the long run. Dejours concurred, suggesting that beyond a certain level and duration, fear leads to paralysis and loss of morale. In addition, the changing nature of work and the marketplace is likely to place strict limits on the success that can be achieved through fear-based management. More and more, organizations are recognizing the need to nurture people's creativity and innovation in order to gain continuing success. Fearful people are likely to focus on doing what is needed to remain safe rather than on being innovative. Teamwork, increasingly important in many organizations, is undermined by fear. The fear-driven workers studied by Dejours used their ingenuity in self-serving ways—to improve their own results, certainly, but frequently to make life difficult in subtle ways for fellow workers or for other teams—so as to elevate their own relative standing.

My main objection to fear-based control is that it stultifies the human spirit, and it's no fun. Perhaps there is a temporary, dismal satisfaction in being the one who maintains control through fear, but it's certainly no fun to be on the receiving end. Often, it's no fun for either party, controller or controlled.

Ricardo Semler (1993) made this point in his book *Maverick*. Semler took over his father's business, Semco, which had been run in an authoritarian manner. For some years, he continued to work in the same way, accepting without question the assumptions of the traditional management style. When things went wrong, he sought the remedy in yet more controls:

> We were so impressed with our statistical abilities that it took us a while to realize all those numbers weren't doing us much good. . . . While I initially liked the idea of a disciplined, hard-driven company run by aggressive managers armed with innumerable statistics, I was starting to have second thoughts. Work hard or get fired. That was the ethic of the new Semco. People were being pushed forward. But how much better to have a self-propelled workforce. (p. 31)

His insights led Semler to make extraordinary changes at Semco, challenging every cherished tenet of management, always in the direction of allowing others more trust and more control over their own lives. The company became even more successful, while morale among the workforce improved dramatically. Although it is just one example, the story of Semco suggests that while fear can work up to a point, love works even better.

What Is This Thing Called Love?

The love to which I refer is not romantic love, or even necessarily affection for people. It is the warm, expansive emotion of moving out toward the world (as opposed to shrinking away or creating barriers, which comes with fear); it encompasses offshoots like hope, curiosity, trust, and delight. I believe this kind of love is in us all and only needs a chance to be released. It may be unnoticed, obscured, or suppressed, but given the right conditions—freedom from fear and space to pay attention—it will blossom of its own accord. Saki Santorelli (1999), an expert on mindfulness and stress, made a similar point in a recent interview:

> We've been reared to believe that we have to be pressured in order to achieve. Sometimes it may be necessary to keep our thumbs on ourselves, since many of us are good at procrastinating, but such pressure ignores the possibility that we human beings are internally motivated, that we love getting the job done, that we want to learn. (p. 33)

Santorelli is suggesting that motivation can arise from the intrinsic delight we take in what we do and what we create. However, I often come across people who believe that we need to be worried, unhappy, or dissatisfied in order to be motivated. A recent example involved a coach who expressed concern about a client's high level of well-being, as measured by a personality questionnaire. "He might not be hungry enough for the job," the coach said. "He might be too complacent to be motivated." The idea that high levels of well-being are a deficit may seem ludicrous, but such perspectives are all too common in the business world.

In *The Inner Game of Tennis,* Timothy Gallwey (1997) described tennis coaching methods that are based on harnessing attention without exciting fear. He asks people to focus on certain objects and avoids telling them in detail what they should do, for example, when learning to hold and swing the racket. Rather than worrying about getting it right, people find the movement that feels right for them. In this way, they are less plagued by what Gallwey calls "Self One"—that is, the part of us that acts as a judgmental overseer. Freedom from the critical attentions of Self One enables Self Two—the body's natural, flowing response—to come through uninhibited. Perfect strokes do not appear at once, of course, but learning is greatly enhanced, and far more enjoyable, than when it is based on a teeth-gritting set of *musts.*

The love I have mentioned has much in common with the response of Self Two. Self Two is the natural learner in us, undaunted by the possibility of failure. Unfortunately, Self One, the part that fears being wrong, is carefully nurtured in most of us throughout our childhood and school days. Nevertheless, most people are able to forget the nagging critic at times and become completely absorbed in a task—a state known as *flow.* D. Goleman (1995) commented on the experience and impact of flow:

> Although people perform at their peak while in flow, they are unconcerned with how they are doing, with thoughts of success or failure—the sheer pleasure of the act itself is what motivates them. (p. 91)

Flow seems to occur when people feel stretched but not fearful—"in that delicate zone between boredom and anxiety" (Csikszentmihalyi, 1986). If, as coaches, we stimulate interest while reducing anxiety, we may be able to help people, including ourselves, experience flow more often. Indeed, the more we create the conditions to experience flow for ourselves, the more likely we are to promote the experience for others. There is a great deal of joy in flow, which I regard as the quintessence of action from a place of love.

My personal agenda in coaching is to promote a person's authority based on this kind of love. Because my aim is to help clients feel freer in their choices, there is no contradiction between my agenda and the agendas of my clients. I may not like some of their decisions, but I believe it is more valuable to help them choose freely and without fear than to impose my view of what they should want. That's the theory and the ideal toward which I work. In reality, I am aware that my own fears sometimes make it hard to tolerate allowing people the freedom to make choices I dislike. I need to be alert to my own need to control.

Fear of Having No Control: The Warning Signs

I used to have no emotional leverage to get clients to face up to the data. They would use all sorts of excuses to tell me why people's views of them were wrong. However, I have begun including objective measures of innate abilities. You can't argue with these. You can either do them or you can't. Adding these measures has given me far more ability to break down resistance and make my clients more effective.

The scene was a conference on executive coaching. The speaker was describing his approach to coaching, an approach that was carefully packaged and trademarked. His slides were very slick, but he seemed to be hiding behind the podium. The overwhelming impression I received was of a frightened man driven to keep things under tight control. He appeared to have little trust in his clients; instead, he acted as if he needed weapons against them.

In the next session, another presenter described her approach to developing "learning communities" of people she had coached. She invited three of those who had taken part in the program to talk about the experience. They began positively, and, after they had continued in this vein for a while, she said, "I find when I come to conferences like this that I learn a lot from the ways other people have screwed up. And I screwed up a bunch of things on this program! I'd like you to talk about what *didn't* work." Her tone was warm and cheerful, and she seemed delighted as the panel of program participants gave examples of problems they had encountered. I was impressed by her openness and sense of partnership with those she had coached. She seemed to trust her clients, to feel she was with them, not against them.

It is not hard to guess which speaker I prefer as a role model, and yet I do not wish to condemn the first one. Doubtless he sought to help his clients, and wanted to "break down their resistance" and "get them to face up to the data" because he believed they were heading for problems if they did not change. Certainly, love does not consist in shielding people from important information about the likely consequences of their behavior. And I would not be justified in feeling smug either, because I, too, have been subject to the kinds of fear he seemed to exhibit and to the desire to make someone see the need to change.

If we as coaches believe that we *must* make people change, the likely result is that we will emphasize problems and deficits—all the ways in which the person is not OK. At the extreme, we may use tactics that undermine an executive's self-esteem in order to help us feel safe. When I notice myself wanting to subdue and subordinate a client, I find fears behind this behavior. I may be afraid that I will not continue to be employed unless I am able to make people change as the organization wants them to change. I may fear that the client will not respect me, or I may be afraid of finding that my ideas and judgment are not so great, so that it is safer to render the person harmless in advance than to risk being questioned. There is a danger of becoming hooked on control. Having seen that a frightening prospect can get someone to sit up and listen, I may be tempted to persist with the tactic until I have driven the person into a submissive state that allows me to wield my power (benign, naturally) at will. "Now," I think triumphantly, "at last! I can really help this person, now that he's like putty in my hands and will really listen to what I have to say."

Of course, if we arrive at a situation in which the person is putty in our hands, we have given ourselves a heavy responsibility. Our message is "Trust me—I have your best interests at heart, and I know what you should do." If we accept this role, we demand of ourselves omniscient wisdom and perfect compassion. Personally, I'm not ready to play such a role yet, and I suspect that if we made perfect wisdom and compassion a prerequisite for entering the coaching profession, we would have few coaches. I know that I need to encourage my clients to trust their own judgment and be willing to question me. However, I have certainly fallen prey to fears that I *should* be perfectly wise and compassionate or that my clients expect this of me.

Other Tell-Tale Signs

In my experience, anger is almost always a red flag, telling me that there is fear in the background. So when I find myself becoming irritated or angry with a client, I have learned to look behind this to find the fear. For example, if I become frustrated because I have just expressed some breathtaking insight, and the client either doesn't get it at all or interprets it in a way that differs from my intent, I find fears behind the frustration. These may range from "I know this is a vital insight, but I obviously can't communicate it, so I guess I won't be able to change the world for the better after all," to "It wasn't brilliant anyway, and I must be nothing but a puffed-up, self-satisfied windbag." The language is extreme, deliberately so, because I find the language of fear to be judgmental, absolute, and uncompromising.

If I can quiet the fears, I realize that my insights will be helpful only if I allow clients to incorporate them into their own body of wisdom, undergoing their own interpretations. My clients' wisdom emerges naturally as they feel safe in the coaching setting, and with the aid of appropriate questions to direct their attention. The extent of their wisdom can itself be a source of threat: "Maybe they don't need me." "What if they're better than me?—they should probably be coaching me!" Such fears could make it hard to listen to clients' ideas and acknowledge their full value.

Perhaps I am alone in experiencing such fears, but I suspect not. I once asked Tim Gallwey whether he had experienced problems in promoting his methods because of coaches' fears that these methods might undermine their expertise and power. He agreed that he had often met with opposition from coaches who seemed afraid that they would become superfluous if they accepted the idea that human learning comes mostly from within.

Shoulds and *Musts:* The Rules for Being OK

All the fears described above are based on internal assumptions about what it takes to be an adequate coach. For example, "I *must* get my client to change in the ways the organization wants," "I *should* have read more books than my client has on the topic we're discussing," or "I *ought* to know what my clients should do in this situation."

These *musts* and *shoulds* represent an internalized authority based on fear—an authority that wields the implied threat that we will not be OK if we break the rules. *Musts* and *shoulds* are especially troublesome when they are unconscious and therefore unavailable for reflective consideration. It is not so much that we need to eliminate such assumptions, but by paying attention and being prepared to notice them in operation, we lessen their power to control us. Awareness sets the stage for us to *respond* rather than *react*—in other words, to make a considered choice of action rather than be stuck in an automatic pattern of reactivity. We cannot ask that we never be afraid. In fact, recent research into brain functioning suggests that we may be unable to prevent fear reactions through conscious willpower because these reactions are evoked first in parts of the brain that are not subject to our conscious control. However, we can affect how we respond to our fear reactions (Saron and Davidson, 1997).

This distinction between responding and reacting was made by Jon Kabat-Zinn (1990) in the context of his work on stress. Kabat-Zinn commented,

> As soon as you bring awareness to what is happening in a stressful situation, you have changed that situation dramatically, just by virtue of not being unconscious and on automatic pilot anymore. . . . This inner change can be extremely important because *it gives you a range of options for influencing what will happen next.* (pp. 264–66)

As we become aware, we have more control. We may even choose to laugh at ourselves (more on this later).

So much for the *shoulds* and *musts* that may assail us as coaches. I believe it is equally important that we help our clients to become aware of these assumptions and to free themselves sufficiently from them that they can make real choices. For example, I recently met with George, a manager who had worked with me in coaching two years before. George was happy; he said that he loved his work and believed it was going about as well as it could. He was even a little concerned about his lack of stress: "Everyone else seems to be stressed all the time. Should I be worried that I'm not?" We decided to set up a meeting with his boss, Susan, to confirm that her perceptions of the situation were in line with George's and my own and to talk about the possibility of George taking on a mentor role within the company. Susan agreed that George was doing extremely well and that the project he was leading was regarded as highly successful. However, she added, "I do think it is important, though, for you two to get together and work out some sort of plan for George's future beyond the end of this project. I know that is three to four years away, but he *must* begin to develop a vision of the future and take charge of his own career."

George looked decidedly uninspired by this prospect. I knew that his natural style tended more toward enjoyment of the moment and living for the day and less toward long-range planning. The pressure to develop a vision of the future could be making him feel anxious and uncomfortable. I also knew that Susan differed from George regarding this issue—for her, looking ahead and making long-range plans were enjoyable and seemed obviously important.

I asked, "Who is it that needs George to have a plan? What are you concerned could happen if he does not develop such a plan?"

"Oh," said Susan, who is no fool. "Perhaps I'm talking about what I would need if I were in his position. But don't you think a plan would be a good idea?"

"I don't really know. What do you think, George?"

Interestingly, as soon as George was freed from thinking that he *must* have a plan, he became quite animated about the idea of considering his future. He confirmed that he had been uncomfortable with his previous conversations on this topic with Susan, because she was telling him he *must* do something that felt inherently impossible to him. Another *must* was involved here—an assumption that if he thought about the future at all, he had to figure out the *right* vision for the future. He had been puzzled and discomfited by reading, over and over again in well-meaning books on personal development, that we must know what we want from life, that we must have a vision, a dream, a sense of purpose.

Knowing that he exerted only partial control over future outcomes, and that he didn't really know how he would feel about them anyway, George could see no way of devising the right plan. When we discussed treating it as a game, looking for avenues to explore and for options that could lead to other options, his interest was engaged. In fact, this was what Susan had in mind anyway—but her use of *must* seemed to imply a rigid process that had made him anxious and disheartened.

Fear and the Need for Certainty

Although it can be liberating to question *shoulds,* it may provoke anxiety as well. To the extent that they provide rules for being OK, *shoulds* give conditional security: as long as you live by the rules, you should be fine. If we begin to question the rules, we may feel as if there is no security at all. For this reason, people often cling to *shoulds* and are hungry for experts in whom they can believe, who will tell them what they should do. We are well primed by schools to believe there is one correct answer and that someone else probably knows what it is. To quote Charles Handy (1994) about his experience in school, "The aim of education was to transfer the answers from the teacher to me by one means or another." In reality, experts are always fallible, and most breakthroughs have come from people prepared to question received wisdom. Handy described how liberating it was to realize that "I was free to try out my ideas, invent my own scenarios, create my own futures" (p. 8).

Kitchener and Brenner (1990) described a model of adult development that is concerned with the growth of epistemic cognition—that is, "an individual's knowledge about the limits of knowing, the certainty of knowing, and the criteria for knowing" (p. 212). The Reflective Judgment model consists of a sequence of stages whereby people's reliance on expert authority gradually gives way to the ability to construct judgments while recognizing the inherent uncertainties of knowing. Handy's sense that the absence of certainty gave him freedom to choose appears to place him at a level of development seldom found in young people, according to research by Kitchener and her colleagues.

Because the proportion of young people among leaders and executives is increasing, we as coaches may often find ourselves working with individuals who believe that there are answers and who want to give or receive them (or both). This desire from our clients may exert further pressure on us to be The Expert, but it is important to resist this role. Resisting the role does not in any way preclude our offering opinions, suggestions, or advice. Learning does not necessarily mean finding out everything for oneself, and one of the wonderful features of human beings is their capacity to extend learning beyond the confines of their own experience by benefiting from the ideas and experiences of others. The key is to be clear about what we are doing—offering ideas and experiences, not telling people what to do. Alfred North Whitehead (1922) regretted the fact that education as typically practiced tended to squash people's questioning curiosity. He suggested that "the only avenue towards wisdom is by freedom in the presence of knowledge" (p. 39).

The way we present information and suggestions can determine whether or not people recognize that they have this "freedom in the presence of knowledge." In an intriguing series of studies, Ellen Langer (1989) and her colleagues have shown that the language in which information is provided has a major influence on the degree of creativity people show in addressing problems. Specifically, she found that people responded more imaginatively to information presented with a degree of uncertainty than information presented as fact. In some experiments, the difference resulted from a simple word substitution—for example, saying an object "*could* be a hair dryer" as opposed to "*is* a hair dryer." Subjects chose to use the objects in novel ways only when the object was given *could be* status. A particularly interesting study by Langer used three conditions: (1) information was provided in absolute terms, (2) information was provided conditionally, using "could be" and "may be," (3) information was provided in absolute terms, but introduced as "one possible model." The group given information in absolute terms was less able to put the information to creative use, and this effect still occurred in group three, which was told up-front that the information was "one possible model." People apparently ignored general statements about the uncertainty of information—if those statements were inconsistent with the way the information was presented. In a coaching context, this suggests that anything we say about not being an expert will be of little use if we then talk and act like one.

Even if we wanted to be experts, our clients' range of knowledge and skills is so vast and changes so rapidly that none of us is capable of mastering all areas. This could lead to our being harassed by another *should*— "I should be keeping up with the literature on everything to do with business and leadership." I've certainly heard that voice in my own head many times. However, coaches come from a wide range of backgrounds, and no two coaches will have the same knowledge and skills. While one coach is confident about providing training in a specific area, such as strategic thinking, another would feel somewhat at a loss—and this is no problem, as long as the coach does not become tense and defensive about it.

Escaping from the *Should* Trap

In reflecting on the way she operates, Noelle, an executive with major responsibility for a high-profile project, attributed her elevated level of stress to the "overseer"—that part of herself that was constantly watching and judging, telling her how things should be done. Noelle elaborated,

> I even know which part of my body is acting as the overseer. I can feel it in my neck and shoulders, like a great weight pressing down on me, telling me, "You've got to do it my way—there's no alternative." It's as if part of me doesn't trust my own competence. No wonder I've been feeling stressed. With each new challenge, my overseer has been saying "Oh, no, I'd better really ratchet up the control now," so I've been getting more and more tense.

"Could you," I asked her, "say to that part of you, 'Listen, I know you're only trying to help, but you really don't need to work that hard'?"

"You know," she said, "I'm going to develop a new image of my overseer; I'm going to see it lying back in a chair, relaxing, and watching me with admiration." The next time we met, Noelle reported that work had begun to flow much more easily and her confidence had increased.

When we and our clients are able to step back from *shoulds* and *musts,* we reclaim our freedom and creativity. *Shoulds* appeal because they provide rules for being OK, which means the ultimate escape is to believe that we *are* OK, now and unconditionally. The more we are able to believe this for ourselves, the more likely we are to support this belief in our clients. *OK* does not mean irreproachable according to some standard—it means OK even with all our so-called imperfections, including any tendency to forget that we are OK!

"You're Fine, You're Just Fine"

As mentioned earlier, the greater our need to feel in control, the more likely we are to emphasize problems and deficits in our clients. The implied message is "You're not OK, and you *must* change." Curiously enough, clients are often willing collaborators in this exercise. Skipping over the positive parts of feedback, they make comments such as "Yes, yes, that's all very nice, but let's get to the meat of it—the things I need to do differently." While it is encouraging when clients are open to criticism, it is a pity that so many appear dismissive of their good points.

Perhaps people who voice such sentiments are working on the assumption that there is nothing to be done about the positives, so they may as well devote their attention to the areas that need change. Negative feedback provides important information, but when people use this as a task list for development, they may take on a new set of *shoulds* that will weigh them down and give them more cause for anxiety. Development becomes another chore or another performance they have to get right.

I try to give the opposite message: "You're fine, and it's up to you whether or not you change." There are no *shoulds*—only choices and consequences. They may prefer some consequences over others, but none will make them OK or not OK because they are *already* OK. My aim is to find out what my clients love to do and then to explore the extent to which they can bring what they love into their work.

I recently worked with David, who told me that his goal was to change his image to more closely resemble the typical successful person in his organization. His initial approach was very serious. He talked a lot about how he should be different, judging himself unacceptable as he was. He was quiet and thoughtful, tended to think things through deeply before taking action, enjoyed theoretical approaches, and sometimes saw things from unusual angles. He said he should be more outgoing and assertive, should take more risks, and he wanted to be seen as a man of action.

I encouraged him to create his own image, borrowing if he wished from the typical image of success, but to recognize that he was fine as he was. He later told me,

> I was very pleasantly relieved to find I could achieve my goal in a manner congruent with myself. During our last session, you said to me, "You're fine, you're just fine," a phrase that I can hear as clearly now as when you spoke it. It has echoed often in my mind's ear. It is especially powerful for me.

Humor As an Antidote to Fear and an Aid to Self-Acceptance

Conversations about change are sometimes a little gloomy, emphasizing how arduous and painful a process it can be. While change can involve painful feelings and difficult situations, it can also be fun. Fear plays an important part in determining the degree to which development is painful rather than fun, and gentle self-directed humor is one of the most effective antidotes. When people take themselves very seriously, they tend to be dominated by *shoulds,* and mistakes become traumatic. It will be helpful for us and for our clients if we ourselves can laugh gently at our foibles and forgive our foolish ways. In doing so, we will encourage a playful attitude in our clients.

Stephen Nachmanovitch (1990) suggested that our curiosity and interest become engaged when we approach development as "serious play":

> To play is to free ourselves from arbitrary restrictions and expand our field of action. Our play fosters richness of response and adaptive flexibility. This is the evolutionary value of play—play makes us flexible. By reinterpreting reality and begetting novelty, we keep from becoming rigid. Play enables us to rearrange our capacities and our very identity so that they can be used in unforeseen ways. (p. 43)

David, the client referred to earlier, found it very helpful to take a playful attitude toward his development. Trusting that he was OK, he felt free to experiment. He revealed that as a younger man, he had been interested in drama, and he was now having enormous fun trying out different ways of being. He was able to quiet his self-critical voices and be kind to himself, finding humor in others' reactions to his experiments. The following is part of an e-mail he sent me after one meeting:

> You would have enjoyed seeing me in a meeting last Friday. I was making a presentation to the VPs, including my boss, her boss, my old boss, my former boss . . . all those bosses in one little room . . . now that's surreal! I thought of you ("be dramatic") and let go. I was marvelous, of course, and at one point my boss's boss winked at me and I winked back at her. Can you picture it? Me winking at the boss?

Which came first? David's confidence that he was fine or his willingness not to take himself too seriously? Laughter tends to dispel fear, but really frightened people will not play. Do we need to help people feel OK so they can play, or do we encourage them to see the humor in situations in order to feel OK? In the end, it probably doesn't matter. It's impossible to say which came first in David's case, but, for him, humor and the belief that he was OK seemed to reinforce each other.

Conclusion

I hope coaches will see the value of helping clients become freer from fear and more able to act from love. If we focus on love instead of fear, we accept the responsibility to take care of ourselves, treat ourselves with love and respect, and pay attention to our own growth and development. As stated early in this chapter, I do not see this commitment as a burden but rather as encouragement to examine the burdens we currently carry and to consider discarding a few of them. The more we can let go of fear, the freer we will be to tap the sources of our own love, joy, and vitality.

So do I write this from the standpoint of a fully joyful person who is no longer troubled by fear? Not quite. The irony is that the dear familiar Self One has been sitting somewhere behind my left shoulder throughout the writing of this chapter, telling me encouraging things like "People reading this will think you're just a woolly-minded idealist with no idea of what goes on in the real world." Oh well. Fortunately, it's not necessary to achieve perfection to be a coach.

Overall, I think we will be most effective as coaches if we can

- Provide a model of authority that is based as much as possible on love, delight, trust, and joy rather than on fear and the need for control

- Notice our own fears in the coaching setting and also pay attention to our reactions to these fears

- Use our awareness to help ourselves and our clients respond, rather than react, to fear

- Pay attention to the *shoulds, musts, ought tos,* and *have tos*—both implicit and explicit—of ourselves and our clients, and be prepared to question them

- Offer our ideas and experience, while keeping clearly in mind that we cannot give The Answer

- Help our clients deal with the discomfort engendered by questioning assumptions and living in an uncertain world

- See ourselves, and encourage our clients to see themselves, as essentially OK

- Use humor and playfulness to make development fun, don't take ourselves too seriously, and encourage our clients to be playful

My happy conclusion is that the more we are able to live in ways that promote joy in ourselves, the more we will be able to release potential and bring out joy in others. Who knows? We may even be able to play a part in nudging the world toward love and away from fear.

Note

1 "A Common Prayer" by Michael Leunig, 1990, HarperCollins, Australia. Reprinted with permission.

References

Csikszentmihalyi, M. (March 4, 1986). Interview. *New York Times*.

Dejours, C. (1998). *Souffrance en France: La banalisation de l'injustice sociale*. Paris: Editions du Seuil.

Gallwey, W. T. (1997). *The inner game of tennis*. New York: Random House.

Goleman, D. (1995). *Emotional intelligence: Why it can matter more than IQ*. London: Bloomsbury Publishing.

Handy, C. (1994). Beyond certainty: A personal odyssey. In P. B. Duffy (ed.), *The relevance of a decade* (pp. 3–15). Boston: Harvard Business School Press.

Kabat-Zinn, J. (1990). *Full catastrophe living*. New York: Delta Books.

Kitchener, K. S., and H. G. Brenner. (1990). Wisdom and reflective judgment: Knowing in the face of uncertainty. In R. J. Sternberg (ed.), *Wisdom: Its nature, origins, and development*. Cambridge, England: Cambridge University Press.

Langer, E. J. (1989). *Mindfulness*. Reading, Mass.: Perseus Books.

Leunig, M. (1990). *A common prayer*. North Blackburn, Victoria, Australia: Collins Dove.

Nachmanovitch, S. (1990). *Free play: Improvisation in life and art*. New York: Putnam.

Santorelli, S. (March/April 1999). Wanting to exhale (interview with Mark Matousek). *Common Boundary*, 30–35.

Saron, C., and R. J. Davidson. (1997). The brain and emotions. In D. Goleman (ed.), *Healing emotions*. Boston: Random House.

Semler, R. (1993). *Maverick! The success story behind the world's most unusual workplace*. London: Arrow Books.

Whitehead, A. N. (1922). The rhythmic claims of freedom and discipline. *Outlook* 8 (Spring 1973): 34–41. (Originally published in 1922.)

[13]

FAILURE AND NEGATIVE OUTCOMES

The Taboo Topic in Executive Coaching

RICHARD R. KILBURG

Have you talked with Nathan?" Mary asked me with agitation in her voice.

I stopped and looked at her carefully. Normally jovial and feisty, she looked as though she had not slept well for several days. The frown lines around her mouth were much more pronounced than usual, and her body seemed to have sagged inward and down toward the floor.

"Not recently. Why do you ask?" I responded, noticing my own anxiety. I knew then that this would not be a normal coaching session with her.

"I want to know whether I should ever talk to you again," Mary began.

Adrenaline surging, I searched for a response that would elicit more information and not get me thrown out of her office. I felt extremely *apprehensive because Mary played a key role in the organization for which I was consulting. For two years, I had worked regularly with her in her role as vice president for operations in a medium-size human services organization. Nathan, her boss and the president of the company, had asked me to coach her as part of a complex intervention plan.*

"Because Nathan took away my job last night, and I want to know if you talked to him about it," she said bluntly.

The announcement surprised me because of its timing. I had discussed Mary's performance and the needs of the organization with Nathan on several occasions. I knew he was disappointed in what she had accomplished; he felt she was difficult to work with in many ways and had fielded a steady stream of complaints and questions about her actions and behaviors during the past several years. Nathan had mentioned that he was considering a change and talked to me about several options, but he had never indicated he was close to a decision.

"As you know, I've talked on and off with Nathan about our work together. I knew he was talking to you about some of his concerns and that he was thinking over his options, but I haven't seen or spoken to him in several weeks."

"So he didn't ask your opinion of this decision?"

"We've had several discussions about the changes he wanted to make, but, no, we didn't talk about this in our last discussion. Why?"

All of my responses were true, but this was one of those difficult moments that occurs when a coach works inside a complex organization and has relationships with several members of the leadership team. Defining zones of confidential and public information, deciding which opinions to share and which observations to keep to oneself, and performing the delicate task of retaining everyone's trust are arduous but necessary components of the work.

"Because I've been thinking that this would be a very short and final meeting. If you knew this was going to happen and didn't tell me, I'd consider it a major betrayal and grounds to never talk to you again."

Mary's anger was direct, as usual. Her challenge to me was equally straightforward. She was asking if she could trust me, whether I had colluded with her boss to deprive her of a position she enjoyed, and whether it was worthwhile continuing our coaching activity.

"As I said, I talked to Nathan on several occasions about you, your work, his response to working with you, and in general terms about what he was think-ing about doing. I didn't know he would be talking to you about this. Do you mind telling me what happened?"

Mary sat down and indicated that I should sit as well. She described her meeting with Nathan the previous evening, when he had informed her that he wanted to make a change in the management structure. He had said he was pleased with much of her work, but her inattentiveness to detail and process, her difficulties in working with certain colleagues, and her in-ability to keep him regularly and thoroughly informed about her areas of responsibility had led to his decision to replace her in the operations job. He had not asked her to leave the organization. Instead, he had suggested that she think about things for several days, and then they would decide together what steps to take next.

As Mary described the interaction, her response, and Nathan's behavior, she oscillated between near tears and rage. She railed against Nathan's cowardice, his inability to be direct, and his failure to provide feedback to her before the fateful meeting. Her list of accusations, injuries, and threats was quite exten-sive, and I found myself swept up in the power of her anger, humiliation, and sadness. It was fully thirty minutes before I spoke.

"What do you see as your options?" I asked tentatively during a brief lull in her stormy speech.

"Well, clearly, I'll look for another job. I can't stay here under these conditions."

"Did Nathan ask you to leave?"

"Of course not. He couldn't say what he wanted me to do. He was his typical wishy-washy self."

"Would you consider another position with the organization?" I asked.

"He said something about taking over one of the operating units, but I would only do that if the conditions were perfect. I'm so sick of trying to do a job with no resources, no support, and no idea of what people want."

We went on to discuss the potential in this other position and what Mary's negotiating stance should be in her subsequent discussions with Nathan. By the end of the hour, she was more oriented to clarifying what she needed to ask of Nathan. We also discussed her emotional responses to the changes and how she might give herself room over the coming weeks, if not months, to adapt to the *pain of altered circumstances, avoid destructive acting-out behavior, and maintain a working relationship with Nathan in the event that the job he had mentioned was one she would consider taking—at least while she looked at her options outside the organization.*

"I guess I'll have to keep talking to you until I'm through with this mess," Mary said as our time came to a close.

The teasing tone in her voice told me that part of our working relationship had been preserved.

"You know I'll try to be as helpful as I can. I'll set up another meeting with your secretary," I replied as I shook her hand.

"You do that, but if I find out that you did talk to Nathan, you can forget the whole thing," she threw at me as I walked out the door.

I begin this chapter with the case of Mary because it illustrates the complexities of coaching executives in large organizations and demonstrates that coaching, like any other form of intervention, does not always work. When Mary and I started our coaching relationship, everyone involved—from Nathan, to colleagues who knew about the initiative, to Mary herself—expressed optimism and the hope that intervention would help her fulfill her potential for leadership in the organization. She was widely known as a bright, energetic, aggressive, but somewhat abusive leader who struggled with her temper and had to work hard to maintain a disciplined approach to management. Part of my initial assessment of the organization revealed both the critical role that she played in operations and the difficulties her colleagues experienced with her.

I found the work with Mary to be quite challenging. She was incredibly smart; intuitively sophisticated about people, politics, and organizations; extremely competent in the core service technologies of the organization; and nationally known in her discipline. However, she also deliberately and at times seemingly gleefully hurt people with stinging criticisms, sarcastic remarks, and huffy withdrawals when angered. The effect on her colleagues was often devastating. Although she was widely respected for her passion, intuition, and technical expertise, they hated to see her enter their areas because of the difficulties she caused.

All these issues were raised in a number of monthly coaching sessions with Mary over several years. She made significant improvements in her interpersonal style, and the frequency of complaints about her decreased. However, she was still unwilling to hold regular management meetings, coordinate the efforts of her staff, or find ways to support their development. Energetic to the point of agitation, she often roamed the halls and seemed unable to stop herself from intruding on her colleagues. She also refused to see it as part of her job to keep Nathan fully informed and organized in his own approach to operations. She often disagreed with my recommendations and suggestions regarding her need to improve her ability to manage up. I coached Nathan to be direct with her about his needs and expectations, and I knew from both of them that he had done so repeatedly. Mary simply did not take these messages seriously. She frequently responded to Nathan's requests by saying that he had a real problem and that I should coach *him*.

Despite my best efforts, Mary made only superficial changes in her behavior. She decreased her unannounced intrusions on staff but held meetings that were unfortunately irregular and largely ineffective, continued to publicly and privately criticize Nathan and anyone else she thought deserved it, and expected the whole organization to adapt to her. To be honest, I felt routinely defeated by her insistence on more or less continuing her usual behavior. As far as Nathan and Mary were concerned, coaching had been largely a failure, yet we continued because of its overall contribution to stabilizing the administration. Nathan told me several times that Mary would otherwise be doomed as a manager. He was especially understanding about my limited coaching success with Mary because he, too, felt that he had failed with her.

The unhappy outcome of my work with Mary has been painful to contemplate. I have repeatedly questioned my judgment, technique, and motivation as a result of what happened. I felt guilty for failing to help Mary and embarrassed whenever the topic came up in the organization. Nathan did not terminate my coaching contract because I had attained my share of successes in other areas, and he continued to value our work together. However, I was anxious and paid close attention to my other coaching activities in an effort to minimize additional negative outcomes.

Coaching Failure and Negative Outcomes

I share this story in order to illustrate one of the most critical issues facing practitioners who want to coach executives. This type of coaching can be difficult and professionally dangerous. Clients are often personally and organizationally powerful and have achieved at least moderate success in their careers. For coaches, failure may mean an end to consultation contracts, diminished professional reputations, and adverse emotional and physical reactions; clients who fail despite coaching assistance may suffer job loss, significant career derailment, family distress, and mental and physical health problems. This point was driven home during a recent, informal conversation with several senior colleagues, during which one of them confessed quite honestly that he always felt a certain sense of terror and fear of failure when he walked into a client organization. Five extremely experienced consultants were gathered around that table, and, in very short order, every one confessed to the same feelings. Consulting is exciting work in a glamorous field, but not only do we occasionally fail, our efforts sometimes make situations worse. Despite the importance of knowing how to manage these issues, there is virtually nothing available in the literature to help executive coaches face these problems.

My purposes in this chapter are to

- Describe and define failure and negative outcome in executive coaching
- Explore some of the factors that contribute to failure and negative outcome
- Provide guidance on how to determine if coaching is in the process of failing or producing negative outcomes
- Briefly delineate some methods to prevent or ameliorate the effects of poor or ineffective coaching

Defining Coaching Failure and Negative Outcomes

It is important to realize that success and failure in coaching exist along a continuum, with complete success at one end and total failure at the other. As coaching approaches complete success, it is unlikely that significant negative outcomes will be experienced by clients, their organizations, or coaches. The opposite is equally true—the closer coaching approaches total failure, the more likely it is that those involved may suffer significant problems.

As in the case of Mary, coaching failure can be partial and still result in negative outcomes. Mary succeeded in modifying some of her behaviors and was using some different skills, but the progress that she had made was judged insufficient. Her boss, Nathan, ultimately ran out of patience and moved to replace her. The emotional effect on Mary was, to say the least, substantial. The physical effect was also significant. Subsequent contact with her revealed that she had gained weight and was being treated for physical illnesses such as stomach problems, back pain, and chronic headaches. After a six-month search aided by an outplacement firm, she found a job running a small human services agency in another city. However, she took a significant pay cut, considered it a step backward in her career, and doubted she would ever reach her professional goal of running a large public agency.

Coaching failure occurs when, in the opinion of everyone involved, the client fails to make substantial improvement in the goal areas for which coaching has been contracted. Some of these areas include

- Enhancing performance of job duties
- Promoting achievement of professional goals
- Improving management and interpersonal skills
- Enhancing the ability to be courageous in difficult situations
- Increasing managerial awareness and self-awareness
- Enhancing emotional maturity and flexibility
- Improving the ability to manage psychological and behavioral conflicts
- Increasing personal well-being, resilience, and vitality

These are similar to the typical goals established by clients and coaches at the outset of an engagement (Kilburg, 1996b).

Negative outcomes can be defined in somewhat more detail, although a careful review of all potential negative results is beyond the scope of this paper. However, major ones include the following:

- Job loss

- Career derailment

- Negative effect on professional and personal reputations

- Financial losses

- Marital and family problems

- Mental and physical health problems

- Loss of professional and personal ambition and motivation

- Increased suspiciousness, decreased trust, and interpersonal difficulties

- Loss of resiliency, vitality, and well-being

Coaching failure cannot bear the sole responsibility for these negative outcomes, but it is vital to recognize that there is a great deal at stake in coaching situations. Clients, their organizations, colleagues, and families seek help from coaches in difficult and often threatening circumstances. The unstated assumption may be that the coach will fix whatever problems exist so that personal and professional advancement can proceed. Guiding our clients toward publicly expressing these assumptions and then negotiating mutual agreement on goals will always be a critical test of coaching competence. Clear and well-understood assumptions among all involved represent a tremendous contribution toward reaching the client's goals. Without them, client and coach may be lulled by a false sense of security, believing that all will be well even if no progress is made.

Factors That Contribute to Failures and Negative Outcomes

Table 10, first presented in Kilburg (1996b), outlines some of the major factors contributing to failures and negative outcomes for both clients and coaches. These factors are discussed below.

Factors Involving Clients

The client's ways of functioning mentally and emotionally constitute five major factors that are of paramount importance to the coaching effort.

First, coaches must always be aware that people can succeed in life and still have serious psychological problems. They should be prepared to assess in general terms the kinds of psychological problems that may be present in

---

Table 10

Factors Contributing to Failure and Negative Coaching Outcomes

In Clients

1. Serious psychological problems

2. Serious interpersonal problems

3. Lack of motivation

4. Unrealistic expectations of the coach or the coaching process

5. Lack of follow-through on homework or intervention suggestions

In Coaches

1. Insufficient empathy for the client

2. Lack of expertise or interest in the client's problems or issues

3. Underestimation of the severity of the client's problems or overestimation of the coach's ability to influence the client

4. Overreaction to the client

5. Unresolved disagreements with the client about the coaching

6. Poor technique (e.g., inaccurate assessment, lack of clarity on coaching contract, poor selection and/or implementation of methods)

---

their clients. Some coaches include psychological tests in their assessment processes in order to make the initial determination. Those who are not clinically trained may find it useful to include psychologists so as to ensure exploration of these areas.

Second, serious interpersonal problems could make coaching difficult for some clients. Coaches are frequently asked to intervene with clients who are having problems getting along with others in the organization. Such clients may be hypercritical, argumentative, mistrustful, mean, vindictive, or simply unskilled. Their colleagues and subordinates might indicate that

291

they have been injured by the person, who also has been impervious to feedback. Clients with serious interpersonal problems often have difficulty forming and maintaining relationships, yet they can do a great deal of good or even excellent work. At times, they are essential to the success of a company but are often widely known as problem people. Such clients will bring their patterns of relating into coaching, and coaches can expect to experience similar interpersonal difficulties. These clients may well need to supplement the coach's feedback with additional learning experiences such as the interpersonal labs provided by National Training Laboratories or individual or group psychotherapy.

In my experience, many of these clients are routinely repeating past patterns of learned relationships and behaviors. If a client starts to treat a coach as though he or she were a significant person from the client's past, it is imperative that this issue be brought to light and explored. I often find it useful to ask my clients if problem people or situations remind them of important passages or characters from their personal lives. This simple question often leads to amazing stories from and insights for clients.

A third factor that can influence coaching outcomes is the client's motivation to change. This quality also lies on a continuum. The ideal client takes change seriously, asks for and performs homework assignments, and seeks additional avenues for growth. At the other end of the continuum, a person who turns every session into a debate, has difficulty adhering to an appointment schedule, demonstrates little or no self-awareness, and seems oblivious to feedback represents a great challenge for coaches. Such clients are often referred for assistance because they have significant corporate responsibilities and have performed some job duties very well but are at risk of career derailment. The best way to motivate such clients is to have their bosses clarify the need for change and explain the consequences of failure. There are many unmotivated clients, and coaches must therefore include these assessments in their initial appraisals.

A fourth factor involves expectations on the part of some clients that coaching will work without their active participation. It is almost as if these individuals believe in the magical powers of the coach. They may well keep appointments, listen and participate enthusiastically, and express great appreciation for the coaching. They believe that such an attitude is enough to guarantee success, and they will rarely think about the coaching activities after a session is over. Another common pattern occurs when a client routinely violates aspects of the coaching agreement. Frequent cancellations or missed appointments and/or failure to follow through on commitments can be major signals that the coaching process is in trouble.

Fifth, the client who does not complete homework assignments or act on coaching suggestions presents a major problem. To be sure, managing their time is a constant source of tension for executives. Leaders are rarely current with their work and face demanding, anxiety-ridden challenges every day. For many executives, coaching looks like just one more appointment in an overbooked calendar. Clients will often make their views known fairly early in the coaching engagement. If a client can barely remember what was discussed in the previous session, uses a busy schedule as an excuse for not following up on coaching suggestions or assignments, or simply seems indifferent to the intervention, you can be reasonably sure that the coaching effort will be arduous and rife with problems.

In these five situations, reviewing the coaching agreement will often clarify the need for follow-through and homework. In my experience, most clients do want to succeed and do not want to waste their time. For this reason, exploring the ground rules, detailing the limitations of coaching effectiveness without some effort on the part of the client, and analyzing the obstacles to better cooperation can correct a difficult situation. In still other cases, you may simply need to provide the client with reminders and notes.

However, full confrontation may be in order for a small number of individuals. On these occasions, coaches should review and clarify the sanctions for their services. If superiors or human resources (HR) professionals are involved in the contracts, coaches are well advised to confer with them before taking action. At times, consultation with an outsider concentrates a client's attention quite well. However, this is a risky type of intervention that may cause resentment and long-term deterioration in the coaching relationship. The ability to face and resolve issues of client motivation is the hallmark of high-level, sophisticated coaching. It is the most difficult aspect of coaching work and requires training, conditioning, support, and courage.

Factors Involving the Coach

As indicated in Table 10, there are a number of ways in which coaches themselves may contribute to failure and negative outcomes. Six factors are discussed below.

First, if a coach lacks sufficient empathy for a client and fundamentally does not care whether he or she improves performance, solves problems, or achieves career advancement, the process will not go well. Nonempathetic coaches may succeed with highly motivated clients simply because their clients will do most of the work. But any challenging assignment is likely to highlight the lack of empathy. Coaches who find themselves having a hard time connecting with a client for any prolonged period should carefully review the assignment in question. This situation can represent a real ethical and professional dilemma because withdrawing from an assignment can be difficult. Nevertheless, withdrawal will be far less damaging than failure or negative outcomes. During the contracting phase, it is crucial that coaches take note of their feelings toward potential clients and the types of problems those clients are presenting. If a coach feels especially anxious or troubled by certain client characteristics, these responses must be explored thoroughly before the relationship continues. In addition, it may be helpful to schedule time during an assignment to assess how much progress is being made and what, if any, negative feelings the coach is experiencing.

Second, when coaches lack either expertise or interest in their clients' problems, it will be difficult to achieve success. Most people who have managerial or executive responsibilities tend to read others fairly well and will become impatient with incompetence. Despite the attractiveness of any particular assignment, coaches should be completely candid with themselves about whether they really can and want to help potential clients before entering into any agreements.

A third and related factor derives from a coach's inaccurate assessment of the client's problems or an inflated view of what he or she may be able to accomplish with a particular client. Accurate reality testing and setting of limits becomes increasingly critical for coaches as the complexity of assignments and organizational contexts intensifies.

Fourth, a coach's emotional reactions to a client may decrease his or her ability to respond effectively. The range of responses from coaches can be quite extensive. Both positive and negative responses lead to problems, but negative responses are most likely to produce failures and negative outcomes. Coaches who notice strong feelings, either before meeting with a client or after the session, should pay close attention. If such emotions are not recognized, correctly assessed, and carefully managed, they can impede the coaching work. In rare instances, coaches who find they cannot overcome their responses may terminate relationships and refer their clients to colleagues.

The fifth factor involves major disagreements between a coach and a client. Disagreements may arise over the client's behavior, demeanor, or responses; the goals of the coaching; or the activities or services the client wants the coach to perform. Unreconciled disagreements can lead to failure, while overt or covert conflicts threaten the coaching relationship and its effectiveness. Coaches must move quickly to bring such disagreements to the surface and then work constructively to resolve or manage them. Otherwise they will threaten the client's ability to make progress, and a coach may need to refer the client to another professional.

The sixth factor has more to do with the present nature of coaching itself than with any individual coaching experience. The subfield of executive coaching as a branch of consulting or organizational development is currently in its infancy. As I described in Kilburg (1996a, b), there are few empirical studies of coaching methods or outcomes. There are no agreed-on standards for practice or sets of competencies required to engage in executive coaching. Many coaching failures may occur because we simply do not know what the best practices are. I believe we must acknowledge that we are learning about coaching in the process of working with our clients and act accordingly. Those of us who are interested in coaching must acknowledge the current state of the field and recognize our possible limitations.

How Do You Know When Coaching Is Failing?

There are a wide variety of ways to determine whether or not coaching efforts are failing or producing negative outcomes. For the most part, coaches depend on their experience to evaluate progress with their assignments. In my experience, there are seven cues that provide early warning of a coaching assignment in trouble.

- A client reports lack of progress or regression on the goals of the coaching agreement.
- Lack of progress is reported by the client's supervisors, subordinates, or significant others.
- Coach and client experience a series of extremely difficult and/or nonproductive sessions.

- The client disregards certain aspects of the coaching agreement by, for example, repeatedly missing sessions with no effort to explain, apologize, or reschedule; not paying required fees; or failing to follow through on or adequately complete homework assignments.
- The client's psychological or physical health deteriorates.
- The client receives negative feedback, reprimands, or discipline from superiors.
- The coach intuitively feels that something is just not right.

A coach who experiences any one of these cues should immediately evaluate the client's response to coaching and the extent of his or her motivation for and/or ability to change. This analysis may lead to discussions with the client, and, in some cases, the coach may find it necessary to confront the client over what has been happening. Interventions that question the progress and effectiveness of the coaching process are very challenging and require a great deal of tact, sensitivity, courage, and dedication on the part of a coach. When a confrontation goes well, a client usually begins to make progress again, but when it does not, the coach should review the viability of the assignment. Evaluation of the coaching situation may lead to the conclusion that the client is not ready to change—at least in this way at this time—and the only option is to withdraw as professionally and tactfully as possible. In the long run, less damage is likely to result.

Prevention and Amelioration of Coaching Failure

Because the field of executive coaching is in an early stage of development and lacks research to guide practice, it seems somewhat presumptuous to describe how to prevent or ameliorate something that is little understood, barely defined, and rarely discussed by practitioners and theorists alike. Nevertheless, the realization that coaches can get into trouble with clients and that some assignments result in failure or negative outcomes has led me to think through these issues in my own practice and adopt some measures that may be useful for others to consider. The following suggestions are offered in that spirit.

First, I believe prevention begins with the coach's level of self-awareness. Helping an executive become more reflective and effective in his or her leadership and management practices presupposes the following conditions:

- The coach understands the tasks involved in coaching.

- The coach is capable of helping a client learn these tasks.

- The coach has the knowledge, skill, and ability to address the myriad types of issues and problems that can arise in an assignment.

This is complicated for anyone, and the ability to be reflective, self-aware, and self-challenging about the work of coaching provides the foundation for everything else. If a coach does not have such capacity, his or her coaching will likely be superficial and largely ineffective. Coaches must examine the methods they use and the frequency with which they engage in their own self-reflective practices. Keeping journals, reviewing notes, talking with colleagues, consulting psychotherapists, taking time for meditation, and seeking supervision can all help maintain sufficient self-awareness.

The second factor, which is closely related to self-awareness, is knowing our limitations as coaches. This kind of self-awareness applies to the point of view that guides coaching activities and incorporates such areas as the level of understanding of organizational, group, and individual behaviors; knowledge of business practices in for-profit and nonprofit organizations; diagnostic and intervention skills; and an understanding of the various leadership and management characteristics required by today's chaotic and competitive global environments. Along with point of view, coaches must know the professional foundations on which their work stands. Although I firmly believe that professionals from a wide variety of disciplines can coach successfully, their approaches, strengths, and weaknesses will flow from their views of the client's world. A coach with a professional base in business tends to proceed differently from someone whose initial preparation was in clinical or organizational psychology. Eventually, both types of coaches encounter similar problems with clients. Business-trained coaches need to acquire some of the knowledge and skills of the psychologist; similarly, psychologists must learn about business and management in order to successfully coach executives.

Third, coaches can avoid a great deal of trouble by exercising caution and sensitivity while negotiating agreements. Careful discussion of goals, clarification of expectations, and thoughtful exploration of potential roadblocks during the first phase of coaching will enable practitioners to refer back to their working contracts whenever difficulties crop up. If a joint review of the coaching agreement illuminates misunderstandings or major differences between coach and client, the contract should be renegotiated and then rewritten. Clarity and agreement on the contract lay the groundwork for a firm and durable foundation of trust and understanding.

Fourth, coaches must be careful about establishing and maintaining effective containment with their clients. Good containment consists of clear, carefully negotiated agreements. It also requires the systematic attention of both coaches and clients to the details of the coaching process (including regular appointments, an empathic connection, and meaningful, in-depth dialogues). (For more discussion of the features of containments, see Kilburg, 1997.) Breaches in the working relationship (such as a series of missed appointments, carelessly expressed feedback from the coach, difficulties in dealing with strong emotions) will generate problems for both client and coach. Although both sides remain responsible for the quality of the relationship, coaches must take the lead in developing, maintaining, and monitoring the coaching relationship and its effectiveness. Done well, the relationship creates a strong and deep foundation for client progress.

Fifth, some sort of formal risk assessment may be useful at the outset of a coaching assignment. On some level, most experienced coaches/consultants already do this by sizing up clients and situations during initial contacts and contract negotiations. Typically, we trust our intuitive feel for organizations and people to guide our decisions, but we may need to be aware of our own tendencies regarding risk assessment. For example, I know from my experience that I tend to be an optimist when it comes to evaluating the motivation and capacity of people to change.

Sixth, it is often valuable for coaches to schedule time for assessing progress and problems during coaching sessions and assignments. Coaches should not assume that everything is fine just because they cannot hear or see anything wrong. For clients, the process of talking about themselves—their strengths as well as the areas in need of development—can elicit strong reactions. Periodic reality checks should be the rule, not the exception. When debriefing progress and implementation problems with clients, management of the relationship becomes a paramount issue. The use of appreciative inquiry and Socratic methods can facilitate these discussions (see Cooperrider, 1996; Hammond, 1996; and Overholser, 1993).

Seventh, unless clients visit coaches in their private offices or coaching takes place exclusively away from the worksite, others will know that coaching is under way. The natural curiosity of human beings generally results in speculation about what might be occurring. Supervisors, HR professionals, and even subordinates may often know that clients and coaches are meeting and why. Other consulting activities may also be occurring at the same time, resulting in a general atmosphere of discussion and speculation. In such circumstances, clients will often be anxious about the confidentiality of their coaching sessions. Crucial questions about the coaching alliance may remain unspoken, especially when coaches have contact with superiors and/or others within the organization. The nature of communications— between coaches and clients and from coaches to organizations—must be clarified at the outset and should be discussed if circumstances change or whenever client or coach has any questions or concerns.

Eighth, coaching in large modern organizations can be very challenging. The rapid pace of change, the chaotic nature of the business environment, and the interplay of individuals, groups, and organizations constantly press on all members of an enterprise, even those who visit only periodically. Under such conditions, coaches must build and nurture relationships within the organizations in which they work. Coaches will be able to provide even more effective services to clients if they have multiple sources of information, are able to check the validity of rumors and gossip, and display the capacity to solve problems within their client organizations. Any relationships, of course, must be conducted with regard to the need for confidentiality discussed previously. However, such relationships, if used carefully, can be of enormous benefit to everyone. By making a well-timed suggestion to a supervisor or HR professional, a coach can create additional development opportunities, reinforce behavioral change, or simply provide support for a client who might be struggling with a new skill. Contact with others in the organization can also help to ensure continued support for coaching, even in the face of other organizational pressures and problems.

The ninth suggestion for preventing coaching failure and negative outcomes concerns the need for ongoing efforts at self-development. We cannot encourage and support our clients in their attempts to grow, learn, and change unless we know the agonies and joys of these processes firsthand. It is imperative that coaches schedule time to read widely, attend conferences at which the latest developments are described and discussed, and network as extensively as possible with other coaches. Such efforts will guarantee that coaching knowledge and skills are continuously developed and refined. Two additional methods may also assist in this process. In some geographic areas, professionals involved in coaching and consulting meet in small groups for peer support and supervision. Such peer groups can aid greatly in managing the isolation that accompanies coaching assignments. Similarly, hiring another person to serve as a shadow consultant during coaching activities guarantees as much support and input as possible.

When a coaching assignment ends with a negative outcome, it can be helpful to debrief the situation, events, and process with a variety of people. Utilize discussions with clients to explore their impressions of what happened and to identify lessons learned from the experience. In some instances, such debriefings have elicited commitments from clients to work further on developing the knowledge and skills they need. Several clients have hired me to continue working with them as they exit one organization and either search for or undertake new assignments in other enterprises. Retaining an organizational consulting assignment after a failure or negative outcome may require additional discussion with supervisors and/or HR managers.

In summary, everyone involved in developing and extending the emerging field of executive coaching should be mindful that it is in the early stages of evolution. Coaching assignments carry risks for every participant, and failures and negative outcomes happen more often than we might like to admit. By paying careful attention to the structure and methods of coaching, we can reduce the occurrence of negative outcomes. However, coaches must be prepared to face up to their failures and use them as growth engines for their own development. If we do, I believe success rates for executive coaching will continue to improve.

Note

Correspondence concerning this paper should be addressed to Richard Kilburg, 5 Barrow Court, Towson, MD 21204.

References

Cooperrider, D. L. (1996). The child as agent of inquiry. *OD Practitioner* 28 (1 and 2): 5–11.

Hammond, S. A. (1996). *The thin book of appreciative inquiry.* Plano, Texas: Kodiak Consulting.

Kilburg, R. R. (ed.). (1996a). Executive coaching. *Consulting Psychology Journal: Practice and Research* 48 (2) (special issue).

———. (1996b). Toward a conceptual understanding and definition of executive coaching. *Consulting Psychology Journal: Practice and Research* 48 (2): 134–44.

———. (1997). Coaching and executive character: Core problems and basic approaches. *Consulting Psychology Journal: Practice and Research* 49 (4): 281–99.

Overholser, J. C. (1993). Elements of the Socratic method, I: Systematic questioning. *Psychotherapy* 30 (1): 67–74.

PART V

SPECIAL
COACHING
SITUATIONS

[1 4]

THE ISOLATED EXECUTIVE

How Executive Coaching Can Help

GAE WALTERS

*It is strange to be known so universally
and yet to be so lonely.*

—Albert Einstein

Mark and Paul,[1] recently promoted to senior executive positions, sit alone in their respective offices a continent apart, similarly troubled, frustrated, and isolated. Both produced impressive results for their organizations and were promoted to lead major divisions with significantly broader spans of control and increased fiscal responsibilities. However, they—like countless other executives—are struggling with a growing sense of isolation that seems to parallel their upward movement in the organization. To these isolated executives, people appear more reluctant to share information, staff members seem less forthcoming about emerging issues, department heads don't engage as openly in dialogue, and colleagues have distanced themselves.

During my seven years as vice president of organizational development for an international luxury hotel company, I was asked by executives all over the world to explain this shared experience of executive isolation. These executives reported that it really *is* lonely at the top, and they often struggled to make sense of their loneliness. Because our hotel company, as the recipient of the prestigious Malcolm Baldridge Quality award, was often used as a benchmark organization, I was frequently asked to share our approach to executive development with other leading organizations throughout the world. With these different executives in different companies, I again found that isolation was a common problem. As a leadership development trainer and executive coach, I have worked with hundreds of executives over the past sixteen years in both large and small organizations (including aerospace, entertainment, law, medicine, banking, fashion, engineering, telecommunications, and information technology). In this chapter, I describe the insights and strategies that have been particularly useful in my work with these isolated executives.

Executive Isolation

The goals of this chapter are to

- Examine the dilemma of the isolated executive and present examples of two executives who became isolated

- Identify a key individual difference—Extraversion or Introversion—that influences the nature of the isolation executives are likely to face

- Describe how *extraverted* executives become isolated and how executive coaching can help overcome this isolation

- Describe how *introverted* executives become isolated and how executive coaching can help overcome this isolation

- Discuss the role of organizational character in understanding executive isolation

Acting Alone versus Becoming Isolated

Leaders must occasionally act alone for good and justifiable reasons. There are times when a decision must be made, and consulting others might be problematic. Effective leaders know when to include others and, more important, when not to include them. There is, most certainly, a time for independent action. Heifetz (1994) outlined three situations in which leaders must act decisively and alone. The first is when the task at hand is so great that it may overwhelm the group and there is no prevailing norm of teamwork with which to tackle the problem. The second occurs when a participative process might further intensify friction among competing factions. And the third is when a crisis situation does not allow the time to engage in a more participative process.

Executives who rise from the ranks of collaborative, team-based organizations quickly discover that one of the hallmarks of this new senior level of leadership is the increased requirement for solitary decision making. In such situations, information may be collected from many people and sources, strategies may be explored and discussed with staff, ideas may be generated in brainstorming sessions, and consultants may be brought in to contribute their particular expertise; however, the senior executive must finally pull away from others, close the door, and decide alone.

The solitary decision making discussed above is situational in nature and is acknowledged and accepted by the organization. However, there are other circumstances that lead to executive isolation. Those working in the field of executive development must first differentiate between the necessary solitary decision making that is a part of senior leadership and the isolation that becomes a source of difficulty for both the leader and the organization.

Two Isolated Executives

The two case examples presented below illustrate how executives can become isolated.

Case Example 1: Mark

Mark, the executive vice president of operations for a worldwide luxury hotel company, was well known throughout the organization for his multitasking ability and action orientation. He began this morning in his customary way, in his home gym with his personal trainer. He had invited two members of his senior staff to join him in the gym so he could combine the workout with a strategy session. When Mark completed both tasks, he drove to the office, making a series of phone calls as he went. He arrived in time to launch a brainstorming session exploring potential international hotel sites. He took several phone calls during this meeting, since he was simultaneously negotiating with the city planner from a Colorado resort community who was balking at an expansion project that was to be announced the following week. Key staff members knew that it was OK to pop in to ask a quick question, and at least three did. As soon as the meeting ended, Mark left the office and drove to the hangar where the corporate jet was waiting. Colleagues who were accompanying him on the trip came prepared to discuss and recommend candidates for the general manager position at the Barcelona property. Mark made his selection, and the announcement was drafted on board and sent electronically. During the trip, Mark enjoyed his time in the various hotels and didn't limit his interactions to his executive colleagues. He always made it a practice to spend time visiting the hotels and restaurants, engaging employees in conversation, and greeting many by name.

Yet despite his outgoing behavior, when Mark devoted time to his own leadership development with his executive coach, he expressed concern about his growing sense of isolation. He wondered why people seemed to be withholding information and distancing themselves from him. He asked, "Why do the people who once came to me about practically everything now talk to me only about the decisions they have made and results they have obtained? They no longer pose questions or suggest ideas to explore." He became frustrated when people informed him of problems only after they were solved, especially when he believed he could have cut through the divisional gulfs that impeded progress and probably had created the problems in the first place. Upset by this turn of events, he asserted, "We've got to function as a team!" Mark's most recent promotion required much more travel. He observed that prior to his promotion, when he was based in the corporate office, he felt "intuitively in sync" with his team. Now, as the head of five regions, he said, "I don't feel a part of *anyone's* team. I'm never anywhere long enough to connect."

Mark's leadership style is fueled by a highly active and interactive approach to his work and his people. He is energized, inspired by, and achieves his greatest clarity of thinking when engaged with the external world. His ability to keep multiple tasks moving simultaneously enables him to initiate and accomplish an amazing array of projects. However, Mark has been described by others in the organization as overwhelming, inconsistent, and exhausting. One of Mark's staff members summed up his style: "When Mark gets excited about an idea, he's red hot . . . but *you* can get burned, and then you learn."

Case Example 2: Paul

Paul was selected to head a large design and development company created by the merger of two previously autonomous organizations. He was confident that his clear vision of what was needed to create a cohesive new organization, coupled with his broad base of experience in the field, made this new leadership role a good fit for him.

Soon after his selection, Paul invited four people to meet with him in a secluded off-site location to devise a plan for his first 100 days in office. He outlined his strategic vision, the challenges he foresaw, the factions that currently existed, and his ideas for reorganizing. Because Paul was an unknown quantity to one side of the newly merged organization (and was not naturally one to seek out people and introduce himself), part of the plan involved a series of brown-bag lunches during which Paul would outline his vision for the organization and answer questions about himself.

At the conclusion of the strategy session, Paul took the written plan with him, refined it, and decided who would fill the newly created positions. When he assumed the presidency, he announced the members of the executive team and began implementing his plan. He executed the steps flawlessly, tracked his performance against the plan, and made adjustments as needed. He met with key people one on one to ensure that they were clear about their responsibilities, goals, and objectives. After Paul's initial series of meet-and-greet sessions, he redirected his energy and time to battles on the corporate front, believing that his vision had been clearly articulated. He had confidence in his carefully selected executive team and didn't want to micromanage this talented group. His interactions with the staff, therefore, became less frequent as he attended to the larger corporate challenges.

People throughout the organization, especially those who had originally been skeptical of Paul and the merger, were impressed. The launch of the new company was extremely successful, and Paul's leadership created a sense of cohesion that was essential to the effectiveness of the merger.

However, this honeymoon period lasted only a few months. The first signs of trouble came during a strategic planning retreat scheduled for Paul and his senior staff at midyear. Now that the organization was in place and project work was well under way, Paul wanted his executive staff to report on the progress of each of their divisions, establish subsequent steps, and design the framework for the year ahead.

The retreat did not go well. Paul's carefully constructed agenda fell apart after the first hour. People brought up issues that were unknown to him and which they felt called for immediate attention. Taken by surprise, Paul said he needed some time to examine the issues before he could respond. He felt that to react immediately would be premature and that more study was needed before conducting any discussions, and certainly before taking action. The retreat continued, but interaction was low and tension remained high. When Paul got home from the retreat, he reassembled the team that had helped him design his original strategy and expressed his frustration and disappointment that what had started so well seemed to have derailed so seriously. He asked, "Why didn't anyone on my staff tell me that these issues were bubbling underneath the surface, ready to explode? We might have had time to design a plan of action." He felt he had been blindsided and knew that there were more important corporate issues on which he needed to focus his attention.

Paul's carefully orchestrated approach to leadership and organizational initiatives grows out of a style that is very different from Mark's. Paul derives energy and inspiration from the internal world of thought and reflection. He is known as a master planner and a visionary leader, extremely thorough and focused. He is seldom caught off-guard and is always ready with Plan B if Plan A meets with resistance. Paul's people, however, report feeling excluded and in the dark. They complain that it takes an inordinately long time to get an answer from Paul and sometimes wonder if opportunities are missed due to lack of action.

A Key Individual Difference:
Extraversion versus Introversion

Mark and Paul are experiencing common, but not necessary or inevitable, forms of isolation. The remainder of this chapter describes a personality characteristic that influences why and how leaders become isolated and explains how executive coaches can help them overcome their isolation.

While all leaders share some basic responsibilities for making decisions and leading people, their styles and behavior can be very different in practice. One key way in which leaders differ is their orientation to the outside world. Some leaders, like Mark, find that decision making is easiest when it is based on wide-ranging discussions with a variety of people. To convince others about those decisions, such leaders seek opportunities for interaction, preferably face-to-face. Other leaders, like Paul, approach their leadership duties differently. For them, decision making is best done in solitude after a careful analysis of essential factors. If they devote sufficient thought, research, care, and consideration to making the decision, it will be right and therefore convincing to others. Either leadership style can be effective—or ineffective.

Carl Jung, in his book *Psychological Types* (1971), identified the two styles as Extraversion and Introversion and identified them as characteristic of a personality difference. Jung's work was expanded by Katharine Briggs and Isabel Briggs Myers, who created the *Myers-Briggs Type Indicator* (MBTI) instrument (see Myers, McCaulley, Quenk, and Hammer, 1998) to help people identify their natural personality preferences. Many executive coaches now use the MBTI personality inventory to provide executives with insight into their typical approaches to leadership challenges, the expected strengths of their approaches, and their possible blind spots. Recognizing and understanding the differences between Extraversion and Introversion are particularly useful when working with isolated executives because Extraverted and Introverted leaders tend to get isolated for different reasons and under different circumstances.[2] Use of the MBTI assessment tool can help executives understand and overcome their isolation.

Defining the Differences

The words *Extraversion* and *Introversion* are often understood as stereotypes and are therefore discounted. Many who hear such words think of the behaviors commonly associated with them (for example, that Extraverts are loud and Introverts are shy). According to Jung, *Extraversion* and *Introversion* really describe how people derive their energy in the world. This process is important because executives use their preferred sources of psychological energy (Extraversion or Introversion) to initiate and sustain information gathering and decision making. All executives collect pertinent data and apply experience, generate ideas and explore options, organize and prioritize the information collected, and make decisions. However, the source of the energy that stimulates and drives these functions of observation and decision making is found in one's preference for Extraversion or Introversion. Executive coaches who can explain Extraversion and Introversion accurately and use these differences appropriately find that they can help executives toward significant breakthroughs in their learning, self-awareness, self-acceptance, and behavior change.

In Jungian terms, Extraverts are people who draw their energy from action and interaction with the external world. They work best with people around them as they talk their way through to new ideas and decisions. They often prefer to learn about things through experience or interactions with others instead of reading about them in books or memos.

Introverts, on the other hand, draw their energy from reflection and contemplation within the internal world of thoughts and ideas. Ideas and clarity develop most readily when the Introvert is being quietly contemplative. Instead of thinking out loud in the external world of action and dialogue, the Introverted leader seeks some degree of solitude in which he or she can hear the quiet inner voice from which Introverts draw psychological strength and energy.

Generally, the leader who functions in the Extraverted attitude tends to trust and be energized by input from the outer world. Mark, the hotel executive, clearly utilizes an Extraverted approach to his work. He is fueled and stimulated by action and interaction. The external world is a source of inspiration. Paul's leadership style illustrates the opposite preference, Introversion. He processes and distills information more efficiently when he can pull away from the world and concentrate on an issue without interruption. He says, "The quieter the setting, the better I think."

How Extraverted and Introverted Executives Become Isolated

Time-pressured executives will naturally seek the most efficient and accessible energy source available in order to drive the high level of activity demanded of them. Executives who understand how their preferences for

Extraversion or Introversion affect their work can become more effective in maintaining their focus and using their energy well. They can anticipate the potential pitfalls inherent in each approach and learn to balance their preferences with alternative behaviors. Those who are unaware of their natural styles and/or fail to balance their inclinations by incorporating other behaviors can experience the interpersonal alienation that leads to isolation.

Leaders become isolated in two ways: through externally created conditions and self-imposed ones. Both Extraverts and Introverts may move toward isolation because their colleagues and staff are pulling away from them or as a result of their own desire to remove themselves from the interactive field. Because of the differences in the natural approaches of Extraverted and Introverted executives, their paths to isolation—whether externally or internally created—can appear quite different.

Extraverted Executives

An executive like Mark, whose psychological preference is for Extraversion, is most likely to find his or her energy heightened or enhanced when acting in or interacting with the external world. Dialogue and discussion with others stimulate and enhance the Extravert's thought processes. New ideas spring forth and grow in an environment that provides immediate feedback, both verbal and visual. The give-and-take of conversation clarifies ideas. Simply being in the presence of others often creates a surge of energy that enlivens and rejuvenates an Extraverted leader.

Extraverted leaders are drawn to interact with the external world for these reasons. They are likely to bring people together to bounce ideas around, to get topics and issues out on the table, and to think out loud. A naval officer compared his preference for Extraversion to a sonar system and explained, "To determine another vessel's position, sonar signals are sent out. As they bounce off objects and return, the vessel's position can be noted and a response formulated. I send out signals to my people, and the feedback I receive helps me determine my course of action." Extraverted leaders send out signals and may recalibrate their actions based on feedback received from the external environment.

Executives with a preference for Extraversion report that not being able to interact with others for long periods of time leaves them feeling listless, irritable, and out of sync.

Externally Created Isolation in Extraverted Executives

Mark discovered that his associates were increasingly reluctant to come to him to explore issues because of his tendency to spring into action immediately. For example, when Janet, a member of Mark's staff, expressed concern about the approach taken by a colleague, Hal, she was hoping to receive guidance from Mark. Mark, however, immediately called Hal and demanded an explanation. Instead of being helped by Mark's input, Janet felt exposed and embarrassed, and soon she and others on Mark's staff learned not to mention interpersonal concerns that they wanted to work out privately. Similarly, when Stephanie shared a preliminary outline of an idea, Mark liked the idea and wanted to run with it on the spot. He pushed for immediate implementation before Stephanie had taken care of all the necessary logistics. As a result, the project failed, and she was held responsible. After observing such incidents, people came to Mark less often with new ideas and instead waited until they had worked out the details themselves.

Extraverted executives have a natural propensity for action. They tend to make quick decisions, proactively seek out information from a wide variety of sources, stimulate exploratory dialogue, and serve as catalysts for energetic discussions. These attributes are generally recognized by the organization as leadership strengths. However, the Extraverted executive may also overwhelm and intimidate people, push staff members and ideas prematurely, unintentionally reveal confidences, and probe inappropriately. It is therefore valuable for Extraverted leaders to be aware of how and when their strengths may become liabilities and why people may begin to distance themselves.

Self-Imposed Isolation in Extraverted Executives

Extraverted executives may also deliberately distance themselves from others. This choice, while uncomfortable, often occurs when the executive discovers that supposedly confidential information has been shared without permission, resulting in feelings of betrayal. If the breach of confidentiality has negative consequences, the Extraverted leader may reevaluate the wisdom of thinking out loud, become increasingly wary, and limit the people to whom he or she expresses ideas and opinions. When such gradual limiting of contacts still fails to stop the flow of information, the Extraverted leader may withdraw altogether and become isolated.

In natural modes of functioning, Extraverted leaders generally believe that the external world provides the most fertile soil for the growth of ideas. Therefore, when an idea is in its early stages, Extraverts will often share and explore their thinking through discussions with others, confident that doing so will be beneficial. Extraverted executives may assume that everyone who participates in this kind of meeting understands its exploratory nature. However, newly appointed leaders may not yet have learned how powerful their words can be. Without an expressly stated request for confidentiality, others may enjoy the bit of reflected power that comes from sharing the inner thinking of a senior executive. Staff members may also interpret ideas as directives and begin to implement them, especially when a person with a preference for Introversion concludes, based on his or her own approach to such a situation, that the boss must have thought the idea through before sharing it.

Extraverted leaders are particularly vulnerable to information leaks and broken confidences. Their preliminary thoughts, whether intentionally divulged or innocently shared, can be thrust prematurely into the larger organizational world. When this happens, the Extraverted leader may become angry and distrustful and may eventually conclude that open dialogue is dangerous.

Extraverted leaders who have been seriously and adversely affected by disclosures of this kind may find their worldviews shaken. What was once a safe place—the external world of open dialogue—no longer feels safe, and, as a result, the Extravert may stop sharing information. Unfortunately, this self-imposed isolation can be immensely difficult for Extraverted executives. They are likely to feel imprisoned and cut off from their source of inspiration, energy, and intellectual vitality.

Coaching the Isolated Extraverted Executive

It's not surprising that an executive at this stage of isolation may seek a safe listener, a person who can be trusted and who will serve as a sounding board. Increasingly, senior executives seek out executive coaches as safe listeners. If the coach understands how the Extraverted executive arrived in this difficult position and recognizes the debilitating effects of isolation, he or she can play an essential role. The coach may become a trustworthy confidant with whom the leader can safely explore strategies, decisions, thoughts, and reactions.

There are three ways in which executive coaches can help Extraverted executives overcome their isolation and become more effective. Each is discussed below.

First, the coach can explain the concepts of Extraversion and Introversion and offer perspectives on the benefits and costs of the leader's natural style. When Extraverted executives are made aware of how their predisposition for action and interaction can lead to resistance from others, they often find the solutions strikingly simple. Because this is potentially powerful information and may help increase interpersonal understanding, it is also beneficial to facilitate a team meeting, with the leader present, to discuss the leadership implications of Extraversion/Introversion. Illustrating that project success rates increase when people are allowed to reflect and work out essential details prior to action is also persuasive.

Second, coaches can help Extraverted executives learn to make optimum use of their Extraversion by identifying specific skills and behaviors that could increase their effectiveness. It is important to remind the Extraverted executive that not all problems are equally urgent and to offer practice in prioritizing. Many executives find it helpful to create a series of questions that must be answered before they pick up the phone and place a call. Extraverted executives also need to learn to specifically express their wish that certain preliminary discussions remain confidential; along the same lines, they should make it clear when they are simply thinking out loud so that their random thoughts are not transmitted to their organizations as new policy directions.

And, third, executive coaches can help leaders develop their less-preferred Introverted side. It is helpful for Extraverted leaders to discuss and practice specific Introverted behaviors that they admire in Introverted leaders and/or that have produced good results for Introverted colleagues. Describing and acting out new behaviors are particularly important for Extraverted leaders when they are developing alternative approaches.

Mark, the Extraverted leader in our case example, solves problems best through interaction and action, so he chose to call a meeting of his direct reports to share what he had learned about his Extraverted preferences. He recounted specific examples that illustrated how his Extraverted approach had created problems for people on his staff. He asked for their feedback and made good on his promise to consider a plan of action before instantaneously responding to an issue. He still invites people to his morning workout sessions and continues to multitask throughout the day. But Mark has learned to lead in a more planned manner and not to react as hastily to external stimuli.

Introverted Executives

When Paul returned from his less than successful retreat, he reconvened his team of consultants and also spent time with the executive coach who had introduced him to the concept of psychological type. Paul explained what was happening in his new position and how frustrated he had become. He had completed the MBTI personality inventory several years ago, and he and his coach reviewed the implications of his Introversion preference and how that might be contributing to his current difficulties.

The road to isolation for Introverted leaders may be easier to understand than that for Extraverted leaders. When Introverts are deep in thought, the external world fades into the background while they attend to their rich inner dialogue. Therefore, Introverted leaders may not even hear the friendly "Good morning" offered by staff or colleagues and may not respond. Introverted leaders are sometimes perceived as cool, aloof, and distant—even arrogant. Introverted executives may not even notice this gradual distancing at first; they may believe that things are running smoothly with all their plans in place. Introverted executives are often shocked to discover that their teams are complaining about their lack of interest or involvement.

If the Extraverted leader's information-gathering system is akin to sonar, the Introverted leader's process of gathering information and deciding direction may be more aptly compared to the guidance system of a Cruise missile. Intelligence is gathered, the target is identified, navigational data are loaded, and the course is set. Once the missile is launched, it is not easily deflected.

Externally Created Isolation in Introverted Executives

Because organizational life is interactive and solitude is rare, Introverted executives typically develop a number of effective strategies for creating solitude even in the midst of a busy day. The resulting behaviors, however, often are misperceived and misunderstood and can lead colleagues and staff to move away from the Introverted executive—creating painful isolation.

For example, Paul's staff noticed that he often broke eye contact and looked away from the person who was speaking. They did not realize that Paul was listening intently and that looking away enabled him to concentrate on the speaker's ideas without being distracted by external cues. In addition, Paul often paused before answering a question or responding to a statement. These pauses occasionally occurred in the middle of a sentence as he scanned his internal landscape for the best example, analogy, or metaphor. His behavior reflected a natural style for an Introvert but was confusing to staff members and led to discomfort and reluctance to initiate interactions on their part. Paul's staff soon learned that they were better served when they submitted information in written form rather than in face-to-face interactions. In such cases, Paul could study and reflect on the request in solitude and then proceed to craft and polish his answer in his internal world. While this was a helpful discovery for them, it had the effect of further distancing Paul from his colleagues.

Self-Imposed Isolation in Introverted Executives

There are a number of ways in which Introverted executives cut themselves off from others. As issues grow in complexity and the consequences of their decisions become more profound, Introverted leaders may be drawn evermore inward. After all, the inner world is the place where they find clarity and craft their decisions. If Introverted leaders don't have enough time and opportunity to access their inner worlds, their frustration and anxiety are likely to increase.

Another source of stress for Introverted executives is the demand for immediate reactions or answers when urgency is unwarranted or when they believe a more studied approach is needed. In describing the advantages of his more deliberate approach, the Introverted senior vice president of an environmental engineering firm explained, "I practically design the entire project in my head first, thereby seeing potential pitfalls and avoiding huge costs and delays before we ever go out into the field."

Introverted executives often experience the strongest demands for immediate responses while participating in meetings, especially those dominated by Extraverts. If no agenda was available beforehand, Introverted executives often learn of the meeting topics on their arrival and will have had no opportunity to research or formulate their thoughts—a situation that is likely to increase their discomfort about making quick decisions or espousing positions. When Extraverted executives begin a rapid-fire give-and-take, with several people speaking simultaneously, Introverted executives may feel relegated to the sidelines. An Introverted executive described her reaction to such a meeting as reminiscent of trying to take her turn in a fast game of jump rope on the elementary school playground: "You want to get in and start jumping, too, but you can't seem to find an opening."

When a meeting appears to be spinning out of control, an Introverted executive may act out of frustration and annoyance by disengaging. At the end of the meeting, Extraverted executives may be heard to remark on how productive the meeting was, while Introverted executives are thinking that it was a waste of time. And the Introvert's disengagement may be noticed by others, who might conclude that the Introverted executive was uninterested or had nothing to offer. These assumptions may lead to further isolation from colleagues who will begin to think the Introvert is not a team player. The Introverted executive is often unaware of these reactions and is usually surprised to discover this perception through feedback.

Coaching the Isolated Introverted Executive
Introverted executives are at first puzzled and then increasingly frustrated to find that their natural style is so often misinterpreted. Since Introverts are not as likely to attend to feedback from the external world, they are frequently surprised (and sometimes hurt) to discover that they are seen as aloof, unapproachable, distant, and even unfriendly. The executive coach must understand Introversion and be free of stereotypical thinking about the preference in order to successfully coach the Introverted executive.

Executive coaches can help Introverted executives overcome their isolation and increase their effectiveness in three ways. Each is discussed below.

First, because Extraversion is often considered preferable by those who do not understand personality types, the coach can make a big difference for the Introverted executive by simply introducing the Jungian concept of Introversion as a positive attribute. When Introverted executives discover this dynamic, many experience a significant sense of relief. However, Introverted executives need to learn that while certain Introverted behaviors can enhance their ability to concentrate, these tendencies can lead to increased isolation and reduced flow of information from colleagues and subordinates. The same behaviors could also create interpersonal discomfort for colleagues and subordinates.

Second, coaches can help Introverted executives balance between their needs with the needs of their colleagues and subordinates. Facilitated discussions on communication strategies, with other team members participating, are sometimes helpful in contrasting the processes of Introversion and Extraversion. Instant recognition, new understanding, and tolerance often result when normal Introverted and Extraverted behaviors are contrasted (e.g., the preference for thinking things through versus talking things out [Brock, 1994] or for pausing versus responding rapidly). Introverted executives might suggest that subordinates provide brief, written overviews prior to their meetings because this will enable the executives to respond more quickly to requests or problems. In addition, it may be helpful for Introverted executives to recognize situations in which updates or progress reports alone represent satisfactory responses. This practice may help reverse the perception of indecisiveness that sometimes arises when Introverted leaders respond to requests for decisions only after they have completed thorough research and determined a comprehensive solution.

Third, keep in mind that "Introverts like to understand things before they try them" (Barr and Barr, 1994, p. 139). Therefore, to be successful, developmental activities must allow for observation and analysis. Introverted leaders may find it valuable to first observe and analyze the behaviors of Extraverted leaders whom they respect and admire. The Introverted executive might want to pay particular attention to the Extravert's body language, facial expressions, allotment of space, intonation, rate and volume of speech, and speed of response. After observing several Extraverted leaders, Introverted leaders should be encouraged to organize these observations into categories and take time to study the data. An important next step would involve mental visualization and rehearsal: Introverted leaders could envision themselves acting in specific ways and, most important, could visualize positive outcomes resulting from these new behaviors. Practicing the new behaviors privately or with their executive coaches can be beneficial. Afterward, the executives can use these Extraverted behaviors in the external world, observe the reactions, and adjust. This final step is likely to require extra effort: Introverted executives occasionally become stuck in analysis and should make a point of practicing their new behaviors externally. With the assistance and encouragement of the executive coach—and the positive reactions of staff and colleagues—this process can lead to a whole new range of behaviors for the Introverted leader.

Paul, our hypothetical Introverted executive, drew up a plan of action that began with a retrospective analysis of leaders whom he admired who exhibited Extraverted behaviors. He focused internally (he described it as "watching videotapes of these individuals in my mind") on the behaviors he felt were particularly effective but were not approaches he would have taken himself. He then practiced these behaviors with his coach and was persuaded to utilize some video feedback. In watching the videotape, he became aware of the importance of facial expression, vocal variety, and posture. He scheduled more "spontaneous" meetings with his staff and planned to spend one hour each day outside his office, seeking opportunities to interact with the general population of the organization. He developed a list of pertinent, open-ended questions to ask during these "impromptu" encounters. He practiced responding audibly and with a bit more animation as people answered these questions. Coincidentally, Paul had recently become a first-time father at the age of forty-seven, and he reported that many of these new ways of responding to people paralleled his way of interacting with his infant daughter. That model of behavior proved to be very helpful as an internal reference.

The Role of Organizational Character

In *The Character of Organizations: Using Jungian Type in Organizational Behavior,* William Bridges (1992) defined organizational character as "the personality of the individual organization" (p. 1). He used Jung's theory of personality types to characterize global differences among organizations. Bridges's work on organizational character can be very helpful in coaching isolated executives because it offers a way of looking at the organization's preference for Extraversion or Introversion. Understanding organizational character is especially valuable when the executive's preference for Extraversion or Introversion is different from the predominant style, or character, of the organization.

Bridges uses Jung's concepts of Extraversion and Introversion to describe an organization's orientation and the primary source of its energy. According to Bridges, Extraverted organizations

Can act quickly, sometimes even before they have taken the time to fully understand what they are up against. They can be impatient with efforts to get more information or to improve on the way it is interpreted. . . . Extraverted organizations depend heavily on conversations and meetings. . . . Written communications are considered unnecessary and tend to be mistrusted. (pp. 12–13)

When an Introverted executive is first immersed in a highly Extraverted organization, he or she can feel buffeted by the power and force of the Extraverted energy system, and if the executive tries to slow the pace to create some time for careful and quiet consideration, the organization is unlikely to understand or respond to the request.

Alternatively, according to Bridges, Introverted organizations

Usually try to avoid sudden actions . . . Their preference is to take in and interpret information carefully and to explore their options in detail before any action is taken . . . Introverted organizations usually rely heavily on written communication, even between people who often see each other face-to-face. Written communications permit more precision and give everyone time to think things over before a reply is made or an action taken. (pp. 12–13)

In an Introverted organization, the Extraverted executive might be viewed as acting too quickly, pushing too hard, and talking too much. If the Extraverted executive tries to prompt others to act or respond, the Introverted organization could become more resistant—and more distant. The Extravert may begin to feel like a stranger in a very strange land.

Both Introverted and Extraverted executives can find themselves isolated from their organizations when these character differences are not clearly understood or appreciated. As a result, introducing an executive to the insightful descriptions and analysis provided by Bridges can be helpful to the executive as well as to the organization.

Conclusion

Increasingly, executives are discovering a partner in the form of the executive coach. The coaching relationship may begin with skills acquisition or performance enhancement; however, if the coach consistently creates an environment in which the executive thinks more clearly, gains important insights into self and others, and explores creative alternatives, the coaching can address issues of greater subtlety and complexity. One such issue involves the degree of executive isolation. The executive coach can play an integral role in helping both Extraverted and Introverted executives avoid or overcome the isolation that can accompany leadership.

Notes

1 Mark and Paul—not their real names—are senior executives with Fortune 500 companies. Both are considered highly effective, as are the organizations they lead. The situations described are compilations of events that have taken place throughout their careers.

2 The MBTI personality inventory includes three other dichotomies: Sensing–Intuition, Thinking–Feeling, and Judging–Perceiving. Each of these dichotomies has a profound influence on a leader's style, and each one (plus the interaction among all four MBTI dichotomies) is very productive in executive coaching work. This chapter focuses specifically on the Extraversion–Introversion dichotomy because it offers the most valuable context and contrast for understanding executive isolation; space did not allow for an elaboration on the influence of all four dichotomies.

References

Barr, L., and N. Barr. (1994). *Leadership development: Personality and power.* Austin, Texas: Eakin Press.

Bridges, W. (1992). *The character of organizations: Using Jungian type in organizational behavior.* Mountain View, Calif.: Davies-Black Publishing.

Brock, S. (1994). *Using type in selling: Building customer relationships with the Myers-Briggs Type Indicator.* Mountain View, Calif.: CPP, Inc.

Heifitz, R. (1994). *Leadership without easy answers.* Cambridge, Mass: Belknap Press.

Jung, C. G. (1971). *Psychological types* (H. G. Baynes, trans., revised by R. F. C. Hull). *The collected works of C. G. Jung,* Volume 6. Princeton. N. J.: Princeton University Press. (Original work published in 1921.)

Myers, I. B., M. H. McCaulley, N. L. Quenk, and A. L. Hammer. (1998). *MBTI manual: A guide to the development and use of the Myers-Briggs Type Indicator* (3rd ed.). Mountain View, Calif.: CPP, Inc.

[15]

COACHING ENTREPRENEURS

BARRY DYM

R. STEPHEN JENKS

MICHAEL SONDUCK

*A*fter the board meeting, Harry was reeling. He asked himself what had happened. After all, in five short years, he had led the company from a rag-tag band of twenty technical people to a leading public company that was well known in the industry. Sales had grown from $5 million when he was brought in as president and CEO to $300 million in the current fiscal year. And, yet, the board had just handed him his hat!

Scenarios like this are all too frequent in the world of the entrepreneur. Often, these otherwise intelligent people neither see their demise approaching nor learn much from the experience. Instead, they tend to look outside themselves for the cause of their downfalls. "It's a strategy conflict with the board," they say, "or a palace coup by the vice presidents. Anyway, as we all know, when the team fails, the coach gets fired." Is it possible to help entrepreneurs learn from such lessons or, harder still, to move toward more sustainable forms of leadership? We think so. In this chapter, we will lay out a conceptual framework that has guided our work.

The chapter will first sketch the distinctive character of entrepreneurs and entrepreneurial organizations and the dramatic transition they must make toward professional management[1]—a transition that includes shared information and decision making and the construction of an infrastructure that operates somewhat independently of the entrepreneur. Next, it will examine the six challenges that we have found most entrepreneurs must face as they move from entrepreneurial to professional management. Finally, the chapter will explain to those who want to coach entrepreneurs the psychology of the change process involved in overcoming the six challenges.

The framework presented in this chapter is based on the authors' many years of experience in working with entrepreneurs (more than twenty-five years each) and observing the issues and paths to resolution that seem to be typical. The bulk of our work has been with entrepreneurs in technology-based businesses, although we also have worked in other fields, such as health care and education, where we have seen the same patterns. Our goal is to articulate those patterns in order to offer a useful guide to the process for those who coach entrepreneurs. While the pattern we identified probably does not apply to all entrepreneurs, we believe it has substantial validity, as we have found it to be common to the many with whom we have worked over the years. The case we use to illustrate the process of coaching entrepreneurs does not represent any one of our clients but is instead a composite of several of them.

The Executive Coaching Option

As coaches, we might hope for a better scenario for Harry. Instead of a board meeting that results in his being offered a buy-out in return for his voluntary resignation, he might begin a successful experience with executive coaching. Our example will explore a more productive path that might have started six months earlier with the following encounter.

One afternoon, Susan, a principal in the venture capital firm that had put up 30 percent of the founding stake and a woman Harry greatly respected, paid him a visit. After a slightly tense greeting, she got right down to business. She was there to report on a private meeting of a few of the outside directors. They were unhappy with his performance, she said. They had doubts about his ability to lead the company through the next couple of years. In her customarily blunt manner, Susan told Harry to get some help. The board wanted Harry to succeed, but their first loyalty was to the company and its customers, shareholders, and employees. If he did nothing to boost their confidence in him in the upcoming months, Susan said, she couldn't be sure that the purpose of her next visit wouldn't be to ask for his resignation. She left Harry with a list of coaches that she and other board members had put together based on similar experiences with other CEOs and suggested Harry give one or two of them a call.

Like many entrepreneurs, Harry didn't have a lot of experience in seeking outside help. The very nature of his personal success led him to rely mostly on his own counsel. But Harry understood the gravity of the situation, and, after a few days of soul-searching, discussions at home, and phone calls with close friends, he decided he'd better at least try to contact one or two of the coaches.

Entrepreneurs generally attribute their success to self-confidence and self-reliance. They trust their instincts, keep their own counsel, and find it difficult to rely on anyone—especially an unknown coach. Their usual response to trouble is to plunge in and work harder, take more control of the situation, and tough it out.

Let's assume however, that Harry accepts Susan's suggestion, calls a couple of coaches, and invites them to meet him. What can a coach do to win Harry's approval in the one hour allotted for the meeting?

First, he or she must demonstrate the capacity and experience to empathetically understand the entrepreneur's worldview, the business itself, leadership and organizational issues, and the personal dilemmas that arise in leading organizations. At the same time, the coach must also bring new knowledge and different perspectives to the situation and must demonstrate a willingness to engage with the entrepreneur in a challenging but unthreatening manner. A tall order!

As Harry sat back and thought about what had led up to this moment, he recalled some conversations he'd had with friends during the past few years. Several times, individuals he trusted had mentioned a "blind side." He had discounted their armchair psychology but now wondered if they were right. Maybe getting outside help wasn't such a bad idea. After suffering the proverbial knock upside the head, Harry could be ready to make the connections between his behavior and the business situation his company faces.

What's Distinctive about Entrepreneurs?

The entrepreneurial journey begins with the personality of entrepreneurs, which, from early on, shapes the organizations they build. The story begins with the willingness of these practical visionaries to shoulder responsibility for almost everything that happens, to take frequent, calculated risks, and to persevere in the face of great odds and almost constant pressure. Entrepreneurs are leaders by virtue of their actions, drive, purposefulness, and apparent certainty—qualities that inspire effort and loyalty in others. Above all, entrepreneurs are very determined people.

At the same time, entrepreneurs are also known to be inconsistent, untrusting, impulsive, and controlling. Visionary leadership sometimes turns to grandiosity. Certainty often masks uncertainty. The willingness to accept responsibility for everything that happens, the desire to be constantly in charge, may become arrogance and obstinacy that eventually isolate entrepreneurs, cutting them off from information and people, the life blood of their organizations.

Entrepreneurs generally form organizations that mirror their personalities: energetic, informal, innovative, driven, independent. At first, profit seems to takes a backseat to growth and the thrill of risk and challenge. Planning tends to be ad hoc, with budgets and financial controls almost absent. Training takes place on the job. Roles and responsibilities are defined by the tasks at hand, often shifting and overlapping one another. When the entrepreneurial organization is small, informality makes it agile, quickly adaptive to market demands.

There is, however, one major exception to the informality: the entrepreneur is in charge. These organizations are hierarchies; power and prestige flow directly from the leaders and from those who enjoy close relationships with them. In the short term, this set-up creates a clear sense of accountability. In the long term, it inhibits the development and retention of strong managers and the capacity for autonomous action. For example, if the leader must dedicate much of his or her activity to positioning the organization in the external world, he or she will have little time to devote to internal operations.

Methods and Approaches for Coaching Entrepreneurs

The executive coach is a consultant, albeit one who plays a special role. As with all consultation, identifying the primary client is a key first step, but the coach must keep in mind that there are often multiple clients. It may seem that the entrepreneur is obviously the primary client, but the situation is not that simple. Board members, other employees, or family members may also be clients.

The coach who sees the *entrepreneur* as the client, and is concerned primarily with the professional development or interpersonal success of this one person, is overlooking a key dimension of the client's success: the importance of the specific organization in which he or she is working. Entrepreneurs are not only managers and leaders of organizations, they often are significant owners, inventors, patent holders, financiers, and chief salesmen. To them, the business is more than a job. It is often their life, or a huge portion of it.

Conversely, when the coach sees the *organization* as the primary client, the focus shifts to improving the effectiveness of the whole company. This may lead the coach to ignore the entrepreneur's needs in favor of those of the larger organization. Unlike other instances of organizational consulting in which executive retention is only one dimension of a company's success, the entrepreneurial organization's success in such areas as customer loyalty, investor comfort, and key employee retention is inextricably linked to retention of the key leader. Larger, stabler organizations may have several leaders, but entrepreneurial organizations typically depend inordinately on the single entrepreneur to overcome business problems. In such a situation, the coach must maintain a careful balance, keeping both the goals of the entrepreneur and the goals of the organization firmly in mind.

The effective executive coach is part therapist, part consultant, and part business problem solver and must learn to balance the three sets of skills. This balancing act is especially important and particularly difficult with entrepreneurial clients because they are identified so strongly with their roles and organizations. Roles, interpersonal style, business goals, relationships, and organizational structure tend to merge, and it is hard to pull them apart in order to work on one theme at a time. In fact, it will be impossible to work on one theme without remaining aware of the larger context.

Coaching entrepreneurs, therefore, calls for versatility and breadth of knowledge from the executive coach. He or she must learn about the business itself, becoming knowledgeable about such factors as its financial, marketplace, and operating circumstances. The coach should form an independent assessment of the entrepreneur's relationships to other key individuals in the organization, including immediate subordinates, board members, and others. It is often useful for the coach to know about the involvement of family members, especially if they are investors or are active in the management of the firm. The executive coach must provide a long view, derived from the experience of seeing many entrepreneurial companies evolve and pass through predictable stages of development. By implication, therefore, we believe that coaching entrepreneurs should be done only by experienced coaches who have worked with executives and other clients in a variety of complex systems.

At the same time, the coach must help the entrepreneur squarely face crisis after crisis. The most important crisis revolves around the question of whether or not the entrepreneur will be able to lead the entrepreneurial organization into a more mature and stabler form. Almost all coaching relationships seek to resolve this apparent paradox: the same behaviors that contribute to an executive's success can, when overextended or misapplied, lead to failure. Simply put, being a powerful person is in itself no guarantee of powerful results. The self-reliance that distinguishes entrepreneurial executives may also be their Achilles heel.

As in any other form of executive coaching, coaches who work with entrepreneurs must identify the psychological, cognitive, and motivational issues or concerns that are exerting such a powerful influence in the direction of either enabling or disabling them. They must also identify the external (organizational) forces, such as culture, goals, and business processes, that are affecting them. In addition, we believe coaches must determine the position occupied by each client in terms of a sequence of challenges that are common to all entrepreneurs. These challenges are described in the next section.

Six Challenges for Entrepreneurs

In order to make the transition from entrepreneurial leadership to professional management, the entrepreneur must delegate authority and introduce planning, consistency, communication, and controls. These steps present the following developmental challenges:

- Perceiving the need to change versus denial and isolation
- Moving toward commitment and planning versus indecision and procrastination
- Accepting the pace of change versus doubt and uncertainty
- Tolerating instability and uncertainty versus regressing to old ways
- Working toward resolution versus fragmentation
- Reintroducing entrepreneurialism versus succumbing to bureaucratic lethargy

Life and business are never this neat, but we have placed these challenges in a developmental sequence because we believe it provides perspective and makes each stage more understandable. In addition, it captures much of the reality of the transition experience and may assist coaches in offering guidance along the way.

Perceiving the Need to Change

To begin the transition, there must be a clear perception of the need to change and a realistic assessment of the extent and effectiveness of the professionalization efforts that have already been undertaken. For example, entrepreneurs often want to do everything themselves. As a result, there are usually no management processes in place, and subordinates do not have the authority to establish such processes. This presents the coach with a "chicken or egg" problem. Should the organization develop a more robust infrastructure that will ease the entrepreneur's fears about letting go, or should the coach approach the entrepreneur at the psychological level first? If the coach looks for a single solution, this may become a never-ending problem. In our experience, both aspects of the situation, individual and organizational, should be addressed at the same time.

For a variety of reasons, entrepreneurs often deny their own perceptions and the urgings of others. They discredit evidence of the need for fundamental change, or the urgent nature of the need, and isolate themselves from those whose opinions differ from theirs. The need for change is frequently underscored by financially oriented people, such as accountants and venture capitalists.

Harry arranged to meet with James, an organizational consultant and executive coach. James was a little unsure of what Harry expected because, when Harry had set up the appointment, he had only said he wanted to meet to explore ways in which James could be of help to him during a phase of rapid growth in his company. James had worked with a number of entrepreneurial executives in the past and suspected there was a good deal more to the story. He hoped Harry would be open with him during the meeting. Harry began the meeting by giving James an overview of the company and its history, emphasizing its tremendous growth and success to date.

When James asked why Harry wanted help, Harry became strangely inarticulate and mildly defensive, finally saying that he had been urged by one of his board members to seek help. James then told Harry that he had been in similar situations with other successful entrepreneurs, and that sometimes a fresh pair of eyes and a different perspective could be useful. He also made clear to Harry that nothing they discussed would be shared with anyone without his explicit prior approval.

Given this reassurance, Harry relaxed and began to tell James some of what Susan had told him. He also revealed his distress at hearing that his leadership style was not effective. James responded by explaining to Harry that almost all successful entrepreneurs succeed initially on their internal strengths, but, as their organizations grow, the very strengths that supported the growth tend to become liabilities. Harry said that he definitely wanted to learn what would make him a more effective leader of a large organization.

Moving toward Commitment and Planning

Once the problems and general solution have been identified through joint diagnosis by the coach, the entrepreneur, and, often, other members of the organization, further progress demands commitment to implementing a plan of action. This may not be as simple as it sounds, especially given the often daunting nature of present demands and the courage needed to risk further expenditures. However, it could represent the first serious attempt to shift the organizational style in a professional direction.

Again, the obstacles are legion. Leaders often languish in indecision, perhaps beginning several times in small ways, then pulling back, or making inadequate or halfhearted efforts at planning. Planning itself tends to be problematic in entrepreneurial organizations. It violates the ad hoc cultural norm and, when done in groups, could appear threatening to leaders. They may react to their sense of unease by hedging their bets; they acquiesce but reserve the right to change their minds. Entrepreneurs do occasionally entrust the planning process to others, particularly those who most clearly perceived the need. Although initially encouraged by their leader's trust and the enhanced position it gives them, they may become frustrated if the entrepreneur rescinds their power. The struggle between entrepreneurs and those who increasingly see themselves as professional managers often begins to pick up steam at this point. What the executive first experienced as an internal ambivalence (between changing and staying put) now becomes externalized. Instead of trying to see the benefits and difficulties involved, each player will take a side and defend it. Such conflicts can lead to procrastination as the battle lines are drawn. When procrastination is lengthy, the organization may flounder, and perhaps fail.

In their next meeting, James provided Harry with a sketch of the six challenges that entrepreneurs face in building their organizations and asked him if the sequence made sense to him. James had tried to phrase the challenges in such a way that Harry would be able to grasp them easily (Table 11). Harry did understand the sequence, and that understanding became the basis of the contract between the entrepreneur and his coach: to explore Harry's journey through each challenge and to help him acquire the perspective and skills to negotiate it successfully. Harry agreed to meet with James on a regular basis, to follow a work plan that they would develop together, and to solicit feedback on his leadership style from his staff.

Table 11

Typical Challenges Faced by Entrepreneurs When Moving toward Professionalizing Their Organizations

- Keeping a clear check on reality without losing hope

- Striking a balance between decisiveness and rigorous inquiry

- Acting even in the face of your own doubts and uncertainties

- Resisting the temptation of returning to familiar ways of solving problems when things don't go as expected

- Consolidating changes into the fabric of the organization and its practices

- Realizing that, even when you've gotten it right, it will need to be done again—organizations are never in a stable state for long

---

Accepting the Pace of Change

The plan of action must be carried out with considerable energy, building and maintaining momentum, leaving little doubt that this is the organization's chosen direction. Change, however, generally proceeds in fits and starts. Because early changes are incomplete and untested, they do not by themselves make convincing arguments for their own viability. This tests the commitment and stamina of everyone, particularly the entrepreneur. It also tests the clarity of the vision of change with which they all began.

At this stage, entrepreneurs may find themselves up at night, anxiously wondering what has happened to their organizations; key managers may also be unable to sleep, wondering if they will retain their jobs. Managers who represent the new methods and culture may ascend the organizational hierarchy, while the "old guard"[2] has to struggle to keep up. As in the stage described above, entrepreneurs may again rescind the authority they had delegated while continuing to hold subordinates accountable for productivity. Others could become frustrated at this point because it may seem to them that the entrepreneur has interfered with their ability to do their jobs. Perhaps worse, change may turn the organizational focus inward. If this happens, customer complaints may rise, leading to a drop in business. In any case, this time of change can make everyone anxious. It is not likely to be easy.

Harry had replaced two of the original vice presidents with executives from much larger companies just before his firm went public. He felt he could strengthen the management team and build for future growth by bringing in people who had more management experience than he did. All too often, however, Harry got into conflicts with the new VPs and tended to resolve them as he had in the past—by making decisions himself. Over time, the new VPs and the remaining original VPs began to have doubts about Harry's leadership ability. They became concerned that, rather than building the group into a team, his management style actually prevented them from becoming a team. His absolute certainty about many topics made it difficult to work together across functions and examine all aspects of difficult situations before taking action.

James worked with Harry to help him understand both the dynamics of the situation and the effect of his behavior on his executive team. Harry invited James to sit in on executive staff meetings and asked him to intervene when he felt he could help the group work together more effectively. James essentially became a coach to the team as well as to Harry.

Tolerating Instability and Uncertainty

This challenge, to tolerate the instability created by the change process, concerns both actual disruptions in work as well as mental and emotional responses to them. Instability is better tolerated if those involved maintain a clear vision of the eventual outcomes while realizing that the conditions are natural and temporary. Disruptions during the change process can actually add to the instability and confusion that stimulated change in the first place because the professional management systems and controls intended to handle the increased workload will not yet be completely in place. At such times, it is tempting to revert to old ways, and leaders and their close managers may begin trying, unsuccessfully, to micromanage every detail of the operation. This tendency is often exacerbated by uncertain financial reports.

James's biggest challenge during this stage was to help Harry maintain a steady hand on the tiller, to understand that the uncertainty he and his team were experiencing with the introduction of changes was natural and would pass as the new infrastructure was fully implemented. The fact that James had been through similar situations with other entrepreneurs was enormously comforting to Harry and his team.

Working toward Resolution

Even as organizations change, they still retain their historic natures. Entrepreneurs who survive the transition, for example, don't suddenly become self-assured managers. The challenge of change is to integrate the best of the old with the new and to stabilize the organization around an innovative, integrated way of doing business—and of understanding itself. The alternative to integration is conflict (between those who represent the ad hoc entrepreneurial style and those who advocate planning and controls) and fragmentation, with various departments and people operating in different, often contradictory, ways. A kind of cold war often evolves between factions, an unstable situation that creates constant tension.

James was able to help the team see that the new infrastructure actually provided a much solider basis for decision making than had the prior method. Information concerning many critical business functions was now based on facts rather than a combination of facts, anecdotes, and gut feelings. However, managers were struggling to trust this new source of information, which they still considered less accurate than their previous ways of viewing the business.

Reintroducing Entrepreneurialism

For purposes of efficiency and order, organizations often kill off the spirit of adventure that built them. After the transition to professionalism, companies must still compete in fast and constantly changing markets with continuously evolving technologies, and they cannot do so if they are sluggish, officious, and conservative—in short, bureaucratic. The challenge at this stage is to put new management practices in service to the entrepreneurial spirit and business goals and not to create management systems for their own sake. Leaders will be challenged to actively lead their management systems for their own allow them the space to exercise their skills, and stabilize the organization, while, at the same time, supplying vision and support.

James devised two ways to help the team maintain its entrepreneurial spirit. First, he asked Harry for his thoughts on where things in the marketplace were going and what, in his opinion, the company could do to maintain its competitive edge. Second, he introduced "blue sky" sessions with the team in which members were encouraged to brainstorm and generate creative new ideas of any kind that could conceivably help the business. Harry was pleasantly surprised to find that, as time went by, many of his team members were coming up with ideas similar to his own. Even when their ideas were quite different, Harry found them interesting and potentially useful. Eventually, the other executives learned that setting aside time for brainstorming was of real benefit in their own departments as well.

Readiness and Change in Executive Coaching

Entrepreneurs must overcome each of the six challenges detailed above by making significant changes in themselves and their organizations. Yet, change is difficult and often evokes defensive responses. In this section, we describe our experience with the psychology of the change process and explain how entrepreneurs proceed through it.

Entrepreneurs can be particularly resistant to feedback, help, and, more specifically, efforts to change *them*. Even the most resistant executive, however, has moments when he or she is ready to change, and it is vital to target interventions to those narrow windows of opportunity. The idea of readiness is as old as time. Traditional religious teachers, for example, often wait years for their students to become ready to receive their wisdom. Nowadays, the importance of intervening when the time is right is a pivotal point in theories of change across many disciplines. Crisis theory, for example, states that the openness and urgency of crises create opportunities for change. The educational theorist Eleanor Duckworth (1987) emphasizes identifying and capitalizing on "teachable moments." Evolutionary and systems theorists such as Gregory Bateson (1972) and Irvin Lazlo (1987) assert that systems in disequilibrium are vulnerable to change. The changes can be unpredictable, but, by attending closely to the course of the process, it is possible to support and emphasize those that align with one's strategies.

Building on these insights, we propose a concept of readiness that offers executive coaches a broad range of options for introducing change. To complement these options, we suggest an array of interventions that are well matched to various "states" of readiness. Imagine for instance, that James, the executive coach in our case, needed a framework to help him determine which of many interventions available to him would be most likely to have a positive effect on Harry. The first part of this chapter focused on the six challenges that entrepreneurs typically face; the following section focuses on the entrepreneur's readiness to hear and make use of coaching suggestions.

Three States of Readiness

In our experience, readiness exists in three different states: responsive, unstable, and forays. Each state requires specific kinds of interventions:

- *Responsive* states of readiness are characterized by curiosity, receptiveness, and determination and are best served by information, advice, and guidance.

- *Unstable* states of readiness are marked by confusion, anxiety, and crisis and are best served by reframing situations to manage anxiety and take advantage of whatever fertile ground may exist to nurture new ideas.

- *Forays* are experiments, often conducted in small pockets of the organization, and when their value is recognized, they are best served by expansion into other parts of the organization.

Responsive States of Readiness

When the relationship between coach and entrepreneur is characterized by essential trust and credibility—hallmarks of a responsive state of readiness—we suggest that the coach begin with straightforward approaches to feedback and change. The first step is to survey organizational readiness by trying to identify the nature of the responsive state.

We have identified three different responsive states: curiosity, receptiveness, and determination. These three states are arrayed along a continuum that ranges from modest interest, to an active desire to learn, to a determination to change.

When entrepreneurs are simply *curious* and are not actively seeking solutions to problems, we have found it best to offer information and a variety of ways to understand a problem, but not to push for change. One approach to expanding the field of vision is future-scenario planning (Van der Heijden, 1996), a form of strategic planning that assumes an uncertain future, imagines several paths to effectiveness, and helps organizations to be alert and agile rather than committed to a particular plan.

In a *receptive* state, people are open-minded, which means they have identified a problem but don't yet have a solution and are ready to hear suggestions about what can be done. Under such conditions, it's helpful to narrow the field by presenting a few strategies with clear recommendations about how to choose among them. Pros and cons are also valuable as are clear preferences backed by experience. When the situation is urgent—for example, if markets are lean or customers are abandoning the company—there is frequently a strong, perceived need to do something and to look for help. In this case, it is useful to make clear, decisive suggestions and to recommend a solution to the problem; multiple suggestions may only cause frustration.

Determined people have identified a problem, are aware that a specific solution is required, and have committed themselves to action. In these situations, we provide specific technical assistance, such as a particular way to implement a program, and get out of the way. Determined entrepreneurs will make immediate use of the assistance and carry through on their own.

Unstable States of Readiness

Entrepreneurs and their organizations are often thrown into states of disequilibrium. For example, a crucial trade show may be approaching, venture capital seems to be drying up, or a key employee leaves abruptly. Conventional wisdom suggests that coach and entrepreneur work hard to mitigate these disruptions and help regain organizational balance. We believe, however, that this unstable state of readiness presents many opportunities—it may "unfreeze" rigid ideas and processes in organizational systems, thereby making those systems more open to new input. These unstable states should be reframed as integral aspects of the change process, and then cultivated as the seedbed of creative thought and action. In effect, such states create fertile ground for change initiatives, particularly when they are seen as normal and not as catastrophic.

We have identified two unstable states of readiness: confusion and anxiety. They are discussed below, with suggestions on how to deal with each.

During times of *confusion*, entrepreneurs may be uncertain about a course of action, such as deciding between creating a more limited product that will get to market quickly or holding to an original, more complex conception. In their isolation, entrepreneurs may feel at sea, unable even to determine who can help them with such questions. Coaches will likely find it helpful to try to name and affirm the confusion. They can then frame it as natural and as a source of potential energy and creativity. Instead of rapidly resolving the confusion in an attempt to reduce anxiety, coaches might decide to help sustain or even amplify it as a way of helping the entrepreneur become more comfortable about living with confusion. In our practice, we have found it useful to allow entrepreneurs to wonder aloud about what's going on and what might be done differently, or we may help them facilitate this process with their employees. These kinds of discussions often unearth curiosity, which is an opening to offering suggestions.

Confusion may turn into *anxiety*, which makes problem solving even more difficult. Anxiety generally turns people inward, away from colleagues, collaboration, and realistic planning. To get anywhere in an anxious climate, we must name the anxiety—not ignore or deny it. It helps to draw out both individual and collective elements by talking with entrepreneurs about what they fear for themselves and their organizations. During times of intense anxiety, it is also important to provide structure. We often temporarily schedule coaching meetings more frequently and supply a similar, highly structured approach for the organization. This might take the form of more team meetings, with, for example, clearly formulated task assignments, work-flow charts, time lines, and the like.

Forays

Forays are changes in thought or action that either have not come to fruition or are not yet sufficiently recognized to exert a strong influence on the whole organization. In effect, forays are experiments in new ways of doing things; they often begin in one part of the organization and, when their value is recognized, can be transferred or expanded to other parts of the organization.

This state is distinguished by the observation or discovery of the many existing or easily created opportunities for change. Unlike the unstable states discussed above, in which change may be destabilizing, forays are best utilized by seizing opportunities and then supporting them. We do this by pushing from behind and taking advantage of the entrepreneur's own incompletely formed ideas and momentum. After specific forays have been identified or generated (as in an experimental behavior that the coach and entrepreneur have designed together), there are many ways to leverage opportunities. For example, entrepreneurs may resolve to delegate more, by getting someone to install a new business system. Change may not happen fully at first and may feel incomplete. Yet each incomplete change represents an opportunity—a readiness for change—if the coach knows how to identify it, intervenes, and leverages it.

For example, when an entrepreneur has successfully delegated some responsibility to an employee, we might suggest broadening that employee's duties or determining who else might be worthy of delegated authority. Where entrepreneurs have initiated informal efforts at strategic planning, we might help them expand these efforts bit by bit, instead of insisting on the type of planning typical in large, well-established organizations.

After the coach has assessed the state of readiness and worked to help support key changes within the organization, entrepreneurial executives—like any other executives—may become resistant to change. Strategies for managing resistance are discussed below.

Managing Resistance

No matter how skillful coaches are at offering feedback and facilitating the change process in other ways, they will meet resistance. Change and resistance go together. Each is natural, pervasive, and universal. Resistance is neither preventable nor bad. As such, it must be managed, not avoided.

Resistance wears many faces. It may look like outright refusal, denial, skepticism, lethargy, incompetence, pessimism, or helplessness. At times, people resist by questioning the competence, credentials, or motives of coaches and by going into a bunker-type mode until the siege of change passes.

Living systems thrive when they balance the need for stability with the imperative for change. To manage resistance effectively, it must be understood as a person's efforts to regain the equilibrium that has been disrupted by change. From this perspective, resistance is feedback about disruptions and the troubles they create. If a coach looks carefully enough, feedback can point out how the relationships necessary to implement change are poorly aligned with one another and with the goals of the change process. Managing resistance means using the information it provides and realigning relationships in order to achieve goals.

We have found these four approaches to managing resistance helpful in our work with entrepreneurs:

- Anticipate resistance
- Explore the meaning of resistance
- Validate resistance, thus empowering those who resist
- Form a partnership to solve the problem indicated by resistance

Each approach is discussed below.

Anticipate Resistance

Evaluation often points out areas in need of change by making clear where present methods or behaviors are not meeting objectives. If evaluation does lead to change, resistance will follow, if not at the beginning, then at some point in the change process. It's important that coaches remember not to ignore or punish it. Coaches must regularly scan the horizon in the manner of a sailor guarding against an unpredictable sea—searching for the many obvious as well as disguised faces of resistance, such as incompetence, canceled meetings, and displays of helplessness.

Explore the Meaning of Resistance

Our experience has shown that it's best for coaches not to try to determine the meaning of resistance by themselves—they should ask the entrepreneurs. We have asked how we might have missed their meaning, acted insensitively, or threatened their interests. As coaches improve at exploring and articulating the reasons for resistance, entrepreneurs will make less use of passive, indirect forms of resistance. The more open the conflict or misunderstanding, the better the chance of resolving it. In fact, the very act of mutual inquiry is the first, major step toward building a partnership capable of solving the problems that led to resistance in the first place.

Validate Resistance

The coach could assert, in essence, that given the circumstances, resistance makes sense. "In your position," a coach might say, "I, too, would resist."

Beneath the manifest resistance, there is important information about how and how not to mobilize people behind a project. By affirming the hidden or deeper meanings, we accomplish two things: we allow entrepreneurs to feel understood, and we encourage them to be direct in the future, so that we can enter productive conversation more easily.

Form a Partnership

When coaches are genuinely interested in validating resistance, they may be able to form partnerships with resistant entrepreneurs. In their joint efforts to reach a common understanding of the problem behind the resistance, coach and entrepreneur sometimes find they have gone a long way toward resolving the problem itself.

Conclusion

We see coaching entrepreneurs as a trickier and more complicated version of executive coaching. The characteristics common to many entrepreneurs often make working with them difficult. Successful coaching ultimately comes down to the quality of the relationship between coach and client. To be successful with entrepreneurs, coaches need a wider range of skills than is required for most executive coaching. Coaches need both knowledge and experience that an entrepreneur will respect. Without respect, the coach's chance to build the necessary trust is seriously compromised. Consequently, we recommend that those interested in coaching entrepreneurs first gain extensive experience coaching managers in less complex situations. If possible, before taking on solo assignments, they should partner with coaches who are experienced in working with entrepreneurs across the entire spectrum of personal and business issues identified in this chapter.

As we coach entrepreneurs, we need to carefully balance the needs of the individual with the needs of the organization and keep both constituencies in mind throughout the process. We must also provide information and support regarding the particular developmental challenges that entrepreneurs face. In addition, to facilitate changes in entrepreneurial organizations, we need to gauge the entrepreneur's readiness for change and offer guidance that is consistent with that readiness. Finally, we should look for—and make productive use of—the inevitable resistance to change.

Even as we keep all of these various factors in mind, we're well aware that coaching entrepreneurs is a tricky enterprise. And we know that, as in any coaching situation, the personalities and interests of the executives involved are key factors in determining coaching success or failure.

To truly succeed with Harry, James will gradually shift from being an active coach, sometimes assuming a challenging posture, to become a sounding board, as Harry learns to shift from being a doer and manager (which was necessary in the early start-up days) to being a leader—able to delegate more, to operate from a systems perspective rather than intuition, and to plan strategically. In our experience, few entrepreneurs are able to make this shift successfully. Coaching certainly can help, but only to the extent that such a shift is attractive enough to motivate them. If James's and Harry's hard work pays off, both the entrepreneur and the organization will be enriched, and Harry will find himself better able to lead his company through whatever challenges lie ahead.

Notes

[1] The term *professional management* includes such factors as the increasingly systematic procedures and more-formalized structures that are necessary as companies mature.

[2] In entrepreneurial companies, people are labeled *old guard* if they've been there longer than a year or so! It is amazing how quickly people get into the mode of defending what exists rather than looking toward what could be. Oddly enough, when it is time for entrepreneurial companies to adopt more professional management practices, the *old guard* sometimes are those very people who want to hang on to the early methods of operations in which there were no rules.

References

Bateson, G. (1972). *Steps to an ecology of mind.* New York: Ballantine.

Duckworth, E. (1987). *The having of wonderful ideas and other essays on teaching and learning.* New York: Teachers College Press.

Lazlo, I. (1987). *Evolution: The grand synthesis.* Boston: New Science Library.

Van der Heijden, K. (1996). *Scenarios: The art of strategic conversation.* West Sussex, England: Wiley.

[16]

COACHING ACROSS COUNTRIES AND CULTURES

KAREN L. OTAZO

A frog in a well only sees his piece of the sky.

—Chinese saying

Executive coaching in any context requires coaches to understand and appreciate the perspectives of different parties (the executive, bosses, peers, direct reports) and successfully help their clients understand, appreciate, and negotiate among those perspectives. There are many possible reasons why perspectives may differ, such as situational circumstances (amount of contact or information), role discrepancies (organizational level or function), and individual factors (e.g., generation, personality type).

Differences in perspective can be substantial and challenging even when coaching takes place *within* a single national culture. When coaching occurs *across* cultures, however, helping executives understand, appreciate, and negotiate differences can be especially complex. In addition to the situational, role, and individual factors mentioned above, coaches will encounter powerful, deeply held worldviews that can affect every aspect of working, communicating, and decision making.

Individual and Cultural Worldviews

As business becomes more global, organizations and their leaders are struggling to be effective in situations that must accommodate the multiple worldviews of key players. Understanding various worldviews is clearly pivotal for business success, and, not surprisingly, executive coaches with cross-cultural experience are in great demand.

While we are often unaware of our own worldview—not to mention those of other people—these comprehensive conceptions shape everything within our understanding. The principal purpose of a worldview is to make sense of reality. Our way of reasoning depends fundamentally on our understanding of the nature of the world and its processes and on our beliefs about the essence and purpose of human beings. These principles form a structure that enables us to interpret reality. They are the unconscious assumptions by which we live.

However, even as worldviews help us make sense of the world, they also unconsciously shape that world. What our minds have not experienced, what is not part of our structure for interpreting reality, sometimes simply cannot be seen. The frog in the well is a good analogy for vision limited by point of view. Although human beings may share universal perceptions of primitive environmental stimuli, certain cognitive patterns, and the ability to generalize new uses of language from existing patterns, we definitely understand reality in individual ways. We unconsciously filter the world through our own paradigms or worldviews and believe that what we see is the only reality.

The converse is also true. Because we think ours is the only reality, other perspectives may appear irrational, naive, or misguided. Essentially, we become blind to other possible worldviews. The ability to understand and articulate a person's or a culture's worldview is one of the keys to coaching across cultures.

It is a complex task to articulate the worldview of another person, but it is even more difficult—and potentially more dangerous—to articulate that of a culture. In describing the nature of a culture's worldview, or "structure of interpretation" (Flaherty, 1999, p. 8), we may oversimplify a dynamic, not a fixed or static, perspective. Moreover, not all members of a culture subscribe to the macro versions of their culture's worldview. Nevertheless, it is still worth deciphering the worldviews of different cultures because the coach is initiating the same process on an individual level with the executive and key organizational players. For example, we could say that certain cultures have animistic ancestral-spirit structures of interpretation or that others depend on a spiritual-hierarchical and fatalistic structure of interpretation. These oversimplified observations are valid to some degree, especially if they help us understand how others structure reality. Yet, even as we contrast cultures, we find it extremely difficult to comprehend that any such processes as reasoning, decision making, and conflict resolution could be radically different from our own.

The Importance of Worldviews in International Business

In this highly international business world, coaches are increasingly called on to help their clients understand not only their own worldviews but also those of a diverse set of players who operate in the same business environment. Good coaches enter into their clients' worldviews and explain those perspectives before exposing them to other ways of conceptualizing and approaching the world. In my experience, coaching has effected some of the most dramatic changes, helping individuals and teams to move from criticizing differences to observing, understanding, and utilizing them to increase their ability to function well in a global context.

I have been an executive coach for sixteen years and have worked with clients from many countries and cultures. Originally from the United States, I have spent a third of my adult life abroad, living for substantial amounts of time in Asia and Europe and learning to speak a number of European and Asian languages. My clients include executives from North and South America, Europe, Asia, and Africa.

In this chapter, I present an extended case study that highlights the rich and multilayered experience of working in a complex international environment. The case involves a chief executive who was trying to find her way as a leader after an unexpected promotion. To succeed in her job, this executive had to navigate the various worldviews of her managers, subordinates, and customers in a multinational retail joint venture. The following pages describe organizational responses that did not work well enough to support the executive as she tried to deal with ambiguity, paradox, and conflicting expectations in the midst of macroeconomic change in her region.

A European Joint Venture in Chinese Asia

Josephine Yu[1] sat across from me at the desk, wearing a stylish silk shorts suit and silk shirt. This beautiful and feisty woman had come a long way, from her first job as a secretary to managing director of Syzygy Furnishings, an Anglo-Swedish joint venture in Chinese Asia (Hong Kong and Taiwan). Josephine had called me in because she was not enjoying the results of her amazing success. Instead, she felt betrayed by the company she had worked so hard to support, thought she might be in danger of losing her job, and was considering giving up entirely and leaving the company. She had called out of desperation, hoping I could help her mediate between the needs of the stores she was running and the demands of the different parent corporations in the joint venture that financed, owned, and supplied the stores.

To deal with a problem in a multinational enterprise like this one, I knew we would have to explore not only specific individuals in the present situation and key players in the parent companies but also the cultural implications of the diverse backgrounds in play. It would be a complex and messy undertaking. I also knew that Josephine was wary of Westerners. I had to gain her trust.

Client Background

In my global coaching practice, I have found that understanding the forces that have shaped my clients' worldviews is of primary importance. In order to understand Josephine, I asked about her history. She explained that she began her career immediately after leaving secondary school in her native Hong Kong. "Hong Kong was struggling," she told me. "My father couldn't support me at college, so I got a job as a secretary. From the outset, I wanted to do more, including my boss's work. I couldn't stand the slow pace of decision making. The urge to do something else, to have a chance to lead, was strong." Looking for an area that would reward hard work, she started selling cosmetics in a department store. Within three years, she was managing twenty employees in department stores and pharmacies across Hong Kong and exceeding all her regional sales targets. When she ran out of levels to conquer, she moved to a company specializing in high-end fashion accessories. She not only loved the product, she also had a knack for understanding the needs of customers—a knack that developed into a set of instincts about Chinese tastes and preferences. It was a heady world of high profit and high pressure. There was also a personal payoff as Josephine traveled and learned the global market. As she put it, "I had to deal with the French and other Europeans. I had to learn how to work globally."

When a British conglomerate acquired her company, Josephine was viewed as a person with marketing but not leadership potential. The British management, therefore, placed her in the number two position at Syzygy, a floundering joint venture. Now in her mid-thirties, Josephine had tasted leadership. Although she was number two in the company, she jumped into the job and started to make changes. The managing director came to rely on her. Within a couple of years, it was obvious that Josephine's boss was in over his head as a leader. He was asked to resign and Josephine advanced to the position of acting managing director.

As Josephine quickly discovered, it wasn't just her worldview that was to shape her experience at Syzygy Furnishings. All companies have distinct worldviews of their own, and multinational conglomerates often take on the worldviews of their parent companies.

The Basis of Cultural Conflict at Syzygy Furnishings

Syzygy Furnishings was the offspring of two parent companies: Skaaka, the Swedish parent, and Empire, the British parent. Families with parents from different cultural backgrounds sometimes disagree over childrearing, values, and allocation of decision-making authority. Children may then be caught in the middle of what are really cultural conflicts; they may also be enriched by the wealth of cultures surrounding them. Syzygy, as the child of two very different parents, was experiencing the conflicts and the benefits of its British and Swedish roots.

Skaaka was an unequivocally Swedish company, privately held and family owned. Because its values could be enforced more thoroughly than could those of a publicly traded company, Skaaka reflected typical Swedish business and family values. As Josephine and I began to sort through the worldviews of the companies, I shared my experience that traditional Swedish characteristics include openness, reliability, directness, unpretentiousness, and teamwork. In their professional lives, Swedes maintain a "long-term business orientation, integrating social concerns with work. . . . They are willing to challenge authority when they believe it is wrong" (Kets de Vries with Florent-Treacy, 1999, p. 64). Skaaka, in full accord with these traditional values, believed that employees and managers—in fact the whole workforce—should enjoy harmonious and cooperative relationships.

Based on this model, Skaaka expected Syzygy Furnishings to adhere to some key business principles. In addition to the core attributes of directness and honesty, Skaaka also wanted all employees to respect its values and concept. Stores were to keep prices down because the Swedish company believed that continually—even ruthlessly—lowered prices—would benefit society and, eventually, make money for the company. Skaaka insisted that all merchandise be purchased through Sweden. Even when some of the products were manufactured near a store in another country (e.g., Hong Kong, China, or Taiwan), the materials were always shipped to Sweden and then redistributed. Finally, it was vital to Skaaka that stores worldwide maintain the company's unique concept. In fact, honoring this concept was more important than turning a profit.

Empire, the British parent, had very different values, and those values were as rigorously protected. I've found that, as a culture, the British appreciate a highly articulate and analytical approach to business. Presentations and numbers matter. After living in the United Kingdom for several years, I would say that although the British believe there are many ways to reach a goal, the bottom line is what matters. Creativity and innovation are valued, but they must pay off. British firms can be flexible about how these results are achieved, and, to a lesser extent than in the United States, they will respect an individual who is following his or her own path. Employers will even tolerate a certain amount of mild disagreement from employees (Hofstede, 1994), but it's the quarterly results that matter.

As a publicly traded company, Empire was most interested in increasing shareholder value, a goal that encouraged both short-term and reactive thinking. Quarterly postings of results tended to drive the behavior of managers and staff. Empire expected its employees to make the numbers, which were calculated using returns on average capital employed. The company relied on its leaders to analyze results and situations rigorously and completely and to be articulate in presentations and written work. Leaders were supposed to be gracious and explain British thinking to the Swedes. And Empire expected to be in charge of the joint venture.

Leading the New Joint Venture

In this complex climate, Josephine found herself thrust unexpectedly into a major role. She was in her late thirties and considered a bit young for her post. Some people thought she just happened to be in the right place at the right time. Her previous responsibilities never involved more than managing several small departments in retail stores, but, in this position, she was in charge of launching six stores and managing another six in three cities in two very different countries.

Although she lacked experience with large stores, she was chosen to lead the new joint venture because she was the only one available. British management placed her in her new position, half expecting that her leadership would fail. In the meantime, they would continue to look for someone more suitable, probably someone more typical, more like them. They viewed her experience base as weak at best, but she had the right marketing savvy for the target markets and "the guts and determination for the dirty work of a start-up," according to her British boss, Elliot Watson. She also had a reputation for getting things done quickly.

When Josephine accepted the position and began taking action, she had no idea about the kinds of cross-cultural currents she'd have to navigate in the course of her work. Simply launching the stores—not a simple task—seemed like enough work to engage her time and attention. While she was aware of the tensions caused by conflicts between British and Swedish ways of running a business, she couldn't have foreseen what would happen when those diverse cultures bumped up against the cultures of Hong Kong and Taiwan.

Josephine's task at Syzygy Furnishings was to accomplish two goals: open stores in urban markets and introduce the Scandinavian-concept store to Chinese Asia, where low-cost furnishings are commonplace. Neither of these goals had been attempted before. Quite carefully, Josephine considered the ramifications of both moves. The company's branches in Europe and America, where land was reasonable and available, could afford to build big boxes containing showrooms and warehouses to create sprawling suburban stores with generous parking. But given rent and space constraints in Asia, Josephine was compelled to create the company's first urban store—with little parking or space. She knew she'd have to reimagine the Swedish concept in another kind of environment and in different cultures. She also knew that the Hong Kong worldview was likely to be quite different from the one in Taiwan. She would have to take this factor into account as well, as she hired her staff and designed her stores to appeal to customers.

Hong Kong and Taiwanese Perspectives

Josephine knew, for example, that people in her native Hong Kong believe deeply in astrology and *feng shui;* pregnant women commonly choose their children's birth dates by consulting astrologers and scheduling cesarean sections with their doctors. They also believe that you are dealt your fate, *yuan fen,* and are allowed nothing more than diligence and hard work with which to make the best of it. In addition, a strong Confucian tradition mandates obedience of child to parent, wife to husband, and employee to manager. Southern Chinese, and Hong Kongers in particular, are very entrepreneurial people and are quite inventive in their approach to getting things done. For example, it is possible to have suits and other items of clothing made in a matter of hours. The pace of life itself is simply faster in Hong Kong. Josephine and I talked about how these beliefs might be affecting her employees and her stores. I have worked in Hong Kong and in the People's Republic of China and know from experience that these beliefs are quite powerful.

British colonial rule also influenced Hong Kong and left a feeling of subservience among the formerly colonized Chinese. At the same time, the British left a legacy of well-run bureaucracy and transparent transactions, which is symbolized by the Independent Commission Against Corruption, a local government body.

Hong Kong employees live in a world heavily influenced by Western products and values. They are eager to be recognized for their work and seek corresponding opportunities for advancement (Hofstede, 1994). They think of leaders as parental figures. Leaders must demonstrate the power to take care of and protect employees; they must also offer specific guidance by indicating goals and direction. Leaders inspire trust and deal with conflict. In exchange, their employees owe them obedience and respect. While it is up to employees to accomplish their tasks quickly and according to their leaders' expectations, in Hong Kong it is unwise to do more than what has been requested by a superior.

According to Josephine, the worldview of Taiwanese employees was somewhat similar to that of Hong Kongers in terms of its strong Confucian values. However, Taiwan is not as modern or fast paced as Hong Kong. Taiwan suffered through a long period of poverty and hardship after World War II, as well as a dictatorship, and, consequently, modernization came later to this island. Life happens at a slower pace in Taiwan. With no colonial legacy, there is also far less of a Western overlay. In addition, transparency of transactions is rare, and corruption in business is much in evidence. Opening stores customarily meant paying special fees to police and fire departments, which Josephine refused to do.

Along with the Confucian expectations of a leader found among Hong Kong employees, Taiwanese employees are used to being told exactly what to do, working regular hours with extra pay for overtime, and leaving any further responsibilities to someone else. It is sometimes difficult to find anyone who will take charge in Taiwan because responsibility is seen as such a daunting burden.

Criticism and Management Crises

In these two different climates, Josephine built her stores. Within six months, through hard work and relying on sheer survival instincts, she raised sales to levels that other start-ups struggled for years to achieve. But despite these remarkable results, both her Empire boss and her Skaaka boss considered replacing her.

British management was concerned about her ability to continue the dramatic growth and profits she had created in a very short time. Elliot, her Empire boss, admitted that her initial insecurity and lack of education were of concern to them. "She is also not easy, doesn't suffer fools gladly, and will not stop until she gets a job done," he continued. "I kept expecting we would have to take her out as a basket case. We were surprised that she made it." But now that Josephine had "made it" quite well, Empire managers were worried that numbers this good simply could not be true. They assigned a

Chinese audit manager to continuously verify her results and a British finance manager to question and critique her numbers each month.

Swedish management, on the other hand, was most concerned with keeping their concept and look alive in the stores—urban or not—and their prices low. Reputation was of paramount importance to them. Josephine's Skaaka boss, Jan, complained that he had been shocked when he visited her retail facilities. The sales figures were wonderful, but the facilities were chaotic and unclean by Swedish standards. He asked that Empire, which had personnel in the area, send in a merchandising manager to help Josephine do it right. He started to worry about Josephine's lack of orderliness and feared that quality controls had been sacrificed for speed. The Swedes did not care if she lost money as long as she represented their company according to their vision.

When Josephine was confronted by the two British experts assigned to her, she interpreted their criticisms as lack of trust on the part of both sets of management. She reacted defensively and did not hear their advice about what needed to be done. They, however, thought their massive criticisms were helpful because the process was basically "for her own good." But she felt attacked. Were they trying to push her out? At this point, she called me as a desperation measure.

She described the hard work of the past six months this way: "They threw me in at the deep end, and I thought I'd drown. I hired people I could trust to work hard and support me. I just kept moving, going back later to fix what didn't work. That was the only way I knew to be successful." There was little guidance from either parent company. She felt she had been tested and emerged a winner in her own eyes.

She did not understand that her strong behaviors appeared more defensive than firm. She also gave off too much energy for the northern Europeans to whom she seemed "out of control." After understanding the complex world in which Josephine operated, I was able to begin working with her, to help her choose new methods and reactions while navigating these rough waters.

Coaching Work Begins

At the beginning of my work with Josephine, I interviewed all the key players in her work life, asking for their views on working with her and how they perceived her effectiveness. Then, we examined the complex context of her work and came up with a set of possible changes that might improve her relationships within the company. One of the first changes she made, after observing the Europeans in meetings, was to be more measured and moderate in her speech and presentation. She also learned how to stay calm and objective when she felt attacked. These changes increased her credibility. In meetings with me and with her closest colleagues, she was free to express herself in her usual manner and practice her new demeanor. With everyone else, she scaled back her energy and emotions.

Josephine's second lesson was to examine her actions from the viewpoints of the parent companies. What did they need to maintain their comfort level with her numbers and performance? As I helped Josephine uncover and articulate the worldviews of the various players in this multinational enterprise, I also found myself paying close attention to her worldview. We discussed those qualities that were most important to her—such as trust, honesty, and filial piety for her boss—and her need to be respected in return.

I sought to understand Josephine's worldview through the individual characteristics I saw in her. For instance, I learned that she sees the world as a place of trust in which to give and receive from others. She places a high value on hard work, wanting to do the best she can, and expects others to feel the same way. Josephine recalled getting assignments in school and being the only one to diligently complete everything the teacher requested. I also looked toward the more linguistically oriented aspects of her worldview. For example, the Chinese language is made up of ideographs, and early training in Chinese emphasizes both verbal and written repetition. With Chinese as her mother tongue, Josephine favors visual learning. This information helped me understand that Josephine would benefit from reports and summaries of our conversations. Similarly, because I knew that there is no distinction in spoken Chinese between the pronouns *he* and *she,* I could see why Josephine tended to mix them up. And with tense being a relatively insignificant structure in Chinese, I recognized the importance of keeping tenses clear in our discussions. Josephine practiced and improved her skills so that grammatical errors would not undermine her credibility. It never ceases to amaze me that Anglo-Saxon companies equate English-language skills with professional competence.

Finally, I tried to observe behaviors that might provide me with a more refined sense of Josephine's worldview. As a typical Hong Konger, Josephine liked a fast-paced approach to learning. E-mail worked extremely well for her, and she preferred an overnight response. I knew I had to be fast and careful to earn her trust. I was also aware that I had to back up my words with actions and be there for her when she needed me. As we worked together, Josephine's comfort with and trust in me grew; in fact, she told me that our relationship helped her develop a new view of Westerners.

Coaching for Business Outcomes

Coaching helped Josephine reconcile herself to the idea that it was necessary to work with both sets of management. When Jan started suggesting ways in which she could improve, she was able to drop her defenses and listen. While she resented his demands for rigid ordering and marketing plans, she adapted when she saw the utility of Skaaka's recommended systems and procedures. "I started to see what was missing in logistics and even in merchandising," she admitted. Overcoming this hurdle helped build her confidence and consequently lessened the insecurity that had concerned Elliot. She was also able to objectively assess the expatriates assigned to her and realized that they might have some merit.

Ultimately, she liked Skaaka's approach and the thinking of Jan and his colleagues; however, Empire's financial and merchandising help was not as welcome. In fact, Josephine was frustrated with the British company's months-long questioning of her figures, and the surprise spot checks at her stores had become a source of great irritation. I challenged her to determine some ways to improve Empire's comfort with the numbers and gain their confidence.

Josephine had developed a comfortable relationship with Kim, the Chinese manager Empire had sent to sent to audit her, so she hired him as her finance manager. That made the British finance manager unnecessary, because Empire had confidence in Kim. It became increasingly clear to Josephine that she could gain credibility by hiring credible key players. Kim had a sterling reputation, was by now well acquainted with the business, and had studied in the United States and spoke superb English. He, instead of Josephine, could defend the numbers. As a further benefit, Josephine had found a capable number two who could be groomed as her successor.

Coaching for Political Capabilities

Now that she was open to the idea of learning from her parent companies and was able to reassure them by hiring credible staff, Josephine was ready to consider coaching for political power as well as business results. She had begun to realize that she needed to tip the balance of power in her organization. She felt that Empire was bullying her because the company had other joint ventures in the region. By this time, she had developed respect for her Swedish boss, Jan. He also seemed to be honest about wanting to help, and not just criticize, her. She worked with me to formulate a plan to ask Skaaka for assistance. Her aim was to convince Empire to call off the British merchandising manager who was still spot-checking her stores.

Josephine was scheduled to tour the Swedish flagship operations in the Netherlands and Sweden. After being exposed to my U.S. business ideas and worldview, she began to consider a move—petitioning the Swedish board for the help she needed to meet their expectations—that had never before been made by a joint venture partner. In the United States, such presentations to boards are common. Josephine had begun to understand Swedish values. Of the ten items listed in Skaaka's values statement, the management rated "strong trust" as number one. This resonated for her, and she appealed to the Swedes to find strong and capable executives whom she could trust, to work for her and do what was needed. "It was so irregular that we said yes," recalled Jan. "Her presentation to the board was unsophisticated and unprecedented, but she opened our eyes with her impassioned pleas for help in areas that were new to her, like store merchandising and retail logistics in a developing country."

Josephine wasn't the only one with a lot to learn. The Swedish home office had not understood the realities of business in Chinese Asia. For example, Josephine came under fire for hiring a 747 to airlift merchandise when it looked as if a newly launched store would be forced to remain closed an extra month because of insufficient stock. It took her personal interactions with the Skaaka executives to make them understand that, due to the astronomical rents in Hong Kong, the cost of leaving the shop closed an extra month was greater than the cost of flying in the merchandise. They finally saw that she had more than made up for the outlay through sales. And, a short while later, they made an enormous concession: they finally agreed that she could source merchandise directly from Asia rather than sending it through Sweden and then returning it to Asia.

In answer to her plea for help, the Swedes sent two Swedish expatriates, seasoned veterans with global experience—one from Moscow and one from Malaysia. At this, British management reacted with concern. They would have preferred their own people in the jobs. Josephine reassured them by pointing out that the Swedes were experts in the retailing field. And it soon became apparent that the new managers were just what was needed to move the entire operation in the right direction. The British concurred, and Josephine's confidence soared as her team went to work to sort out the operation. Securing support from Skaaka and gaining the new managers were master strokes. She was now able to refer any questions about her incredible profits to a seasoned expatriate who spoke the language of retail and finance—not to mention the English and Swedish—that her bosses understood. She grew to like her new reports so much that she started hiring seasoned expatriate talent for her new stores, to start them out with experienced staff. Her bosses could not have been happier with the results.

End of the Coaching Engagement

As I had done at the beginning of the coaching engagement, I conducted oral feedback sessions with all the key players in Josephine's working life: staff, supervisors, suppliers, and colleagues. I asked for their perceptions of Josephine and her position. Through their words, Josephine was able to observe herself working with them, meeting with them, giving direction, and becoming frustrated. As a result of her sincere attention to these other views, she learned to observe herself without judgment and to ask those she trusted to do the same for her. This sort of observation was not easy; she had to consciously ignore her own constant internal self-criticism— criticism that was much like hearing her father's voice in her head.

Josephine learned a great deal from her experiences managing the cultural crosscurrents of her joint venture partners. While she was negotiating their cultures, she also had her hands full operating within two Chinese cultures, one perhaps fifty years behind the other in business sophistication and transparency of operations. In the process of seeing the world as others saw it, she also had to reexamine her own strongly held values of total trust and honesty. She came to understand that trust and honesty meant different things to the other key players. She also struggled to find a way of communicating her ideas without provoking strong reactions. Coaching had shown her that even small issues can sometimes seem large within another structure of interpretation. Josephine learned that she had to shape her message to fit the listener's worldview. Her enormous effort paid off; she was more successful than she had ever dreamed possible. As our initial coaching engagement came to an end, I asked Jan what one thing would make Josephine better at her job, and all he could think of was, "Speak Swedish!"

Further Insights

Yet, six years later, in spite of her enormous progress, Josephine felt that there was still so much to be done. She also realized that, in resolving more problems than she cared to remember, she had given up her life to make the job work. She was beginning to ask herself if her dreams were still the same as those of the joint venture companies. Would she always be pulled between the cultures of her two European managers?

As Josephine put it, the managements of Empire and Skaaka "came from two different planets." One mandated a 12 percent return to shareholders. The other wanted to protect its retailing concept and continue to lower prices at all costs. Mediating between the two consumed much of her time and attention, and she knew that her next task was to pass along to *other people* the cross-cultural skills they would need to mediate between the two companies. Josephine now understood that it wasn't enough to hire good people at the retail marketing level, although that was ostensibly the main focus of her work. Having learned the complexities of conducting business in multinational settings, she knew she needed to hire and develop leaders who could survive the cross-cultural stresses at Syzygy Furnishings.

Josephine recalled the extraordinary difficulties she had experienced in developing the ability to step outside her own worldview to understand the worldviews of others. She knew now that it was necessary for the business climate in which she operated. However, with the help of coaching, and through her intellectual curiosity and willingness to work hard, she had shown that it was possible to learn—and thrive—in a multinational environment.

Conclusion

My experiences living, working, and coaching in a variety of countries and cultures has given me a great interest in—and a profound respect for—different worldviews. Experience convinces me that in order to be helpful in multinational environments, executive coaches must be able to accept and perceive through disparate worldviews. In these situations, effective executive coaches are those who can take on more than one role. One role may involve revealing the worldviews of the different players and companies involved and encouraging executives to act in ways that both support and expand those worldviews. Another role could be to assist the client in resolving the cultural dilemmas inherent in mediating among multiple cultures (Hampden-Turner and Trompenaars, 2000). To succeed, executives like Josephine must be able to sustain all the tensions of balancing these dilemmas while they are running businesses in complex financial and political environments. It is often hard for corporate executives to understand the pressures felt by people in positions such as Josephine's. So an additional role for the executive coach is to educate those corporate executives who are out of touch with the challenges faced by executives at the edges of their far-flung enterprises. Being flexible enough to play many roles comes with the territory of coaching across countries and cultures.

Note

[1] This case study is real and is used with permission. The names have been changed for legal reasons.

References

Flaherty, J. (1999). *Coaching: Evoking excellence in others.* New York: Butterworth Heinemann.

Hampden-Turner, C. M., and F. Trompenaars. (2000). *Building cross-cultural competence: How to create wealth from conflicting values.* Chichester, England: John Wiley & Sons Ltd.

Hofstede, G. (1994). *Cultures and organizations: Intercultural cooperation and its importance for survival: Software of the mind.* London: HarperCollins Business, Hammersmith.

Kets de Vries, M. F. R., with E. Florent-Treacy. (1999). *The new global leaders: Richard Branson, Percy Barnevik, David Simon and the remaking of international business.* San Francisco: Jossey-Bass.

INDEX